# BURMA/MYANMAR

## WHAT EVERYONE NEEDS TO KNOW

# BURMA/MYANMAR

## WHAT EVERYONE NEEDS TO KNOW

### Second Edition

## DAVID I. STEINBERG

OXFORD

UNIVERSITY PRESS

# OXFORD
UNIVERSITY PRESS

Oxford University Press is a department of the University of Oxford.
It furthers the University's objective of excellence in research, scholarship,
and education by publishing worldwide.

Oxford   New York
Auckland   Cape Town   Dar es Salaam   Hong Kong   Karachi
Kuala Lumpur   Madrid   Melbourne   Mexico City   Nairobi
New Delhi   Shanghai   Taipei   Toronto

With offices in
Argentina   Austria   Brazil   Chile   Czech Republic   France   Greece
Guatemala   Hungary   Italy   Japan   Poland   Portugal   Singapore
South Korea   Switzerland   Thailand   Turkey   Ukraine   Vietnam

Oxford is a registered trademark of Oxford University Press
in the UK and certain other countries.

Published in the United States of America by
Oxford University Press
198 Madison Avenue, New York, NY 10016

Library of Congress Cataloging-in-Publication Data
Steinberg, David I., 1928-
Burma/Myanmar: what everyone needs to know / David I. Steinberg. — 2nd ed.
p. cm.
Includes bibliographical references and index.
Summary: "Taking into account the dramatic changes the country has seen in the past
two years—including the establishment of a human rights commission, the release
of political prisoners, and reforms in health and education—David I. Steinberg offers
an updated second edition of Burma/Myanmar: What Everyone Needs to Know."—
Provided by publisher.

ISBN 978-0-19-998168-7 (pbk.) — ISBN 978-0-19-998167-0 (cloth)
1. Public administration—Burma.   2. Burma—Politics and government.
3. Burma—Colonial influence.   I. Title.
JQ751.A58S84 2013
959.1—dc23
2012041007

1 3 5 7 9 8 6 4 2
Printed in the United States of America
on acid-free paper

*To my family*

*Ann Myongsook Lee*
*Alexander Lee Steinberg*
*Eric David Steinberg*

*who sustained me*

# CONTENTS

## 3 The Colonial Era's Importance in Understanding Burma/Myanmar Today    27

## 4 Independence and the Civilian Government (1948–1962): Mixed Heritages    41

## 5  The Military Coup, the Socialist Period (1962–1988), and the Perpetuation of Military Rule                                       63

## 6  The SLORC/SPDC Era (1988–Present): Continuation of Military Power                          82

*PHOTOS FOLLOW PAGE   105*

# ACKNOWLEDGMENTS

With gratitude, I would like to acknowledge three groups of people who contributed to the production of this volume.

The first are those unnamed individuals worldwide who unwittingly and unceremoniously assisted in the writing of this work. Instructed by the publisher that there were to be no notes, I have uncharacteristically and with a considerable degree of guilt mined without citing the works of many distinguished scholars and others concerned with Burma/Myanmar, using their materials, ideas, and data. Without their silent participation, this could not have been written. To them I offer profuse apologies, and I promise to make their critical contributions to the field more publicly known in other fora. It is small recompense that the Suggested Reading section contains many of their works.

To my friends and acquaintances in Myanmar, whom I dare not publicly name, I thank you for indulging me over some fifty years. Your friendships and advice have been critical to whatever contribution I may have made to knowledge about this country and to me personally as well. If I have misrepresented or misinterpreted your country and culture, I apologize and assure you that it has not been intentional.

To those who helped me by commenting on drafts and correcting my egregious errors, many thanks. They include commentators such as Andrew Selth, Mary Callahan, John

Brandon, Matthew Daley, Dominic Nardi, Lin Lin Aung, Zarni, and some unidentified readers. My class on Burma/Myanmar at the School of Foreign Service, Georgetown University, had access to an early draft and commented on it. I alone, however, am responsible for sins of commission or omission. To David McBride of Oxford University Press, who commissioned this work from me, I express my thanks for his initial confidence, his Herculean efforts to make this more readable, and in shortening my Proustian sentences that sometimes seem, even to me, interminable.

Southeast Asia (redrawn from a map produced by the U.S. Central Intelligence Agency in 2004)

Administrative divisions of Burma/Myanmar (redrawn from a map produced by the United Nations in 2008)

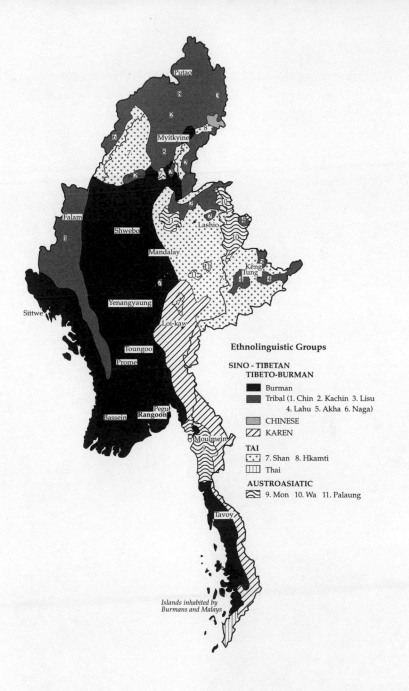

Ethnolinguistic map of Burma/Myanmar (redrawn from a map produced by the U.S. Central Intelligence Agency in 1972)

# PRELIMINARY NOTES

## Personal Names

All names in Burma/Myanmar are personal—there are no surnames, even within the same nuclear family. When Burmese nationals publish or travel abroad, one of their names may be used as an unofficial surname for practical purposes. Names may be one to four syllables. Female names often have a double syllable (e.g., Lin Lin Aung). Names are normally preceded by a title based on a family designation:

*U* (uncle) for a mature male
*Daw* (aunt) for a mature female
*Ko* (elder brother) a male somewhat older than the speaker
*Maung* (younger brother) a more junior male
*Ma* (younger sister) a more junior female
*Bo* (military officer)
*Bogyoke* (supreme commander)
*Thakin* (lord) used by British in the colonial period and
    adopted by some Burmese in the nationalist movement

Western titles are also used: Doctor, General, Senior General, Brigadier, and so on, as are Christian names (certain titles have become embedded in the name in foreign usage; e.g., U Nu, whose name is simply Nu, but when he began writing, his work was authored by Maung Nu).

Sometimes these words (U, Ko, Maung, etc.) may also be part of the name, and not a title (a male with a name of Oo Tin, might be known as Maung Oo Tin as a youngster, Ko Oo Tin as a college student, and U Oo Tin as a middle-aged man).

Names in the text are either spelled according the U.S. Department of State Board of Geographic Names or the personal preference of the individual. The following list of names are for those who appear in the book frequently.

Aung Gyi (b. 1919–) Brigadier, retired

Aung San (1911–1947) Architect of Burmese independence

Aung San Suu Kyi (b. 1945–) So named by her mother to remember her illustrious father; this is not normal Burmese usage

Khin Nyunt (1939–) Lt. General, Prime Minister, under house arrest (2004–2012)

Maung Aye (1937–) Deputy Senior General

Maung Maung, Dr. (1924–1994) President, August–September 1988

Ne Win (1920–2002) Generalissimo. Variously, President, Chair BSPP, Prime Minister, Minister of Defense

Nu (1907–1995) Former Prime Minister

Nyun Tun (1954–) Commander-in Chief, Navy, 2008–1012; Vice President, 2012–

Saw Maung (1928–1997) Senior General, Chair SLORC 1988–1992

Sein Lwin (1924–2004) General, President, July–August 1988

Than Shwe (1933–) Senior General, Chair SLORC/SPDC 1992–2011

Thein Sein (1945–) General, Prime Minister, 2007–2011; President, 2011–

Tin Aung Myint Oo (1950–), General, Vice President 2011–2012

## Names and Terms

Many countries have changed their names (Siam–Thailand, Ceylon–Sri Lanka, etc.), but none has caused as many problems as the Burma–Myanmar split, which has unfortunately become the surrogate indicator of political persuasion. In July 1989, the military junta changed the name of the state to the Union of Myanmar, from the Union of Burma. Myanmar was the official written designation and an old usage, and this change was insisted on by the military to lessen (in its view) ethnic problems. The military has assiduously used *Myanmar* for all periods of Burmese history and does not use *Burma*, *Burmese* (as an adjective, for the language, or for a citizen), or *Burman* (the majority ethnic group, the military uses *Bamah*). This has not been accepted by the political opposition, and although the United Nations and most states have accepted the change, the United States did not, in solidarity with the opposition. The Burmese government sees this as insulting.

In this volume, both *Burma* and *Myanmar* are used—*Myanmar* for the period since 1988 (the start of the military government) and *Burma* for all previous periods, and Burma/Myanmar is used to indicate continuity of action. *Burman* is used for members of the majority ethnic group; *Burmese* is employed here as a designation of all citizens of that country of whatever ethnicity or linguistic predilection, as the official language of the state, and as an adjective. This usage should not be construed as a political statement. Place names are generally selected in accordance with traditional usage. The name of the state has evolved: The Union of Burma, The Socialist Union of Burma, The Union of Myanmar, and, as of March 30, 2011, the Republic of the Union of Myanmar.

Other names have been changed. The older form will be used in the text because of enhanced familiarity, but some of the revised spellings are listed here.

| Older Form | Newer Form |
| --- | --- |
| Akyab | Sittwe (City) |
| Arakan | Rakhine (State) |
| Chindwin | Chindwinn (River) |
| Irrawaddy | Ayeyarwady (Division/Region and River) |
| Karen | Kayin (State, ethnic group) |

Magwe         Magway (Division/Region)
Maymyo        Pyin-U-Lwin (City)
Mergui        Myeik (City, Archipelago)
Moulmein      Mawlamyine (City)
Pagan         Bagan (Old Capital)
Pegu          Bago (City and Division/Region)
Prome         Pyay (City)
Rangoon       Yangon (City)
Salween       Thanlwin (River)
Tenasserim    Tanintharyi (Division/Region)

**Acronyms**

AFPFL         Anti-Fascist People's Freedom League
              (1948–1958)

ASEAN         Association of Southeast Asian Nations

BCP           Burma Communist Party ("White Flags"—
              or CPB, Communist Party of Burma. In
              some volumes, CPB is used for "Red Flag"
              communists)

BSPP          Burma Socialist Programme Party
              (1962–1988)

KMT           Kuomintang, Chinese Nationalist
              Government

MEC           Myanmar Economic Corporation (a
              military-controlled conglomerate)

MEHC          Myanmar Economic Holdings
              Corporation (a military-controlled
              conglomerate)

NCGUB         National Coalition Government of the
              Union of Burma (founded in December
              1990)

NCUB          National Coalition of the Union of Burma
              (founded in 1992)

NLD           National League for Democracy

SLORC         State Law and Order Restoration Council
              (1988–1997)

SPDC          State Peace and Development Council
              (1997–)

| USDA | Union Solidarity and Development Association. Spawned Union Solidarity and Development Party (USDP) |

**Burmese Words**

| *Ana* | coercive power |
| *A-na-de* | of not wanting to embarrass or cause difficulty for another person |
| *Awza* | influential power, charisma |
| *Hpoun* | (also *pon, hpon*) glory, a type of power |
| *Karma (Kamma)* | retribution for good or ill for past actions in previous reincarnations |
| *Nat* | animate spirit; often of a person who has died a violent and untimely ("unripe") death |
| *Sangha* | Buddhist monkhood |
| *Tatmadaw* | Burmese armed forces |

## Currency

The kyat (K.), on independence in 1948, was equal to the Indian rupee. It is divided into 100 pya, but inflation has eliminated their use. The official exchange rate has been K.5.8–6.8 to the U.S. dollar (based on an International Monetary Fund basket of currencies). This was used only in certain government calculations. There are also other exchange rates for foreign trade, official conversions, and so on. The unofficial rate has varied, but in the summer of 2009 was about K.1,000 = US$1. There are also foreign exchange certificates supposedly at a par to the U.S. dollar but slightly discounted at about K.950 in April 2009. In the spring of 2012, the government changed the official exchange rate and "floated" the currency at about K820=US$1.00. In the summer of 2012, the rate was approximately K.870=US$1.00.

## Administration

Myanmar is divided into seven divisions (provinces, but called regions in the 2008 constitution) and seven states (also provinces), the former indicating essentially Burman ethnic areas, and the latter minority regions. There are a multitude of ethnic and linguistic groups, subdivided into various dialects. The Burmese call them "races," which is a translation of the Burmese *lu myo* (lit. "people type"), which can mean ethnicity, people, race, or nationality. The government maintains there are 135 such groups.

Under the constitution, in 2010, and in addition to the seven states and seven regions, there are also six ethnic enclaves that will have some modest degree of self-governance. The "self-administered [ethnic] zones" are Naga, Danu, PaO, Palaung, Kokang, and a "self-administered division" for the Wa. The boundaries are not ethnically delineated. There are 65,148 villages in 13,742 village groups, 63 districts, and 324 townships.

## Ethnic Groups

| Indigenous | (% of population, 1983 official figures) |
|---|---|
| Burman (Bamah) | 69.0 |
| Shan | 8.5 |
| Karen (Kayin) | 6.2 |
| Kayah | 0.4 |
| Chin | 2.2 |
| Kachin | 1.4 |
| Mon | 2.4 |
| Arakanese (Rakhine) | 4.5 |

These figures are subject to dispute. There are a variety of other important minorities, such as the Naga, Wa, Palaung, and so on, who are not separately calculated in the 1983 census. The Rohingya in the Rakhine State near the Bangladesh border are considered stateless. The following table indicates the foreign ethnic groups resident in Burma/Myanmar (from the 1983 census).

| Chinese | 233,470 |
|---|---|
| Indian | 428,428 |

Pakistani              42,140
Bangladeshi            567,985

A new census is planned in 2013 with UN technical assistance.


## Population

Estimated in 2008, Burma has a population of 53 million. Other figures range from 47 to 58 million. In preparation for the referendum on the constitution in 2008, the official figure was 57,504,368. But this is likely to be spurious specificity.

Rangoon population is estimated to be 5 million, Mandalay 1.3 million, and Moulmein, 600,000.


## Other Statistics

The gross domestic product per capita in 2006 (at the free market rate of exchange) was variously calculated at US$210 to US$300, at purchasing power parity in 2010 about US$426.

Myanmar's official exports in 2007/2008 (the Burmese fiscal year begins April 1) were US$6.043 billion, of which natural gas was US$2.590 billion, agricultural products US$1.140 billion, gems and jewelry US$647 million, forest products US$578 million, and fisheries US$366 million. Due to extensive smuggling, both import and export figures are likely to be grossly underestimated. National debt was US$7.176 billion (December 2008). Real GDP growth rates were 0.9 percent in 2008 and 0.3 percent anticipated for 2009. The nominal GDP was US$26,488 million in 2009.

Buddhist monasteries in 2008 number over 56,839, monks over eighteen years of age over 246,000, novices over 300,000, and nuns over 43,000.

In 1988, there were purportedly 66,000 insurgent troops.

## 2<sup>ND</sup> Edition
## Other Statistics

The gross domestic product per capita in 2011 at purchasing power parity was US$1,300, or about US$850, below every country in Southeast Asia. The nominal GDP in 2012 was US$46,050 million, and GDP growth rates were 5.0 percent in 2012 and 5.4 percent anticipated for 2013. Approximately 32.7 percent of the population in 2007 lived below the poverty line.

Myanmar's official exports in 2011/2012 (the Burmese fiscal year begins April 1) were US$8.255 billion, and imports were US$7.481 billion. Principal exports are natural gas, agricultural products, gems and jewelry, forest products, and fisheries. Due to extensive smuggling, both import and export figures are likely to be grossly underestimated. Inflation in 2012 was 9.7 percent. Foreign exchange reserves in 2011 were US$3.9 billion, and foreign debt in 2011 US$5.8 billion.

Buddhist monasteries in 2008 numbered over 56,839, monks over eighteen years of age over246, 000, novices over 300,000, and nuns over 43,000.

There are said to be over 50,000 insurgent troops in Myanmar.

## A Note to the Statistically
## and Policy Perplexed

"Data are very unreliable. Facts are negotiated more than they are observed in Myanmar." There are no notes in this volume, as specified by the publisher, but this does not indicate a lack of sources. Although the interpretation and conclusions are those of the author alone, the statistical bases for these opinions may be found in a variety of official and unofficial documents. Statistics, however, are often imprecise or manipulated, caused by internal political considerations or insufficient data, and biased externally by a lack of access to materials. Some opinions stated are from residents of Myanmar, who for obvious reasons must remain anonymous. For additional material, the reader is referred to the Suggested Reading section.

# Geography

Burma/Myanmar is the largest of the mainland Southeast Asian states (261,970 square miles, 678,500 square kilometers), about the size of Texas. It is the fortieth largest country in the world. Burma/Myanmar is some 1,275 miles long from its northernmost mountainous region near the Tibetan border to the mangrove swamps on the Bay of Bengal at the Thailand border. From its eastern extreme on the Mekong River bordering Laos to the Bangladesh border on the west, it is some 582 miles wide. It has a littoral on the Bay of Bengal of 1,199 miles. Its highest point is a mountain on the China/Tibetan border (19,295 feet). The border with China alone is 1,358 miles, that with Thailand 1,314 miles, India 857 miles, Bangladesh 152 miles, and Laos 125 miles.

If we think of Burma/Myanmar in ethnic terms, around a central geographic core of lowlands inhabited by the majority Burmans, two-thirds of the population, there is a horseshoe of highland areas inhabited by minority peoples who also live across the frontiers in adjacent states. Starting from the southwest, they are the Muslim Rohingya, the Chin, the Naga, the Kachin, the Wa, the Shan, the PaO, the Kayah, the Karen, and the Mon. There are many more groups. The government claims 135 such entities (the Chin alone are said to have 53 groups), but this is a calculation from the 1931 colonial census that counted ethnicity, language, and dialect in an obscure methodology.

Major rivers flow north to south, the most important of which is the Irrawaddy, navigable from Bhamo, about sixty miles from the China border to the Bay of Bengal. The Chindwin River feeds into the Irrawaddy from the west in central Burma and is also navigable. The Sittang River is of smaller size; the majestic Salween River's headwaters are in southwest

China in the Tibetan plateau. It bifurcates the Shan State, and empties into the Gulf of Martaban, part of the Bay of Bengal.

## Repetition

I assume that readers will not read this book through as they would a novel (although the charge of fiction in the absence of reliable data is an interesting one, and happy endings are lacking). There is considerable planned repetition of information so that readers who look up a question of interest in the table of contents do not need to scour a set of other related questions in order to receive a reasonable answer.

# INTRODUCTION

This introduction was written and the first edition published prior to the inauguration of the new government on March 30, 2011. From the inaugural speech of the new president, former general and former prime minister U Thein Sein on that day, a series of reforms have been initiated that promise extensive progress. The mood of the society has shifted with a degree of openness not seen in Burma/Myanmar in half a century. This new edition, written in February 2013, attempts to capture that change and the hopes that have thus been engendered.

* * *

They know the foreign visitor is discreet and is not a reporter looking for sensational comments. He will not quote, and thus endanger, anyone. In Rangoon (Yangon) or even up-country, one must be cautious in talking with people about the current situation in Myanmar. Often in such conversations there seems to be a type of quiet, almost silent, understanding that there will not be requests for anything mundane or anything explicit. Yet one senses a longing for an optimistic future, some kind words indicating that the outside world understands and has not forgotten those innocents caught in the Myanmar miasma. Often, a tentative question is asked: can you give us some hope? Not a solution, not manna rained down, but the simple feeling that things may get better...sometime.

It is sad and also embarrassing to admit honestly that one cannot offer an early way out of the present set of crises. Humanitarian assistance should be provided for the neediest, of course, but this is not a solution. It is only an amelioration, no matter how badly it is needed for those endangered. Advocating that people rise up to the barricades—asking others to expose themselves and their families to harm when, as a foreigner, one is physically removed—is morally unacceptable and in any event foreign involvement would undermine the legitimacy of the cause in which they believe. On the other hand, exhorting isolation exacerbates the very issues one would like to overcome, and plunging in with support to the regime retards positive change. Even external analyses have had little immediate effect.

That change will come—is coming—seems evident. In less than a year a "Saffron Revolution" (that was neither saffron in color nor a revolution in politics, but so named analogous to other "colored" demonstrations elsewhere) started and was destroyed; a new but flawed constitution was approved in a pseudo-referendum; the greatest natural disaster ever to befall Burma/Myanmar in historic times occurred; and elections are in the offing. This is certainly not progress, but the forces that will be unleashed, including an invigorated civil society, and their effects will move Myanmar, perhaps in unknown ways, and will affect international relations and attitudes.

But whatever progress is made will be by the Burmese peoples themselves in a manner that is acceptable to them, rather than externally imposed. Foreign formulae, even when they may be well intentioned, are largely extraneous. The unique history of Burma/Myanmar, as outlined in this short volume, calls for unique solutions to rather common international problems that many states share, although those in Myanmar are exacerbated. The facts connected with these crises may be soundly articulated abroad, their historical antecedents evident, but solutions will come from within. Years ago, when something was to be done, the cry was, "Do it *bama-lo*," in the

Burmese manner. The government surely would approve of the sentiment much as they would disapprove of the language, decreeing that what was needed must be done *"Myanmar-lo,"* in the Myanmar manner.

Either way, the outside world can sympathize with the plight of the peoples, can provide some emergency humanitarian assistance, can attempt to convince the authorities of the need for progress and humanity, can reiterate and call for adherence to the kingly governmental virtues of the Buddhist canon, and can invoke the Buddhist concept that change is inevitable.

Within that construct, the external world can educate itself to the complexities that are Burma/Myanmar and some possible avenues for alleviating its problems. So when the time comes, as it surely will, outside communities will be able to appreciate the nuanced issues and step forward with the sensitivity necessary to help intelligently, in contrast to many less effective responses of the past. We on the periphery should minimally follow the physicians' code: do no harm.

This volume is a small effort in that direction.

This introduction was written and the first edition published prior to the inauguration of the new government on March 30, 2011. From the inaugural speech of the new president, former general and former prime minister U Thein Sein on that day, a series of reforms have been initiated that promise extensive progress. The mood of the society has shifted with a degree of openness not seen in Burma/Myanmar in half a century. This new edition attempts to capture that change and the hopes that have thus been engendered.

# BURMA/MYANMAR

## WHAT EVERYONE NEEDS TO KNOW

# 1

# THE CRISES THAT ARE BURMA/MYANMAR

This chapter and those that follow, all written before the change in government based on the elections in November 2010, are left intact to encourage the reader to reflect on how the state was perceived both by its inhabitants and external observers at that time. The final chapter will discuss the changes that have occurred, and how these changes have affected views toward the state and its leadership, and how the future may evolve under a new, partly elected regime even if reminiscent in part of the old.

## What is Burma?

Burma/Myanmar is, after North Korea, probably the most obscure and obscured state in the contemporary world. It seems to appear on the world stage only in moments of crisis, but its problems are both enduring and tragic. Its future influence will be significant. Its strategic importance, natural resources, size, location, potential, and even its attempts to encourage tourism and foreign investment should have made it better known, but Westerners are only vaguely aware of it. It is on many powers' policy agendas, yet never in the top tier. It has been called in the United States a "boutique issue." Concerns over its autocratic military government and the plight of its peoples are widespread, yet there is no international consensus on how to approach and relate to Myanmar. Indeed, there are stark differences. This modest volume attempts to explain the reasons the world should be interested in that state and the many, often subtle factors that have positively or negatively affected both its internal affairs and foreign responses to them. Rudyard Kipling presciently wrote, "This is Burma, and it will be quite unlike any land you know about."

### Why are we interested in Burma/Myanmar?

Burma is an anomaly. There are probably more people today outside that state who know the name of one famous Burmese than who know the new name of the country in which she lives, even though they may not be able to pronounce either correctly. The continuing house arrest of Nobel Peace Prize laureate Aung San Suu Kyi in Myanmar, formerly known as Burma, has generated both concern and admiration for her throughout the world. For many abroad, she has come to personify the Burmese crisis: its need, so long delayed, for human rights, democracy, and economic development. Concern for her is compounded by perceptions of her vulnerability and protection for her safety.

World concern has also focused both on the failed Saffron Revolution—the demonstrations by Buddhist monks in the fall of 2007 that were brutally suppressed—and the tragedy of the May 2008 Cyclone Nargis, which killed about 138,000 people with over 190-km winds and a 3.5-meter tidal surge in the Irrawaddy Delta area of the country. Over 2.5 million people were affected, and many lost their homes. These countless immediate personal tragedies impinge on our consciousness. But we should not only consider the longer-term decline in standards of living among the afflicted, many already suffering from malnutrition and disease. The affected Irrawaddy Delta region is the rice bowl of the state. It produced 65 percent of the state's rice, 50 percent of its poultry, and 40 percent of its pigs. The cyclone's impact has spread far beyond its immediate range.

These issues, with such stark statistics, are pressing and acute, but focusing on them alone offers only limited analytical insights into that country. Burma/Myanmar presents many more complexities, challenges, and crises, some of which have greater worldwide significance than is first apparent. Its problems are difficult to ameliorate or solve. We would do well to be attentive to that little-known state, for its history, geographic setting, diverse social systems, cultures, and influence extend far beyond its frontiers; its regional and global relations influence the present. It will likely affect the future in even greater measure, for it is positioned at the nexus of potential China–India power rivalry.

### Why should we be interested in Burma/Myanmar?

As valid as our immediate concerns about Myanmar may be, a far broader range of issues should prompt our interest in that unfortunate land. We have been more concerned about political repression's impact on human rights than human rights issues arising from endemic poverty, yet the latter is equally important. Myanmar is currently one of the poorest states in the world. Humanitarian assistance is needed not just to alleviate poverty or assist cyclone victims but to deal with the entire decaying social infrastructure: health, education, agriculture, and nutritional services, especially for infants and the very young. High infant mortality rates and malnutrition deny a future for a burgeoning population of over 50 million diverse peoples who a half-century ago were predicted by many to become the wealthiest and most developed in Southeast Asia.

Myanmar's tragic present is not confined within its borders but spills over its frontiers and littoral to neighboring states that have attracted the downtrodden: refugees, the minority poor, dissidents, and others who feel they no longer can face political, economic, or conflict conditions at home. Some bring with them diseases, such as malaria, tuberculosis, and HIV/AIDS. Some are exploited for economic or sexual reasons. Some become involved in international criminal activities, such as the narcotics trade, and many sell their labor for jobs that neighboring populations consider demeaning. The Myanmar administration seems to be unwilling to address or perhaps incompetent to solve these issues. Adjacent states, especially Thailand and Bangladesh, are consequently under stress in dealing with these problems and peoples. Regional concerns thus mount.

Myanmar is also geographically strategic. Sandwiched between the great and growing cultural, economic, and military powers of China and India, and contiguous with U.S. ally Thailand, Burma/Myanmar's numerous indigenous minorities spill over into these and other countries. Former Prime Minister U Nu once said, "We are hemmed in like a tender gourd among the cactus." Historically, Myanmar's internal Chinese and Indian (those from the subcontinent) minorities have been economically powerful, creating tensions and antagonisms with the majority Burmans. Burma's neighbors have both sought to influence it and to gain access to its natural resources. As a consequence, Myanmar has become an important element of regional power rivalry—the nexus on the Bay of Bengal. China has penetrated deeply into it, which in turn has prompted India to shift policies. Myanmar also remains a major concern to Thailand and ASEAN (Association of Southeast Asian Nations—the ten countries of the region). The country is a central actor in the region, and both its resources and support are coveted by neighboring nations even as its policies are condemned from a distance. As one eminent Southeast Asian said of Myanmar relations, those states around Myanmar have "the burden of proximity," whereas those farther afield have the "luxury of distance."

This role is not simply regional. Myanmar connects to the western approaches of the most strategic natural waterway in the world—the Malacca Straits. This is the critical strategic and commercial link between the Middle East and East Asia, which depends on Middle Eastern oil reserves. It is the strategic supply route west between the military bases of the United States in the Pacific and its Middle Eastern bases, such as Diego Garcia, in the Indian Ocean. It is the trade route east for India. Its impact is also important for such states as Japan, which regards China as a potential rival. Bypassing the Malacca Straits and shipping oil and gas directly through Myanmar to southwestern China—a significant Chinese policy objective—is seen by Japan as inimical to its national interests.

Since July 1997, Myanmar has been a member of ASEAN. Myanmar's politics have proven to be something of an embarrassment to the other member states, although none have had immaculate political histories or spotless democratic reputations. Its influence extends beyond that critical regional body, however. Through the ASEAN Regional Form (ARF), ASEAN has relationships with the European Union, Japan, China, the United States, Australia, New Zealand, and other countries. Whatever these states may think of Myanmar, they are linked to it through ASEAN's umbrella.

We should also be interested in Burma/Myanmar because of its thousand-year history as an important realm in the region. Powerful kings expanded the state from its core in what is now central Burma to incorporate the frontier regions that are now part of Burma/Myanmar. They were also aggressive against all neighbors. Neither the Thai nor the Burmese have forgotten that in 1767 (and in 1564 and 1569) the Burmese destroyed the Thai capital of Ayutthaya, which is still the name for Thailand in Burmese, and controlled parts of what is now northern Thailand for decades. A classical Burmese dance is still called by that name, and the Thai continue to make movies about their valiant defenses against the invading Burmese. After conquering Burma in World War II, the Japanese gave Thailand areas of Burma's Shan State, which were returned after the war. The Burmese view with deep concern the Thai and American annual joint military exercises called Cobra Gold, which some Burmese believe is a prelude to armed intervention, and deplore America's virulent anti-Burmese junta rhetoric. Burmese officials view Thailand, which has a security treaty relationship with the United States, as its surrogate.

On its western frontier, Burma also invaded Manipur and East Bengal, leading to the first of three Anglo-Burmese Wars (1824–1826, 1852, 1885) and a long, bloody period of pacification. Incorporated into the British Empire as a province of India until 1937, Burma was governed on an inappropriate Indian model with dire consequences. It declared its independence on January 4, 1948, following India and Pakistan.

Burma's border regions, which have been porous and ethnically arbitrarily determined since the colonial era, have weakened the central state's authority and compounded its problem of legitimacy. Mark Twain is famously supposed to have said that if history does not repeat itself, it often rhymes. The Bangladesh border arbitrarily splits a Muslim population, and Burmese military actions have forced two massive migrations in the past thirty years. Northeast Indian Naga rebels, as well as those from a variety of other ethnic groups in that poor region, have sought refuge in Myanmar; eliminating this threat was a factor in changed India–Myanmar relations. Historical memories in any case are long, and sometimes bitter.

Burma has extensive, underutilized natural resources, including oil, gas, teak, gems such as rubies, jade, copper, and a variety of metals and minerals as well as hydroelectric potential that are coveted regionally and internationally.

Burma has also a rich cultural heritage—remarkable art and architecture that was influenced by, but also affected, the region. Its experience with Buddhism, too often overlooked in the concentration on more accessible states in the region, may offer insights into its roles in Southeast Asia and Sri Lanka. Burmese Buddhist shrines attract devout pilgrims from Asia and beyond; World War II graves still prompt visits of relatives and descendants of those fallen—both Japanese and Allies.

### What can we learn from Burma/Myanmar?

Burma/Myanmar is unique and not easily comparable to other states. Its historical experiences preclude simplistic transference of its lessons abroad. It presents an array of issues that, considered in comparative focus, may help us understand not only Burma/Myanmar but other states that face a set of similar (albeit not identical) dilemmas. Indeed, it has much to teach us about intractable social and political problems throughout the world. Such inquiries may also contribute to our theoretical understanding of a number of those conundrums that bedevil other states. Internal conditions in Myanmar as well as foreign responses to them may provide lessons about the efficacy of such approaches in and to other countries.

Burma/Myanmar features many of the problems facing multicultural states and raises a basic question: how might societies with disparate ethnic and linguistic groups achieve national integration without destroying local cultures—creating nations and not just states? Should there be a uniform state school curriculum in the national language, or can other local languages be taught, and if so, at what levels? Civil–military relations are also an issue in many developing states, and in Burma the Burmese military has retained effective power since 1962—certainly one of the longest such reigns in the modern era. Political and social pluralism is important in many societies, and Myanmar may offer lessons on the effect of the presence or absence of various components of civil society on its people and the political process. We could draw from Burma's sad experience with economic development how better to encourage equitable and sustained growth that spreads across a diverse population. The military's opening to foreign investment and the expansion of the local private sector have not met economic expectations, and one might ask how rent-seeking and corruption affected the attempt to reform a rigid socialist system.

We should question how international and indigenous political legitimacy symbols and attitudes may differ and may be perceived, and what effect these views have on both internal and external state actors. What does it take in Myanmar for a government to be considered legitimate by its various peoples and the international community?

We need to know what kinds of foreign policies toward Myanmar have proven to be effective or ineffective. International organizations can learn valuable human rights lessons from the Burmese situation that will help the international community—individual states, international institutions such as the United Nations or ASEAN, and international nongovernmental organizations—improve conditions there. The Myanmar case may help us understand whether the international community can effectively promote democracy, pluralism, and better governance elsewhere, and if so, over what period and to what extent.

Individual states and international institutions have employed an array of policy instruments. Sanctions, isolation, engagement, military, economic, and humanitarian assistance—all have been tried at various times by various organizations in recent years. Politics and influence groups within foreign states affect policies in dealing with Myanmar or other "difficult" states. Is Myanmar a "failed" state, a "weak" state, a "fragile" state, a "rogue" state, a "pariah" state, a "thuggish" state? These are terms used by foreign powers and institutions, but what do they mean, and what effect does their use have on Myanmar itself and on its relations with others?

The junta that rules Myanmar does not allow public analysis of its problems and is highly sensitive to alternative views. Orthodoxy is required; censorship of all publications and media, including imported books and journals, is ubiquitous. Many Burmese living abroad, including exiled intellectuals, are often under constraints because of citizenship worries or because families are still within the country. To criticize the regime or veer from the approved dogma could bring trauma or jail. In addition, few Burmese, foreign scholars, or policy makers outside of that country can afford to invest the time and finances to study that unique set of cultures. Jobs are scarce, remuneration meager, interest limited, and any but individual psychological rewards are minimal. So Myanmar is often considered an enigma. *Inscrutable* used to be the term applied by the West to societies that were culturally different, but the word really reflected our own unwillingness to try to comprehend the actual conditions abroad.

## Why is learning about Burma/Myanmar so difficult?

Should one have the temerity to try and study this fascinating land and its peoples and cast inscrutability to the dustbin of history, the obstacles are extensive. Myanmar is opaque in research terms. Access is limited except within a few nonpolitical fields. Some geographic sections of the state are off-limits. Although tourism has been officially encouraged by the government for over a decade, it is discouraged by the political opposition—the National League for Democracy and many foreign human rights groups. In 1988, Thailand had 100 times as many tourists as Burma; Nepal had 10 times as many. The media is rarely allowed in, and reporters that enter often do so under the guise of tourists. The bureaucracy is usually reluctant to assist scholars because any negative views they might later express abroad could have dire consequences for those who originally approved the research. Survey research, interviews, and fieldwork are carefully scrutinized, and those who cooperate with foreign researchers may be subject to harassment and/or interrogation. Telephones are tapped; scholars are sometimes followed.

Orthodoxy is required not only in the military government but among the opposition, the dissident expatriate Burmese community, and even in the corridors of many Western and Asian governments. Even the suggestion of alternative hypotheses or approaches becomes anathema. There is not only fear within Burma, whose citizens are subjected to pervasive intelligence surveillance, there is also palpable fear in expatriate communities where political heresies can result in social exclusion. Criticizing political icons becomes difficult at best.

Data are unreliable. Those who control its flow shape it to impress Myanmar's rulers. The result is akin to a Potemkin village designed to impress those at the top of the political ladder. Positive figures are often inflated, negative facts diminished, and unpleasant realities ignored. Some data are simply not available, more are unreliable. Much of Burmese society operates outside of the formal economy—some say most of it does so.

Other difficulties abound. For foreigners, Burmese names are an enigma. There are no surnames, so relations among even nuclear families requires highly specialized and personal knowledge because every family member has their own, different name. Many Burmese also have the same name (the initial syllable is dependent on the day of the week one was born), and foreign confusion abounds. Events take place based on astrological or numerical calculations that are incomprehensible to the outside world, although obviously not to the Burmese. The Burmese language (part of the Tibeto-Burman group) is difficult to learn. It has its own script and is unrelated to other major Southeast Asian languages. Learning it requires a great deal of time and a significant intellectual investment.

Even the name of the country is an enigma—and in the West, it has become a surrogate indicator of political persuasion. In July 1989, the ruling junta changed the name of the state from Burma to Myanmar, an older, written form dating back centuries, claiming that it was more ethnically inclusive and without colonial baggage. The United Nations and the world generally accepted that change, on which the military has assiduously insisted, using that name for periods and events dating back into Burmese history. The Burmese political opposition, and the United States and a few other states, did not do so and argued that this change was the product of an illegitimate military government. With nationalistic fervor and to rid themselves of a colonial taint, the military also changed the names of many cities (e.g., Rangoon to Yangon) to conform to Burmese spelling patterns, as well those of many rivers, place names, towns, and streets (see the Preliminary Notes section). Some 600 names have been changed.

## What are the crises facing Burma/Myanmar?

In spite of the difficulties of access and the unreliability of data, we need to use the tools we have to analyze the multiple crises in Burma and their contexts. Western-oriented conceptual models and limited comparative studies make this even more difficult. Studying Burma/Myanmar is often neither science nor social science, but more akin to art, where truth is in the eye of the beholder. Consequently, different interpretations abound. The myriad problems facing the state are so diverse that if asked to provide lists of the most challenging issues, different observers would point to different examples. Yet there would be no disagreement about the seriousness of the problems selected herein. Those listed are broad categories as seen through the eyes of one foreign observer who has experienced and watched that diverse society grow, stagnate, and deteriorate over some fifty years. These issues are enumerated in greater detail later in the text; they are included here to give the reader an impression of the breadth of the internal problems the leadership and the people face.

We concentrate on the internal problems facing the society. Those that are generated from abroad, such as questions of international acceptability, foreign relations, externally perceived legitimacy, and other issues, are considered separately.

The internal crises facing the state may be divided into a number of convenient and interpenetrated compartments for discussion. These are:

- A socioeconomic crisis. It has intensified with one-half the population below or at the poverty line (significantly, a line defined by the World Bank but not accepted by the Burmese government). Even primary schooling (most register but half drop out) is often too expensive for significant proportions of the population, health care is the second worst in the world, inflation eats into meager wages with 73 percent of income going for basic foods, and 35 percent of children under age five are malnourished to some degree. Landlessness has mushroomed, and internal debt exploded. Myanmar is one of the world's poorest countries. Per capita income is variously estimated to be about US$290 in 2008. Cyclone Nargis intensified the growing rich–poor gap. This is, in effect, a crisis in human security.

- A youth crisis. Social mobility is controlled by the military junta; jobs are scarce and unrewarding, many of significance are occupied by the military, and others are closely controlled or monitored. Many people desire higher education, but universities have been sometimes closed for long periods, and higher degree programs are said to be weak and are not internationally recognized. There is no correlation between a degree and a good job. Military control is ever present and constitutes a state within the state. A pervasive dissatisfaction and frustration have caused some 1 percent (an educated group) of the total population to escape Myanmar, either legally or surreptitiously, to foreign lands, their sense of hope for the future markedly diminished. This is, in effect, a long-term crisis of human capital that will negatively affect development.

- A crisis of the minorities, comprising one-third of the population. This is likely to be the most difficult and enduring issue facing any Burmese administration: how in some manner and degree acceptable to the diverse Burmese peoples are power and resources to be shared equitably and fairly in Burmese terms among the various ethnic groups of that state? Each ethnic group regards the protection of their individual languages, customs, cultures, and real or mythic histories as important to its identity. Significant portions of the major minority groups have been in active revolt against the Burman state at some time. Senior General Saw Maung estimated that a million people have been killed in the multitude of insurrections since independence. In eastern Myanmar alone, some 540,000 minority peoples have been displaced from their homes. The military has established some "free fire" zones. Some estimates calculate that Burma/Myanmar has experienced 236 "conflict years," or 40 percent of all those in Southeast Asia, and 30 percent of all conflict casualties. Many minority armies now have negotiated cease-fires, but some are still active and one, the Karen rebellion that started in 1949, is the longest in modern world history.

- A crisis of governance. There is an intractable political crisis, characterized externally and simplistically, as one between democracy and totalitarianism, between the military and civilian leadership. The world has focused its attention on Burma/Myanmar mostly because of this issue. The validity of elections (those of 1990 and those planned for 2010), a referendum, a new constitution, the promises for a roadmap to what the leadership calls a "discipline-flourishing democracy" have all become part of the search for a political solution to a generation-long political stalemate.

- A crisis of administrative competence. In spite of the regime's pride in extensive infrastructure construction that remains externally unrecognized, governance is enmeshed in a rigid hierarchy in which individual actions and initiatives are retarded by fear. Complicated by personal loyalties and entourages with resultant rent-seeking and corruption, initial bureaucratic inertia was aptly illustrated in the ineffective early response and management of the Cyclone Nargis crisis of 2008.

- An environmental crisis. The government and various cease-fire and present insurgent groups have unconscionably stripped the country of much of its unique teak forests and other hardwood resources. They have exploited its extensive mines without concern for pollution and have constructed (and planned) dozens of hydroelectric projects that dammed previously free rivers and forcibly evacuated thousands. More generally, the regime disregards modern environmental policies and guidelines.

- A crisis of fear that permeates society. The population fears the state's administrative control mechanisms and military power. The military administration itself fears and mistrusts foreigners and is anxious about a possible invasion that some foreign rhetoric seems to imply. Military disdain and mistrust extends to their own civilian citizens and ethnic minorities; they are concerned that a return to civilian rule would lead to the break-up of the state. Fear leads to official censorship and even self-inflicted restraint as a defense. Myanmar is listed as having one of the world's most controlled censorship regimes— 164th out of 168 countries.
- A private sector crisis. The state's 1988 reforms, the most ambitious since 1962, were to encourage the private sector through attracting foreign investment and spurring local industry and trade. It has, however, prompted widespread rent-seeking and corruption with meager results for the people, no matter how much the administration has benefited from exploitation of its natural gas and other reserves.
- A crisis of distribution. In 1988, the pauperized government that was on the cusp of the coup had only about US$30 million in foreign exchange reserves. In 2008, it had over US$3.1 billion but has not used these resources to improve the quality of life or standard of living of its diverse peoples.
- A crisis of internally perceived legitimacy. How the people of that state perceive the legitimacy of its administration is in question. Indigenous cultural-religious factors affect these views and their expectations of the state's obligation to deliver goods and services. Foreign influences and opinions on the nature of political legitimacy may also affect these internal perceptions, but among what groups beyond the internationally oriented elite and to what degree is uncertain.

The scope and complexity of the problems facing the state and its peoples are set forth here to allow a context to begin considering what factors have influenced the generation of these problems. We can start to analyze the causes and historical context of these questions; the various Burmese governments' attempts to cope with equity, growth, history, legitimacy, and international relations; and how the external world, in an age of globalization, has reacted to them.

To do this, we need to review historically the contemporary residual influences of four ages of Burmese history: the precolonial era of the monarchy (until 1885) in chapter 2, the colonial period (1885–1948) in chapter 3, the civilian government (1948–1962) in chapter 4, and military rule under the socialist government (1962–1988) in chapter 5. Each has had extensive impacts on current events (chapter 6), and each influenced and is reflected in the state's social and political structure (chapter 7) and will likely influence the future (chapter 8). Chapter 9 covers the events from the elections of November 2010, through the formation of the new government on March 30, 2011, to January 2013.

# 2

# IMPORTANT RESIDUES FROM THE PRECOLONIAL PERIOD

The Burmese look with increasing pride on their precolonial history. No group has more assiduously made contemporary use of the record of approximately 1,000 years of Burman hegemony of the region we now call Burma/Myanmar and some neighboring areas than the present State Law and Order Restoration Council (SLORC)/State Peace and Development Council (SPDC) military government. They have used the past to justify the present, even employing prehistory to support their nationalistic (sometimes chauvinistic) claims to legitimacy. Members of the military consider themselves custodians of national unity and sovereignty, denying to any other institution or group that claim. The regime believes, and have emphasized in their newly written histories, that they are in the direct line of the great Burman kings, military leaders who unified the state. Their larger-than-life statues dominate the parade grounds at their new capital Naypyitaw, their images enshrined in the massive Defense Services Museum in Yangon.

### How does Burmese history relate to contemporary events?

Citizens of Burma/Myanmar have ample justification for pride in the history of their country. The three major dynasties that have controlled what we know today as Myanmar have contributed much to world culture through sponsorship and support of Buddhist activities and knowledge, as well as art and architecture. They have also played important roles as expansionist rulers in the region.

Administrations around the world use and reinvent their national histories to explain, justify, and/or enhance their contemporary roles—their "imagined communities." The *tatmadaw* (Burmese armed forces) is no different, although they have to a major degree rarely seen elsewhere invoked the past and in part rewritten it to surround themselves with what they regard as an impermeable nationalistic mantle.

In the new capital of Naypyitaw (literally, the royal national site), some 240 miles north of Yangon and on the verge of the traditional Burman central region called the dry zone (in contrast to the coastal regions where rainfall is two to three times as heavy), there are three gigantic statues of Burmese warrior kings (each thirty-three feet tall) who unified the state by conquering local kingdoms and expanding Burmese military power to neighboring lands. Anawrahta (r. 1044–1077), Bayinnaung (r. 1551–1581), and Alaungpaya (r. 1752–1760) are the administration's heroes and by implication the precursors of the present regime, which is the fourth (in their view) protector and unifier of the state. Rumors abound that at least one Burmese general (Saw Maung, chair of the SLORC, 1988–1992) considered himself (or was considered by some of his underlings) the reincarnation of King Kyansittha (r. 1084–1113) and is said to have dressed in royal regalia and performed traditional regal rites.

The invocation of the past is not simply limited to recorded history. Prehistory has been used for the glorification of both the state and the leaders who have fostered such research and who may believe they have inherited this mantle. Under this administration, a site has been found that the leadership claims contains the world's oldest humanoid remains. Thus, today Myanmar becomes unique in human history, and indeed, its present leadership politically benefits from archeology and its sponsorship. Other, later prehistoric remains have been found that are claimed to indicate that Southeast Asian civilizations emanated from what is now Myanmar. Ironically, North Korea has similarly claimed the predominant role in early Northeast Asia by finding the "tomb" of the legendary founder of the Korean "race" in Pyongyang. Perhaps authoritarian regimes seek legitimacy in this prehistorical manner.

The return to the aura of the precolonial period is in part not only to overcome the shame of having been colonized but also to provide a direct link from the past and its glories to the present military, whose leadership is Burman. Significantly, one of General Ne Win's multiple marriages was to a descendant of the last Burmese king. It is also an indirect effort to demonstrate the unifying powers of the Burman majority over some minority groups that had significant kingships. The Mon Kingdom (1287–1757), centered on what is now Pegu (Bego), was Buddhist and had wealth that was noted by early European travelers to the region, until it was conquered by the Burmans. Another coastal region, the Arakan (Rakhine), had kingdoms subject to Indic influences that existed from about the ninth century until overcome by the Burmans in 1785. Burman hegemony extended over various tribal areas and smaller local states in the Shan region. Significantly, to enhance the past and thereby accrue legitimacy to the present, the regime has rebuilt the royal palaces in Mandalay, Pegu, and Shwebo, compromising authentic architectural styles for contemporary visual and metaphorical effects.

Conquest was not simply for booty. It was inherent in the concept of the world-conqueror Buddhist king (*cakkravatti*), sometimes considered an embryonic Buddha, who invaded not for land but to validate his universalistic religious status. Southeast Asia, however, was land-rich but population-poor. Monarchs forcibly relocated people, and slaves taken in conquest were needed to increase agricultural production, and thus state revenues, and to build and maintain the pagodas necessary for legitimacy. Regimes transported back to the Burman capital Buddhist symbols, from statues to white elephants to scriptures, providing physical evidence of the monarch's prowess and religiosity.

Wars and conquests were endemic. The modern concept of national boundaries that extend to a designated line did not exist before the Western conquests of the region; thus, control was contested. Rather, a *mandala* system of sovereignty was the norm, in which power radiated from the Burmese king, and indeed from the throne itself, in a series of concentric circles to almost indefinite distant regions. In those areas, local rulers might owe allegiance and pay tribute to the Burmese king and also to one or several nearby more powerful kingdoms and even to the Chinese emperor in Beijing. This was not considered illogical or inappropriate, but it did foster disputes.

The capital was the center of not only the state but the world, and the legitimacy of the king depended on his being in harmony with the cosmic order. This concept may sound anachronistic, but the attitude that control of the capital itself is crucial and that the capital is the symbolic center—Burmese dynasties often moved their capitals for both political and astrological reasons—may have played some role in the military movement to Naypyitaw in 2005 (see chapter 6).

### How did Burmese kings view governance and authority, and is this relevant today?

Even though the titles and technology changes may mask past practices, many traditional attitudes and predilections continue today, modified only in part. Under the veneer of modernity, there are remnants, as in most societies, of primordial or deeply embedded concepts and attitudes that still affect both the rulers and the expectations of many of those ruled.

Some scholars have cogently argued that since 1962 the military has in fact acted very much on the model of the Burmese kings. In many traditional societies, including Burma, power was conceived as finite. This is in contrast to modern administrative theory, in which power is viewed as essentially infinite, so that it can be shared or delegated to the potential advantage of all involved. This has not been the case in Burma/Myanmar, for to share power (from center to periphery, between leaders, etc.) results in automatic loss—a zero-sum game. In these circumstances, power becomes highly personalized. Loyalty thus becomes the prime necessity, resulting in entourages and a series of patron–client relationships. Those outside of this core group may therefore be considered potential adversaries—a "loyal opposition" thus becomes an oxymoron. The potential for diminution of one's power (*ana*, in Burmese) by sharing it results in information that is carefully guarded (in the modern era, censorship has been the result). Even sharing plans might diminish authority, as could a fixed system of succession, which did not develop. These tendencies continue in the modern era.

Administration was personally (not institutionally) determined. A trained, tested, and permanent bureaucracy never developed, as in China and Korea, resulting today in an administratively weak state unable to manage effectively a socialist economy.

The authority of the state (the kings or modern rulers) extended to economics as well. All wealth and power in the society were under his domain. Oil production, teak forests, and foreign trade were monopolies of the monarchy, so the introduction of tempered socialism on independence under a moderate civilian government and virulent socialism under the military after 1962 had historical precedents. They were also reactions to colonial and foreign control over the economy. Even under the SLORC/SPDC, which has espoused a free market system since 1988, the state has been extremely interventionist.

Monarchs had undifferentiated power. They combined executive and judicial functions, and in theory their rule and authority were absolute, although in practice these were mitigated by high-level Buddhist monks, who often were ministers. Modern leaders are said to have exhibited these same characteristics.

This traditional need for personally defined loyalty and entourages continues and is not confined to the military; it permeates groups on the right and left, public and private institutions, and among pro- and antigovernment organizations as well.

### What were Burma's relations with internal peoples, regions, and neighboring states?

Contemporary historians often claim that the early colonial histories inappropriately treated ethnicity as the salient feature of Burmese history. It is true that the British divided that province of India into Ministerial Burma, which was under direct British control and was largely Burman, and the Frontier Areas (earlier known as the Scheduled Areas), which were the home of many minorities and were more loosely governed. This was, in fact, the Indian model of British governance. Indeed, the *tatmadaw* (armed forces) has continuously claimed that the British instituted a policy of "divide and rule" among ethnic groups that resulted in today's mistrust among the Burmans and the minorities. The military has claimed that historically the ethnic mélange that is Burma/Myanmar lived together peacefully "in weal and woe," a peace disrupted by the evil colonialists. Both groups seem to have overstated their cases. Ethnicity did become a critical feature affecting British rule, as we demonstrate in the next chapter, but the contemporary animosities exhibited by the ethnic nationalities (called "races" by the Burmese) stem as much from Burman internal imperialism as from the colonial heritage.

As mentioned, Burman kings conquered and established monarchies within the territories that are now Burma/Myanmar. As they were internally expansive, they were also externally aggressive. Chinese–Burmese relations were (and continue to be) especially salient. The Yüan Dynasty (the Mongols) destroyed the Burmese capital at Pagan (Bagan) in 1287, but later Chinese invasions (there were four between

1765 and 1769) were defeated. In 1644, Ming Dynasty troops fleeing from the new Chinese Qing Dynasty tried to find refuge in Burma, as did Chinese Nationalist (Kuomintang, KMT) soldiers escaping from communist forces in 1949. Both times China eliminated the threat to their government. Some claim that Chinese southward population expansion stopped in Yunnan Province because the lower-lying border areas of what became Burma had a particularly virulent strain of malaria that especially affected the Chinese. Due to the mandala system of multiple sovereignties, the court in Mandalay paid tribute to Beijing. On the British annexation of upper Burma in 1885, the British agreed to continue to pay the Burmese tribute (such tribute was to have been taken by Burmese, not by the British), but never did so. One Burmese king has been known as "the king who fled from the Chinese," and today relations between the two states are exceptionally close. Some feel that the modern close Sino-Burmese relationship is in fact a variant on the traditional tribute system of states within the Sino-centric sphere of influence.

Thailand, however, has historically been the major rival of Burma. Some of these residual attitudes continue today, exacerbated by contemporary issues in spite of appropriate diplomatic relations. Aggressive Burmese kings continuously fought the Thai, until they destroyed the Thai capital Ayutthaya in 1767. Minority groups occupy both sides of the ethnically ill-defined border. The Shan people in Burma's Shan State are ethnic and linguistic cousins of the Thai. Many from these groups, some of whom have been in revolt against the central Burmese authorities, have sought refuge in Thailand from Burmese military action. These rebels have been used by the Thai to insulate the conservative Bangkok regime from the "radical" Burmese. Thai attempts to foster buffer zones (essentially ethnic rebel areas) were unstated policy until 1988. These traditional animosities have been ameliorated by more recent regimes in Thailand, but relations can again deteriorate into regional conflict over border disputes, as they did in 2002.

Narcotics produced in Burma/Myanmar have been a major thorn in bilateral relationships. Opium, which is refined into morphine and heroin, was produced in the hill areas of the Shan State and transferred abroad, largely through Thailand. Although opium production is now very limited and has been replaced by production in Afghanistan, a new surge is likely due to a lack of markets for alternative crops. The newer scourge of Burmese-produced methamphetamines has become a major political issue in Thailand. In spite of these negative factors, in the twenty-first century Thailand officially became Myanmar's largest trading partner and largest foreign investor.

It is significant that today the junta regards the border with Bangladesh (formerly East Pakistan) as its most vulnerable frontier. Burmese expansion in the early nineteenth century into what was then East Bengal and fears of a Burmese conquest of Dhaka and even Calcutta led to the First Anglo-Burmese War (1824–1826) and the British seizure as reparations of two coastal areas of Burma–Arakan to the west and Tenasserim to the east. The Burmese also conquered the kingdom of Manipur on its western flank, threatening the British position in Assam, but the coastal area was of greatest concern. Because western Arakan and the Bangladesh border are both heavily Muslim and culturally related, populations have mixed and moved across these traditionally undefined frontiers. The Burmese do not recognize the citizenship of these people, who call themselves Rohingyas and are in effect an unrecognized cultural minority. The result is that the Rohingyas in Myanmar are stateless today. In January 2009, the Burmese government denied that Rohingyas who were attempting to flee Myanmar to Malaysia by sea were a "national race," and referred to them as Bengalis.

After the Indo-Pakistani war that led to Bangladesh's independence, in 1978 over 200,000 fled across the frontier to escape Burmese police and military raids. Although repatriated by the United Nations, a similar exodus took place in 1991–1992, when 250,000 fled. Some 15,000 or so remain in camps in Bangladesh.

As the minorities straddle the Thai frontier to the east, the Muslims, the Chin, and Naga peoples to the west and north of the Burmese border also inhabit the Indian frontier regions, as do the Kachin of northern Burma/Myanmar and Yunnan Province in China.

Early Burmese kingdoms had contacts with the Portuguese and the Dutch, as well as the British. Their colonial period will be covered in more detail shortly, but the lure of China trade as well as fears that the Burmese court was making overtures to the French, who were also interested in the Yunnan trade through their conquest of Vietnam, finally led the British to end the Burmese monarchy in the Third Anglo-Burmese War of 1885.

The ethnic complexities that are endemic along the frontiers of Burma/Myanmar have played critical roles in monarchical and colonial Burmese history; their influence has also been important in contemporary Myanmar.

### What was the role of Buddhism in traditional Burma?

There is no other single institution in classical Burma more important than Buddhism of the Theravada (or Hinayana) school. Buddhism is the most central of all the primordial values that define a Burman (and some of the minorities as well, such as the Shan and the Mon). The latter strongly influenced the Burmans and the Burmans adopted much Buddhist influence from them. Built onto an indigenous animist base that is still vital and alive, Buddhism permeates the government and peoples' lives and values. Buddhism in the classical period defined political legitimacy, and every king tried to regulate the *sangha* (monkhood), purify practices, reform various sects and scriptures, and build pagodas. At Pagan alone, there are several thousand pagodas, many still in use and some of massive proportions and architectural importance and beauty. The classical prestige of the *sangha* continues into the contemporary period.

The monarch was the patron of the faith, and his close entourage and advisers were often composed of senior monks, for entrance and exit from the ecclesiastical order was easily accepted. The *sangha* influenced the monarchs and tempered their reigns, for the just ruler was defined by Buddhist principles. The king ruled because he was morally superior to the people by virtue of his karma. But the monarch had an obligation to help improve the livelihood of his subjects so that they in turn could improve their karmas. Order was a singular need in the society, but too strong or repressive an order could result in the rise of a usurper, who, if he succeeded, then had a better karma.

The monks had an even greater role. They educated the populace, and all schools in the precolonial period were in Buddhist monasteries. To be devout was to be literate and be able to read scriptures. Early British observers claimed that Burma was the most literate state between Suez and Japan, and one British traveler in the early nineteenth century believed that Burmese women had a higher percentage of literacy than British women.

The British, to avoid charges of favoring Buddhism and to open avenues for Christian missionaries, eliminated the position of the most senior monk, the *thathanabaing*, thus in essence demoting and denigrating Buddhism by depriving it of its administrative cohesion. The introduction of secular education further undercut Buddhist influence. Instead of being destroyed by these actions, however, Buddhism became the surrogate indicator of Burmese nationalism when political activity was banned by the British, and monks were martyrs to the nationalist movement and often led it.

The relevance of Buddhism to beliefs and legitimacy in the postcolonial period is still central and permeates Burman society. In the civilian period (1948–1958, 1960–1962), U Nu employed Buddhism for political purposes, making it the state religion following the elections of 1960. Today, in virtually every edition of the controlled Burmese press, the military is pictured as attending to Buddhist needs and customs. Even though the *sangha* lacks the taut administrative structure of the *tatmadaw*, it is the only institution in the country that rivals the *tatmadaw* in size, influence, and national presence. The opposition has also illustrated its religiosity, both in the failed Saffron Revolution of young Buddhist monks in 2007 and also in the public actions of Aung San Suu Kyi when she has been allowed out of house arrest. Under modernization in contemporary Myanmar, how much the Buddhist concept of karma—that the status of individuals reflects their past good or evil actions— makes a Buddhist society more tolerant of poor leadership is unknown.

# 3

# THE COLONIAL ERA'S IMPORTANCE IN UNDERSTANDING BURMA/MYANMAR TODAY

The colonial period lasted a relatively short time in its domination of the whole country—only from 1885 to 1948. Its impact, however, has been of far greater significance than one might expect from only two generations of foreign rule, the shortest of the colonial experiences in Southeast Asia. (The French were in Laos from 1893 to 1954.) This significance lies elsewhere than in the ostensible modern institutions that continued after the end of colonialism. Rather, traditional patterns of power have become reestablished in spite of the new institutions of authority evolving from the colonial domination and contemporary international politico-economic trends. Many of these new forms of governance operate in part within traditional patterns of authority. The most profound impact of colonial rule is not simply found in these new institutions (legislatures, voting, constitutions, the judiciary, the bureaucracy, etc.) but in the strong nationalist reaction to that era and its foreign domination. This profoundly and emotionally influences contemporary Burma/Myanmar, and indeed, may be said virtually to confine the administration of that state within emotional anticolonial strictures.

*What led to the three Anglo-Burman wars of the nineteenth century?*

The three Anglo-Burmese wars (1824–1826, 1852, and 1885) resulted from Burmese westward expansionist moves into

British-administered East Bengal and Manipur (1824–1826); greed—access to the natural resources of Burma proper and commercial disputes (1852); and French influence and potential economic expansion—if not direct colonization—of Upper Burma and control over the potentially lucrative trade with China through Yunnan Province (1885).

The British and the East India Company's presence in Dhaka and even Calcutta was perceived by the British to be threatened by an expansive Burman empire that only a generation earlier had taken over the kingdom of Arakan, bordering on East Bengal. The Burmese had also conquered Manipur. Profound cultural differences also made meaningful negotiations difficult. The most publicized was the footwear issue. The British refused to take off their shoes in the palace and in pagodas, thus insulting the cosmological order (the palace as Mount Meru—the center of the world) and the primordial value of Burman society—Buddhism. Regulations for removing footwear in Burma/Myanmar are today the most stringent of such laws in all Buddhist societies. British arrogance toward a culture for which they had no respect was thus illustrated and was also stimulated by reports of monarchic atrocities against members of the extensive royal family who might be pretenders to the throne (succession was not fixed in law or custom). Because the Burmese may have bested their neighbors in warfare, monarchs perhaps believed their grandiose, archaic royal titles translated into modernized power. In spite of British technological superiority, the Burmese fought bravely in the first Anglo-Burmese War, as British reporting indicated. The British were ill prepared to fight a tropical war; more of their troops died from disease than in battle.

The second war, in 1852, evolved from a dispute over British commercial interests in the teak industry. It resulted in the British occupation of central lower Burma, thus uniting the whole coast of that country under British rule, as they had seized the western province of Arakan and the eastern region of Tenasserim as reparations from the first conflict. The third war was designed not only to facilitate the possibility of trade with Yunnan but to deny the French, who had occupied Vietnam and were controlling Laos and Cambodia, from solidifying their growing influence at the Burmese court. This effectively would have resulted in the denial of the southwest China trade to the British. Anglo-French rivalry in mainland Southeast Asia was important to both. The independence of Thailand as a buffer state between the two was a result of this regional balance of power. There was resistance to these wars in British Parliament, but the media, fueled by merchants who wanted access to the raw materials of the state and to the potential China trade, essentially carried the day.

Trade potential in the colonial era thus pointed north. The British explored in the nineteenth century the possibilities of trade with China in Yunnan and beyond with mule trains beginning at Bhamo on the Irrawaddy River. Now, China views Myanmar as its market and avenue to the Bay of Bengal and the Indian Ocean. That country is exploring the possibility of using Bhamo as a base for southern economic expansion down the Irrawaddy to the Bay of Bengal and beyond.

### What was the role of India in colonial Burma, what are its residual influences, and why are they important?

The British occupation of Burma largely used troops from the subcontinent to suppress discontent. Administrative convenience (if not acumen) led the British until 1937 to govern Burma as a province of India in spite of profound cultural differences. The Indian pattern of control became the model. As the British ruled India both directly and indirectly through the princely states and certain designated peripheral areas (such as the Northwest Frontier Province), so Burma was eventually divided into Ministerial Burma (also called Burma Proper), that core of the country essentially inhabited by Burmans and directly ruled, and the peripheral regions that were indirectly administered. The Burmese continuously claim that the divide-and-rule policies of the colonialists are the cause of their minority problems today. The colonial period helped reify ethnicity, resulting in minorities becoming more cohesive entities that had not before existed. This led to ethnic nationalism and the demands on the state for specialized rights.

Because Burma was administratively integral to India, various types of immigration were approved and sometimes subsidized. At the administrative acme, Burma was governed by the Indian Civil Service, at first composed of the British. Only much later were Indians included. After 1937 and the administrative separation of Burma from India, the Burma Civil Service was established. The Burmese called the BCS the "heaven sent," as they were on the highest rung of the Burmese social ladder at that time. Because the British did not trust the Burmans, who had resisted their rule, those recruited into the Burma army who were not Indian were essentially from the "martial races." Thus, minorities formed the majority of the troops: the Karen (27.8 percent), Chin (22.6 percent), and Kachin (22.9 percent), who were organized into ethnic military units, such as the Karen Rifles. Only about 12.3 percent of the Burma army was composed of Burmans at the start of World War II. Burman antagonism against the Karen was exacerbated by the Karen participating with the British in the pacification of the Burmans.

The lower levels of the administration—clerks, peons, and others—were often recruited from the Indian community, for these people knew the British ways and administration and spoke English. As modern medicine and education were also introduced, Indians came to staff many of those professional positions. Some fields of urban manual labor, such as dock workers, were largely Indian. By the 1930s, Rangoon was essentially an Indian city, with Burmans in the minority, in spite of the attractions of the venerable Shwedagon Pagoda, the most important Buddhist pilgrimage site in Southeast Asia.

As the economy of Burma expanded and became monetized, Indian labor was recruited, in many cases as a type of indentured servitude (to pay off transport costs and debts). This became especially important in the development of commercialized rice agriculture. With the growing commercialization of the Burmese economy under the British, the Indian subcaste of Chettyars from Madras moved into the money lending field, which they soon dominated. The Burmese, unused to the legal implications of credit and repayments, often overextended themselves, using land as collateral. When the Great Depression dropped the price of rice on the world market after 1929, many Burmese lost their agricultural land, which was 80 percent mortgaged, mostly to the Chettyars. This and the Indians' preferential position in Burma caused great resentment against all Indians that to a large degree persists today.

The British tried to mitigate the problem of rural indebtedness as early as the end of the nineteenth century through the establishment of cooperatives. These were top-down efforts, in contrast to those evolving out of the European experience. These government-controlled cooperatives continue today under an official ministry; they have been one element of state control over the population and the economy.

The influence of India was not all negative. The Indian nationalist movement and the activities of Mahatma Gandhi and the India Congress Party had a positive impact of the rise of Burmese nationalism. As the Burmese became more assertive through strikes in the central oil fields and student demonstrations (1920, 1936), the British considered separating the administration of Burma from that of India. There was considerable ferment in Burma over this possibility—some felt that separation might delay self-governance and later independence, whereas others wanted the autonomy from Indian administration. Separation finally occurred in 1937, although the Government of Burma Act was passed in 1935.

The British adopted a means for localized control at the village level. In traditional Burma, the village headman (rarely a woman) was the leading authority in the village and in a sense represented the village to the world beyond. His job was to keep government away from the village. As the Burmese proverb states, government was one of the five evils, along with fire, flood, thieves, and enemies. The British overturned this concept and made the headman the lowest representative of the Crown, reporting up the bureaucratic ladder and charged with enforcing government regulations. This change was continued after independence, allowing greater state control of rural areas.

### What economic development programs did the British introduce?

The goals of colonial administration in Burma were multiple. The British could concentrate on imposing law and order so that the province could pay for its own administration. They had denied French influence. Thailand was essentially politically neutralized to the east. The British controlled the west, and a weak China to the north posed no potential threat. To encourage control and trade, the British expanded communications, built roads and railroads, and developed ports, as well as riverine transport (the Irrawaddy Flotilla Company is a prime example). Burma held the world's most extensive teak reserves (much in demand for building because it was impervious to termites). The British developed a sophisticated and much renowned Burma Forest Service, said to be the best in the world, to protect this valuable resource (up until the degradations of the past generation).

Burma had mineral wealth. The traditional oil wells of central Burma, formerly under royal monopoly, were modernized, and Burma became, before World War II, a modest oil exporter (the Burmah Oil Corporation). Annual production in the 1930s was 250–280 million gallons. The Bawdwin-Namtu mines (producing silver, lead, zinc, copper, and gold) were renowned. The Mawchi mine was the largest tungsten mine in the world. Tin and other minerals were exported. The traditional exploitation of the world's finest jade and ruby mines and sapphires all contributed to the export-led growth of colonial Burma.

By far the most important economic innovation was the development of the Irrawaddy Delta as the world's premier rice-growing region. The delta was transformed from a lightly populated swampy area, largely inhabited by the Karen, into the world's rice basket. Although such development started after the second Anglo-Burma War of 1852, the opening of the Suez Canal in 1869 expanded European markets. The Irrawaddy Delta was the site of the greatest global agricultural investment at that time. Just prior to World War II, Burma became the largest rice exporter in the world, shipping some 3.123 million tons in one year alone. There was substantial migration from central Burma to the delta to work the land because the poorer regions of central plain (called the dry zone because it required irrigation for rice cultivation) offered fewer economic opportunities even though it was the seat of Burman culture. (The Irrawaddy Delta was devastated by Cyclone Nargis in 2008.) The Japanese conquest of Burma in World War II was prompted not only by the wish for a route for the invasion of India but also to glean the state's natural resources. The scorched-earth policies of both sides, however, destroyed about half of the Burmese infrastructure and industry.

### What was the role of Buddhism during this period and what social changes affected the society?

"To be Burman is to be Buddhist," as the saying goes. Buddhism was the primordial value of Burman society. The rites of social passage, the functioning of education, the prestige and glory (*hpoun*, in Burmese; a monk is known as a *hpoungyi*, "great glory") was related to the *sangha*, the Buddhist clergy, which was controlled by an administrative hierarchy with the *thathanabaing* (supreme patriarch) at the apex. Education was monastically fostered at the village level, and the monks had the most prestige. The monarchs all built pagodas, the king's advisors were often monks, and some monarchs themselves had been monks. Virtually every Burman male had become a novice or monk at some time in his life. Every morning, offerings were made to monks who circulated through towns and villages, providing opportunities for the populace to gain merit. Contrary to Western popular opinion, they were not begging but providing a religious service to the people. Success in life—from position to wealth to health and family—were attributed to one's good karma, built up through the work of previous incarnations.

The British eliminated this formal structure and undercut the position of Buddhism. They abolished the position of *thathanabaing*, so that the *sangha* lost administrative cohesion. They introduced modern secular education in both English and Burmese, thus not only truncating one of the important monastic functions in many areas but establishing alternative avenues of economic mobility that were not dependent on Buddhism. Those who had traditional educations could not compete for modern positions.

The monastery still was the center of village life. The monk had great prestige, and people offered up appropriate gifts to the members of the *sangha*. Still, the great title of respect for an individual was *payataga*, the builder of a pagoda. But society had changed. Because the Burman areas lacked a hereditary gentry, there was a fluidity of mobility. Some Burmans went to England and were educated as lawyers and doctors. Others went to prestigious mission schools in Burma and were taught in English. Others went to the University of Rangoon. The education of some minorities was encouraged; a high school (Kanbawza College) was established in the Shan State for the sons of the hereditary rulers—a kind of princely school along the English public school (i.e., private school) model. But Burma was treated as a plural society, unintegrated with parallel economic and social systems.

The Burmans had lost control over their own economy. Large corporations were often European owned; the Indians dominated much of the trade and were followed by the Chinese, who emigrated into the country both over land and by sea. From the Burmese perspective, the Burmese were being deprived of their own heritage. Beginning in the 1930s and continuing beyond independence, there was an increasing demand to get the economy back under local control, meaning Burmese state control, that is, socialism. Although the communist movement began among intellectuals in the late 1930s and early 1940s (the party was founded in 1939), the ideological spur to socialism was more rooted in local reaction to economic disassociation than to international ideological stimuli, except among a modest intellectual minority. A moderate socialist civilian government was followed by a more radical military socialist government (1962–1988) until its collapse through incompetence in 1988. This issue of who controls the economy resonates even today, for the economic ascendance of the Chinese under the present administration has created nationalistic disquiet. If the Burmese were to feel that the Chinese (no longer the Indians or the Europeans) were in obvious economic command, there could be severe consequences.

## How did Burmese nationalism develop and what have been its effects?

With the end of the monarchy in 1885 and the exile of the king and his family to India, a period of intense but scattered rebellion and dacoity (armed robbery by gangs) developed in much of upper Burma. It took the British about ten years to pacify the country and establish their authority (there was also a war with the Chin 1917–1919). This was done in a brutal manner in which whole villages were destroyed and many were killed. As noted, even more important was the gradual downplaying of Buddhism through the elimination of its structure of authority and the development of alternative means of education.

The British banned political activity. But when the Burmans saw the inroads that Christian missionaries and institutions made on the population, especially those non-Buddhists among the minority groups, early Buddhist leaders saw the need to emulate

Christian activity. On the model of the Young Men's Christian Association (YMCA), the Burmese established the Young Men's Buddhist Association (YMBA) in 1906; because it was religious, the British did not ban it. It was in fact both a religious and political organization. Later other Buddhist groups were organized, such as the General Council of Buddhist (Burmese) Associations in 1920, with political objectives in mind.

The link was thus established early between Buddhism and nationalism, and that link is still strong, although the issues may be somewhat different. Buddhist monks were active in the nationalist movement; two prominent ones went to jail, and one died in prison (U Ottama, 1879–1939). Both are considered martyrs to the nationalist cause. The educational marginalization of Buddhism together with economic deprivation, especially after the Great Depression of 1929, led to economic jealousies and frustrations that spilled into the streets, with monks leading demonstrations against Muslims, most of whom had migrated from the subcontinent, as a result of perceived insults against Buddhism.

Because the monarchy and Buddhism were so intertwined, some of the rebellions against the British to try to reestablish the monarchy had a religious element. The most important of these was the Saya San (Hsaya San) rebellion of the early 1930s that was finally put down by the British with extra troops imported from India. Saya (teacher) San was a sometime monk who was later captured, tried, and executed. He established a jungle palace and advocated combined traditional Buddhist, magical, and astrological teachings. Most Western historians regarded the rebellion as a return to mystical fanaticism, but it was an atavistic reaction to conquest exacerbated by the depression that lowered international rice prices, and (as we might say today) globalization, akin perhaps to the Boxer Rebellion in China at the end of the nineteenth century. Both Burmese and some foreign historians have reevaluated its significance, and under the SLORC/SPDC, Saya San is considered a nationalist hero, and his portrait is on the Burmese currency.

*What was the impact of World War II on Burma, and what effect did Japanese conquest have on Burma and its future?*

World War II changed many elements of Burma. It destroyed much of the infrastructure and industry as scorched earth policies were applied as the British retreated and later as the Japanese did the same. Only some thirty years later did the Burmese per capita income reach pre–World War II levels.

The war caused the exodus of large numbers of Indians, who fled from the Japanese back to India. Lacking food and water, many of them died on the jungle tracks as they tried to walk out of the country. The war also exacerbated tensions between some of the minorities and the Burmans, for the Karen and the Kachin sided with the Allies and sometimes acted as guerrilla forces behind Japanese lines assisting the Allies (such as Wingate's Raiders, Merrill's Marauders, Force 136, Detachment 101, etc.). Until March 1945, the Burmans were officially in league with the Japanese. Burmans massacred Karens in Myaungmya in the delta area in May 1942, an event that is still remembered.

The role of Japan in Burma during World War II and the defeat of the Allies there and elsewhere in Asia hastened the end of colonialism and spurred the development of nationalism. It also established a bond between the Japanese and Burmese. This bond is compounded by sadness for the great losses the Japanese suffered in Burma, the mutual compassion of Buddhism (even if the two states adhere to different versions, Mahayana and Hinayana), and the suffering and poverty of the Burmese people. It later led to Japan becoming the largest donor of reparations and then economic assistance beginning in the 1950s.

Perhaps most important, it destroyed the illusion of Western and British invulnerability and boosted the rise of Burmese nationalism. Under the Japanese, Burma became titularly independent on August 1, 1943. It was a pseudo-independent state with a Burmese dictator, Ba Maw, with its capital called

Rangoon Naypyitaw. Its specious autonomy soon became apparent to the Burmese. Although there are still a few Burmese military alive who were trained under the Japanese and who reminisce fondly about their relationships, the Japanese military treated the Burmese with cultural disdain and a brutality that is largely forgotten. World War II also fostered the growth of ethnonationalism as some minority groups asserted what they considered their rights as part of the Allied war effort.

Although there were many British and a few elite Burmese in the safety of Simla in India or London who planned for the return of British-dominated government, World War II effectively ended the colonial era, even though it lingered for three more years. It also brought into prominence young Burmese who had been in the nationalist movement in the late 1930s who became the leaders of the independence movement and the new government. They included Aung San, U Nu, Ne Win, and others who played important later roles in contemporary Burma.

### How did the Burma army develop during the colonial period and under the Japanese?

When Burma became separated from India in 1937, there were no Burmans in the regular army (one company had been employed in the Middle East in World War I). As noted, a small number (12.3 percent) of Burmans were eventually recruited, but the army was essentially composed of minority groups. When the Japanese invaded Burma in 1942, many Burmans deserted and joined Aung San in an anti-British Burma Independence Army and were deployed with the Japanese invaders. This group was later disbanded by the Japanese, under whose auspices a smaller Burma Defense Army was formed under the command of Aung San; Ne Win commanded one of its three battalions. When Aung San became minister of defense under the puppet Japanese-controlled government, Ne Win became military commander under what was then called the Burma

National Army. In March 1945, Aung San (who had secretly been in touch with the Allies) and the Burma National Army turned against the Japanese and helped liberate Burma with the British. Some Burmese military officers as late as the early twenty-first century have expressed affection for the Japanese, some of whom maintained contact with their former Burmese colleagues.

A critical result of the early Burma military experience was the role of the Fourth Burma Rifles. Ne Win was its commander, and as he rose in prominence in later years, many of his officers and enlisted men assumed positions of authority. These included Aung Gyi, Sein Lwin, Saw Maung, and many more. The Fourth Burma Rifles under Ne Win became a type of entourage system, so important in Burmese political culture. It ensured that Ne Win's influence would be felt in Burma/Myanmar long after he left official positions.

### How do the Burmese today consider the colonial era?

The colonial period is generally deplored, especially by the military, and cited as the root cause of most of the problems facing the state. Minority rebellions and difficulties are attributed to British policies of divide and rule and the development of only a relatively minuscule industrial base serving foreign interests. The Burmese, including many outside the government, consider the policy of unlimited Indian immigration a major social and economic deterrent to Burman development. Many feel the racist and segregationist elements of British rule contributed to the degradation of Burman culture. Burmans often criticize the role of Christianity in minority conversions and the educational marginalization of Buddhist monasteries. The military has specifically decried the subjugation of Burman women to foreign exploitation as unpatriotic and an attempt to dilute the Burman race. They cite the marriage of Aung San Suu Kyi to a British academic, Michael Aris, as disqualifying her from leading the country. This colonial issue, as exemplified in Rudyard Kipling's poem "The Road to Mandalay" (and its paean to Burmese women who had relations with British soldiers) and George Orwell's *Burmese Days* (whose hero had a Burmese mistress), thus continues today.

There are probably few alive now who personally remember the colonial period. During the civilian era, however, when things were not going smoothly, many elderly did remember and appreciate certain aspects of life then, even if they deplored colonialism as such. Burmese would complain that the telephones worked better during the British days, trains were more comfortable, and there was less robbery and more law and order. More Burmese were trained under British rule than inhabitants of many other colonial states.

The British legal system was generally admired under the civilian government. Many colonial laws continued and are still used, some as instruments of control and coercion. The U Nu government could arrest individuals under a British public order law and hold them indefinitely, and the military more recently employed British laws from the early twentieth century to employ forced, unpaid labor (*corvée labor*) for local construction. Every administration has used those measures supportive of its purposes. Every one has discarded those politically inconvenient.

How Burma might have developed independent of colonial rule is a moot point. Claims that Burma/Myanmar would have remained a premodern state, and thus colonial rule was important, cannot be substantiated. Independent Thailand gradually adapted to Western pressures and influences and may be the closest example of what might have been. In most societies emerging from the colonial experience, the degradation of inferior status naturally rankles, often resulting in an exuberant nationalism that colors the past and present and is likely to influence the future for a considerable period. Burma/Myanmar is no exception.

# 4

# INDEPENDENCE AND THE CIVILIAN GOVERNMENT (1948–1962): MIXED HERITAGES

The civilian government, which lasted from independence in 1948 until the military coup of 1962 (with a military interregnum in 1958–1960), has variously been resurrected as a positive or negative guide to the political future of Myanmar. Many observers believe that the representative parliamentary democratic government formed under the 1947 constitution is precedent and a guide (if not a model) of what Myanmar needs in the future. Others believe that this period can be neither a guide nor a model, and the democracy that was instituted had severe problems and limitations. Whichever position one holds, it is evident that the Burmese military played a far more influential role under Burmese civilian rule than in most modern Westernized states. One scholar claimed that the whole civilian governmental period was a cultural aberration, a colonial residue, and that independence in a Burmese manner really started with the coup of 1962 because it resembled precolonial concepts of governance. All the leaders from this period have since died. The analyses of the efficacy of governance in this period are salient in the contemporary debate on Myanmar's projected and/or desirable future.

### How did independence come about?

London essentially determined Burmese independence, although the cry for an independent Burma by the Burmese was long, loud, and clear. Following World War II, there were thousands of Burmese with arms who might have made retention of British control very tenuous. Winston Churchill said he was not about to see the dissolution of the British Empire, but the Labour Party won the postwar elections. India was bound to become independent, and Burma would certainly follow. England was exhausted by the war; holding onto their colonies in the face of rising nationalism seemed impossible. Inevitable independence, then, should be gracefully granted. What kind of independence, and whether independent Burma would be divided between Burma Proper and a separate minority area was unclear. Some in England wanted to try Aung San as a traitor because he backed the Japanese before and during most of the war, and others regarded him as a criminal for killing a headman; he, however, negotiated independence. This resulted in the Aung San–Atlee Agreement of January 27, 1947, calling for independence within one year. Through his leadership of the second Panglong Conference (the first was in 1946) and the agreement of February 12, 1947, which brought together minority groups and Burmans, he was able to convince the British that the minority areas should not be separated from Burma Proper. Some Karen leaders felt betrayed, as some unofficial British may have promised the Karen an independent state for their support during the war. The Karens were only observers at the conference.

The Burmese military has written that they alone fought for and brought about independence. This seems to be an exaggeration, although they joined with the Allies and fought against the Japanese in March 1945 toward the end of the war. The nationalist movement had been important during the colonial era, the Japanese occupation destroyed British credibility, and India was to be independent. All of these events contributed to the pressures for freedom. Eventual independence was certainly inevitable, a product of London and Rangoon. The exact timing, however, of 4:20 A.M., January 4, 1948, was based on Burmese astrological calculations as to the most auspicious day and moment.

## What was the role of Aung San?

Aung San (1911–1947) is considered the father of modern Burmese independence, the terms of which he effectively dictated. He was a vigorous, magnetic, young nationalist leader whose forceful personality was critical both to negotiations with the British and to encouraging the minorities to keep within what became the Union of Burma. He was trusted by the minorities; no other leader at that time or since then has played such a role. He advocated some type of federalism with the minority areas and suggested sharing the state's resources with them. This has been variously interpreted by some of the minorities but since ignored by all governments.

His assassination on July 19, 1947 (along with a number of his proposed cabinet), by a disaffected Burmese politician named U Saw silenced a widely trusted personality. He was not a democrat, but rather wanted socialism, national unity, and a single, dominant political party. He became the icon of the civilian period. His picture was on the currency and in virtually every public office and in many private homes. The government officially and annually remembers his martyrdom. The room in which that deed took place in the old colonial secretariat building remains a type of shrine. In the popular view, he has become almost a *nat*, a spirit of a powerful person who died a violent and untimely death. Politicians carefully invoked his language to suit their political needs of the moment. The Anti-Fascist People's Freedom League (AFPFL, the civilian ruling coalition party) used him for their purposes, as did Ne Win following the coup of 1962, selectively quoting him to demonstrate the legitimacy of a particular policy or action.

Later, following the coup of 1988 and the political ascent of his daughter, Aung San Suu Kyi, his image was intentionally downplayed. His ubiquitous pictures were removed from offices and the currency (and from private homes) to prevent the aura of Aung San being transferred to his daughter. Her name was rarely used by the junta; she was referred to simply as "the lady."

### How did Burma deal with political and ethnic rebellions?

Burma was plagued with what seemed like myriad rebellions over time. Only two advocated the overthrow of the government; one was the Red Flag Communist Party, which revolted even before independence. It had split in March 1946 from the White Flag Communist Party (the Burma Communist Party, BCP), which also had advocated overthrow and had revolted some months after independence. There were also a variety of Peoples' Voluntary Organizations (PVO), which were often not more than bands of armed undisciplined men in revolt. Aside from the Kuomintang (the Chinese Nationalist Party, which had been defeated by the communists) troop remnants, which essentially wanted to exploit narcotics production and trade for their own enrichment, different groups demanded independence or greater autonomy at various times. More recently, many have advocated a federal system of government. This is a concept that the military has continuously and conceptually rejected since at least 1962.

The military tried repression and then cooption for a period in the 1960s. They enabled some groups to keep their arms as a kind of militia (that program was abandoned in 1973) as long as they did not fight against the government. It enabled them to engage in their traditional occupations, which in some cases involved opium production. The few attempts at negotiations did not produce results. After the 1960 elections, passage of legislation making Buddhism the state religion, and the coup of 1962, the ethnic rebellions spread as military control continued. In the 1980s and 1990s, there were about forty of them. Some element (sometimes more than one) of almost every significant ethnic group revolted at some period. It was only after the State

Law and Order Restoration Council (SLORC) came to power in 1988 that a large number of cease-fires were negotiated with most organizations. They were not, however, peace treaties but usually verbal agreements under which the rebels held certain territories and were able to keep their arms, supposedly until a constitutional referendum, before which they would surrender their weapons. (This vote finally took place in May 2008; they have yet to surrender their arms as of this writing.) Final solutions to the rebellions have yet to be negotiated. Whether the leadership of these groups reflects the views of their ethnic constituents is unclear, because none were elected. Those in active rebellion at any time have been a relatively small percentage of any ethnic-linguistic group, although among those groups there are many sympathizers.

These rebellions were often supported or used by foreign states, exacerbating the isolation, suspicion, and concern among Burmans over both their minorities and foreign powers. Some British had supported the Karen; East Pakistan (and then Bangladesh) backed the Muslim Rohingyas on their border with Middle Eastern funding. The Indians were said to be involved with the Kachin and Karen. The Chinese assisted the BCP, the Naga, and Kachin rebels. The United States supported the Kuomintang, and the Thai a wide variety of rebel groups, essentially creating buffer states or zones to insulate conservative Bangkok from what they regarded as radical Rangoon.

For obvious reasons, then, even in the civilian period the central government was suspicious about foreign involvement with their minorities.

## Why didn't Burma join the Commonwealth?

In contrast to India and Pakistan, Burma did not join the British Commonwealth because of implicit internal pressures from the Burmese left wing. A Constituent Assembly met in May 1947 to draft a constitution, and the text proclaimed that Burma was to be "an independent sovereign republic," thus eliminating joining the Commonwealth. There seemed to have been strong internal pressures on the planned government. If Burma had joined the Commonwealth, both the legal and illegal left could charge that the new government, soon to be decimated by the assassination of Aung San and his colleagues, was not really independent. The Red Flag Communists made this charge even before independence when they actively revolted. To demonstrate the autonomy of the civilian leadership and appeal to nationalist sentiment, this break in ties seemed the least costly means to deal with the left. The development of the Commonwealth-sponsored Colombo Plan to provide assistance to developing states, however, allowed the Burmese to participate and receive British assistance through this multilateral mechanism. Burma joined in 1952 but did not request assistance until 1954. Technical training was an important component of such aid.

### How did the Chinese nationalist incursion affect Burma?

The Chinese communists gradually defeated the forces of the Nationalist government (the Kuomintang), backed by the United States, during the Chinese revolution in 1948–1949. The Kuomintang evacuated its government to Taiwan, where it remains. Some forces, however, retreated from Yunnan Province into the Shan State of Burma. In this instance, history did rhyme, for in 1644 when the Manchu Qing Dynasty defeated the Ming government, Ming troops also fled into the area now known as Burma to take refuge.

In the fervor against the spread of communism, these forces were supported not only by Taiwan but surreptitiously by the United States through the Central Intelligence Agency. The unrealistic expectation was that these troops, a relatively small number of perhaps 16,000 at their peak, would advance back into China. Although their strength could not defeat the regime's army, their supporters thought they could spark a popular counterrevolution against the communist government. Seven attempts were tried, but all failed. Eventually, after the Chinese established their People's Republic in 1950, the Chinese troops twice crossed into Burma to control the very modest threat to their regime. Finally, in 1961, Chinese communist forces of some 20,000 quietly crossed into Burma and with the support of 5,000 Burmese troops and effectively eliminated the Kuomintang remnants.

Because of the weakness of the Burma army and the rise of other rebellions against Rangoon, these Kuomintang troops occupied a wide swath of the Shan State and could not be dislodged by the Burmese army alone. As this clandestine occupation became widely known in Rangoon, the civilian government, under pressure from the left, protested to the United Nations and in retaliation forced the closure of the U.S. economic assistance mission to Burma in 1953. Eventually, a large portion of these troops were evacuated by air to Taiwan, and others crossed into Thailand, where they established themselves in areas only titularly controlled by the Thai government. Some remained in remote parts of Burmese territory.

One of the major effects of the Kuomintang incursion was the spread of opium production in that region. As a means to sustain and arm itself, the troops remaining in Burma encouraged the growth of the opium poppy, its conversion into heroin, and its export, which in that period occurred mainly through Thailand. Although opium production had been encouraged by the British and taxed by local chieftains (*sawbwas*, maharajas), before independence it was a local (not international) problem, and its use seemed largely restricted to the Chinese minority in the region. The Caretaker Government (1958–1960) abolished the legal production and sale of opium.

The enduring effect of the Kuomintang period was not only the increase in opium production, which early on became the source of about 90 percent of that drug's importation into the United States. More important was the effect on the Burma army. Because local authorities could not deal with the incursion or even conduct local administration in parts of the Shan State, the Burma army took over direct administration of local government in some areas. Combined with their positive role in the Caretaker Government of 1958–1960 (see below), the military developed a strong belief in its capacity to govern the whole state. This confidence may have contributed both to the coup of 1962 and their belief in the military's capability to govern the country. From 1962, the military planned for perpetual control both directly and through their civilianized persona.

### What were relations with the United States?

The United States recognized the independence of the Union of Burma very early. With the conquest of China by the communists, the outbreak of communist-inspired rebellions in Burma, Malaya, the Philippines, Vietnam, and Indonesia, and then the Korean War in 1950, there was palpable fear that the East Asia region was about to become communist-dominated. The essential U.S. policy in East Asia since the nineteenth century had been the prevention of control of that region by any hegemonic power; in the mid-twentieth century, the Sino-Soviet bloc was so perceived by the United States.

The United States dispatched a team to Southeast Asia to determine what was needed to prevent communism from spreading. The result was a U.S. foreign assistance program in Burma and other countries. There were a variety of specific projects and also technical assistance in economic planning. As a protest against the U.S. supply of arms to the Kuomintang, the Burmese government canceled the aid program but kept the economic advisors and paid them with Burmese government funds. After a hiatus of several years, the program was reinstituted.

The government of the AFPFL, a broad-based coalition, contained left-wing elements. In opposition to the AFPFL was an above-ground communist-oriented party, the National United Front (NUF). There were also two underground communist insurrections. Thus, the moderate socialist government under U Nu had to walk a fine neutralist line in the Cold War. This vehement neutralism allowed both the Soviet Union and the Western states to vote for U Thant (then ambassador of Burma to the United Nations) to become secretary general of the United Nations (1961–1971). He became Burma's most famous citizen.

Although U Nu had written an anticommunist play, "The People Win Through," he had to balance delicately the United States, the Colombo Plan, the Soviet Union, Eastern European states, and China. State scholars and military officers were sent abroad, mainly to the United States and United Kingdom. Various governments, including the United States, had information centers and libraries, and the British Council, the Ford Foundation, The Asia Foundation, and the Fulbright Program as well as Johns Hopkins University all provided various types of aid and training. Burma received economic assistance from all of them in various forms, but consciously U Nu was most concerned with China and Burma's long, indefensible border with it. As one author wrote, Burma was carefully neutral but always in China's shadow.

### What were relations with China?

Burmese relations with China were mutually cautious at the beginning but improved later. In an act of self-protection against an overwhelming neighbor, Burma was the first noncommunist country to recognize the People's Republic. China, however, was skeptical at first. Revolutionary doctrine at that time stipulated that all noncommunist states controlled by capitalists or former colonial lackeys had nefarious plans or attitudes toward the new People's Republic. Recognition by such countries was not automatic, as in normal diplomatic practice, but was treated with suspicion and had to be negotiated. Chairman Mao, who at that time was visiting Moscow, cabled to Beijing to reinforce that point when the Burmese relationship was being discussed. After several years, relations warmed, and there were numerous high-level visits by Chinese leaders, including Chou En-lai, to cement the relationship called *paukpaw* (variously translated as cousins, brotherhood, or a relation based on kinship). Burma was the only country for which that term was used, and it indicated a special association but one that was not always smooth.

At the same time in the 1950s, the Burmese military, perhaps in contrast to the civilian government, recognized that the only potential external enemy of the state was China. Military planners advocated expanding the Burmese army with three infantry and one armored division. They recognized that such augmented strength could not halt a Chinese invasion but could only perform a holding operation against it until the United States, as in the Korean War, came to its assistance. U Nu believed the plan too expensive for so short a duration, and instead opted for closer Chinese ties as insurance. (Illustrating a vast change in attitude, in the 2000s the State Peace and Development Council [SPDC] wanted to train a paramilitary force as a holding operation against the Americans until the Chinese came to their aid.) A border agreement was eventually signed with the Chinese, each side making modest concessions, but early communist Chinese maps continued to demark northern Burma as Chinese territory, as had Chinese Nationalist maps before them. This has since ceased.

China provided various types of foreign economic assistance, usually popular and visible projects. Trade with China was limited, and overland trade was both illegal and spotty. Various insurgencies controlled many of the natural border crossings and a large area of the Shan State, called the Wa State, was inhabited by that ethnic group, some of whom (the "wild Wa") had a reputation for dealing severely with outsiders (occasional headhunting for fertility rites). China began its support to the BCP only in the late 1960s, when the BCP, defeated in central Burma, began its own long march to the Wa area on the China border, where it established itself and recruited locally. Deng Xiao Ping famously said that state-to-state relations were separate from party-to-party relations, so this dualism of close national ties and close insurrectionist ties existed for some time. China armed and trained members of the BCP and operated a clandestine radio station from Yunnan for the BCP.

It was only after the Cultural Revolution spilled over from China into Burma in 1967 with Chinese students demonstrating in the streets and espousing Mao's revolutionary slogans that official relations became temporarily strained. Anti-Chinese riots occurred, although perhaps the Burmese authorities were relieved to see economic frustration vented onto Chinese merchants rather than against the government. Many were killed, but these deaths were officially unacknowledged. Ambassadors were withdrawn for a period. Since the coup of 1988 and the Tiananmen incident of 1989, however, Myanmar's international relations are closest with China (see following discussion).

### Was Burma communist or socialist, and what were the ideological influences on the society?

As already noted, there were two communist parties that followed various international revolutionary slogans. The Burmese government, however, was fervently anticommunist and tried to ensure its image of neutrality by taking economic assistance from all sides. A left-wing legal party, said to be the legal arm of the illegal BCP, did operate and expanded its influence in the civilian period. The communists were intent on regime change, and U Nu was expressly opposed to communism. The military during the Caretaker Government produced a volume by its psychological warfare arm called *Dharma in Danger*. Dharma, Buddhist doctrine and law, was portrayed as threatened by communism. Since that time, and even after the collapse of the BCP in 1989, the military has invoked the danger of communism to the state to justify some repressive measures.

Socialism, however, was the hallmark of most politicians who wanted to get the economy back under indigenous control.

The socialist party was founded in the late 1930s and became an integral part of the AFPFL. U Nu equated the egalitarian elements of Buddhism with socialism. Capitalistic greed, he said, was not a Buddhist virtue. During the civilian period, socialism was of a moderate variety; following the coup of 1962 it became a rigid doctrine encapsulated in the "Burmese Way to Socialism" (1962) an eclectic mixture of socialism, Buddhism, and humanism. It was further expounded in what became the philosophical basis for military rule, *The System of Correlation of Man and His Environment* (1963). These were taught as dogma to civil servants and in the universities.

When a retired Burmese military officer was asked whether the head of state, General Ne Win, was an ideological socialist or simply interested in power, he replied that Ne Win would be a socialist when Mao Zedong learned to play golf.

### What were the government's plans for economic development?

Burma's early economic planning was strongly influenced by international socialist trends. Shortly after independence there were two communist parties in revolt, as well as a legal left-wing party. Democratic socialism was not only internationally fashionable at that time, it was generally viewed in Burma as necessary to get the economy back under Burmese control.

In essence, the government was financed through extraction of materials and their sale overseas. Tax collections and import duties were meager, and private remittances from abroad were absent. In addition to teak exports and some minerals, the government bought paddy (unhusked rice) from the peasants at a low price, milled and exported it, using the difference to finance the state. The insurgencies not only drained resources but also denied the government access to much of the mineral and natural wealth of the state, which was in unsafe areas.

The first economic plan was the Pyidawtha Plan (literally, cool, comfortable, or pleasant land) that was moderately socialist in concept. It was based, however, on a false assumption: that the price of rice (Burma's largest export at that time) would remain as high as it had been during the Korean War. This proved to be incorrect, and much of the plan could not be implemented.

The government was concerned about social welfare more than profit, and such endeavors were rarely cost-effective. A pharmaceutical factory was established to provide vitamins; book translations into simple Burmese were distributed through the Burma Translation Society. To save foreign exchange, a steel mill was built by Germany to operate on scrap iron, which was in abundance from war wrecks in central Burma, but it cost more to ship a ton of goods from Mandalay to Rangoon than from London to Rangoon, and the operation was never economical.

Although Burma tried to get more Burmans into business, and import and export licenses were limited to citizens, the firms often had a titular Burman president but in reality were owned and operated by Chinese behind the scenes. This was not unknown in other countries as well.

Efforts were made to increase agricultural production, but short-term credit was insufficient (and often politically manipulated), fertilizer was expensive and in short supply, and irrigation was mainly a means to prevent economic disaster from a failed monsoon. Because the state owned all land (and still does), peasants did not have the incentive to invest in infrastructure improvements for the property they farmed.

The pre-World War II standard of living of the Burmese was better than that of many developing countries. But the scorched-earth policies of both the British and the Japanese as they fought over the whole state, together with inappropriately conceived and inadequately administered economic policies, prevented reaching that level again until the early 1970s.

### What were the effects of the 1947 civilian constitution?

The 1947 constitution, adopted prior to independence, was an attempt to develop a parliamentary democracy in a multiethnic state. It was written by fifteen Burmans, some of whom had British legal training, and was a product of compromise between the Burman majority and the minorities, but power rested effectively with the majority. It had a bicameral legislature composed of a Chamber of Deputies, representing the whole country and holding financial control, and a Chamber of Nationalities, providing a voice for the minorities. Each constituent state (Shan Kachin, Kayah, Karen somewhat later, and the Chin Special Division) had its own government but was dependent on the center for financial support. As one eminent Burmese consultant to the process noted, "Our constitution, though federal in theory, is, in practice, unitary." It had all the usual provisions for the protection of cultural and other rights, although as with many constitutions, these were often ignored. It stipulated elections, which were held with credible results in noninsurgent areas. It avoided establishing a state religion, although it gave special place to Buddhism (the faith of some 89 percent of the population). It established a judiciary that was more independent than that of any government since then. It was a reasonable effort to translate Western parliamentary practice into a non-Western context, but it was quickly prepared. It was generally regarded at the time as forward-looking.

### How did the AFPFL operate and govern?

The AFPFL was a loose confederation of political parties and local influential leaders and strong men. Its membership ran the gamut of left to left-center political opinions that were socialist to some degree. More important, the AFPFL included a broad array of individuals reflecting the essential personalization of power; each leader had a power base and his own entourage, and sometimes armed supporters. These entourages were reflected in mass organizations that were affiliated with the AFPFL: a workers' association, a peasants' association, and a variety of specific groups, like veterans. The police were also organized along political lines, and various ministerial positions were allocated to factions within the AFPFL. Spoils were allotted in accordance with personal loyalties. Ideational differences were less important than personal ones.

Because loyalties were highly personal, splits developed between leaders that on April 28, 1958, became formalized into two opposing camps; one was known as the Clean AFPFL and the other as the Stable AFPFL, each attempting to keep the cachet of the AFPFL name. The degree of tension was so high that the military feared civil war. This led to the constitutional coup of 1958 that the Caretaker Government instituted to avert this probability.

## What caused the military "Caretaker" Government, how did it function, and what was its legacy?

Since independence, the military has had an honored position in Burmese society. It had sided with the Allies in March 1945, and Aung San had negotiated independence with the British labor government. The military had fought off the Red Flag communist rebellion that started even before independence, the White Flag communist (BCP) rebellion that started shortly after that date, various PVO paramilitary groups that sometimes became bandits, and the most severe, the Karen rebellion, which advanced to within what are now Rangoon suburbs. At its lowest point, the government commanded perhaps 2,000 troops. As we have noted, the military also had some experience in administering territories threatened by the Kuomintang.

Serving in the military was a desirable career, attracting the sons (and a few daughters) of many in the elite. The Burma army during the civilian period grew to about 110,000 men and since 1949 was commanded by General Ne Win, who was also minister of defense and occasionally deputy prime minister.

Given the personalization of power in Burma/Myanmar, various AFPFL leaders were jockeying for position. As a consequence, there was the possibility that paramilitary forces and the police might be used and civil war might develop. Elections scheduled for late 1958 could have led to bloodshed or communist control.

The military was not about to let this happen. On September 24, 1958, key military leaders went to U Nu, who was prime minister, and said a coup was necessary to avoid civil war and to preserve the Union. Faced with an illegal coup, U Nu opted instead to invite the military to govern constitutionally for six months through passage of appropriate legislation. They stayed eighteen months, voluntarily withdrew, and allowed a free election to take place that brought U Nu back into power, although the military had favored his opposition. This act has sometimes been called a constitutional coup or a coup by consent; it was the first of three quite diverse coups in this country (the others were in 1962 and 1988).

The military articulated three objects of their transitory government: restore law and order, eliminate "economic insurgents," and prepare the country for civilian elections. For eighteen months the military unilaterally ran the state, making all major decisions through officers placed in the various ministries and organizations; the mayor of Rangoon was one such pivotal figure. Quick decisions were reached, and the military performed very well during this short period. They were not corrupt and forced lower prices in the bazaars (believing that the merchants, who were often foreign, were gouging the people). They instituted law and order, cleaned the cities, moved squatters to the outskirts of Rangoon (as did the SLORC in 1988 and 1989), and negotiated some border agreements. The military passed a universal conscription law for all males and females on an Israeli model, but it was never implemented because volunteers exceeded demand. They eliminated the legal rights of the Shan sawbwas as well and outlawed opium production.

The military expanded the Defense Services Institute, a type of military post exchange for the army that began in the early 1950s and became the first Burmese conglomerate. It had some fourteen different corporations that included an international shipping line, a bank, a printing press, department stores, trading companies, and a restaurant. They were considered eminently successful businesses, but this was problematic because it was run by the military and cost accounting of the use of military personnel and facilities were not included.

This period, however, gave the military confidence that it could manage the Burmese economy and was probably instrumental in its belief, coupled with its administration of parts of the Shan State, that it could manage the whole country. At the close of the temporary military rule started by the legalized coup, the military published a volume on its accomplishments entitled *Is Trust Vindicated?* This compared their work to Hercules cleaning out the Augean Stables.

The militaries and their regimes around the world, as some of the social science literature of that time argued, were the hope of development. Even if they were autocratic (and because they were anticommunist), they were regarded as rational, goal-oriented, uncorrupted, and nationalistic, and seemed to perform better than civilian governments. The Burmese military in the period of the Caretaker Government was in a sense a model for other countries, and it was often cited as such. In retrospect, however, it might be argued that this praise for the military worldwide was a convenient finding from an anticommunist world perspective.

The military's success was lauded by both Burmese and foreign observers, for not since the British period had the state been run so well (if undemocratically). But the sad aftermath of the second military coup in March 1962 obliterated in foreign and domestic eyes the early progress that the military had brought to the Union of Burma.

### How did the minorities fare under the civilian government?

The Union of Burma was a fragile artifact, a product of the Panglong Agreement of February 12, 1947, that was led by Aung San, who, by the force of his personality, provided the trust that wove the Union together. The patchwork was a Union composed of the (essentially) Burman areas and a Shan, Kachin, Kayah, and later Karen State. In addition, there was a Chin Special Division (province). Under the 1947 constitution, the Shan and Kayah States could opt to leave the Union after ten years and a plebiscite. The Kayah State was an anomaly; it had been recognized as independent by both the British and the Mandalay courts in 1875, but on independence this was ignored. Only later under the military were the Mon and Arakan States constituted, although U Nu had earlier promised their formation.

The minorities were represented in a separate bicameral legislature, and each has its own government but very limited resources. To placate the minorities, the president of the Union ethnically rotated. The first was a Shan, the second a Burman, the third a Karen (who had been a Christian but was said to have espoused Buddhism). Had not the coup of 1962 intervened, the fourth would have been a Kachin. It was assumed that anyone in that position would be a Buddhist. Power, however, resided with the prime minister, who for most of the civilian period was U Nu, a devout Buddhist who also knew how to use his faith for political purposes. During the civilian period, there were significant Christian populations among the Karen (perhaps a third), the Kachin (today over 95 percent), and the Chin (today some 80–90 percent). Conversions to Christianity were not uncommon among animist peoples, but they were rare among Buddhists. Minorities staffed the various ministries and the bureaucracy, and there seemed to be little discrimination as long as one played by Burman rules—that is, identified with the majority of the population. Ability was more important than ethnicity.

To ensure state solidarity, official education was in Burmese, and local-language textbooks and materials were not officially allowed (except for some Chinese publications). Local languages were taught in after-school hours and private institutions, such as churches, but the official curriculum was mandated by the

Burman center. On Union Day, the anniversary of the Panglong Agreement, various minorities were brought together in a festival of costumes, song, and dance, but this was primarily symbolic. Although the 1947 constitution (and subsequent ones) called for the protection of local cultures, this was not backed by effective central government support.

The constant complaint among the minority governments was that the central government did not allocate sufficient resources to them. Aung San once said that if the Burman area got one kyat, the minorities would get one kyat. This was variously interpreted as resources would equally be shared between the Burmans and all the minorities, or that the Burmans would get one share while each of the minority areas would also get one share. In either case, this did not happen. They were all administratively and fiscally under central (Burman) control. They often claimed that even if their populations were smaller, their land area was larger and most of the natural resources of the state were in minority areas, and they did not receive sufficient funding. Some of the minorities wanted to negotiate directly with foreign aid agencies for support, but this was denied by the center, perhaps fearing foreign connivance in secession efforts. In fact, the minority issue (ostensibly) prompted the military coup of 1962. As one scholar argued, before 1948, Burma had unity but not independence. After 1948, however, it has independence but not unity.

### How did the 1960 elections affect Burma?

The elections of February 6, 1960, following the Caretaker Government, were regarded as free and fair. U Nu, leading his faction of the AFPFL, renamed the Union Party, won against his Stable AFPFL opponents, although the military would have preferred to see the latter victorious. U Nu won in large part because he received the majority of the Buddhist vote. He promised to make Buddhism the state religion. He was known as extremely devout, almost monk-like, even picking saffron (the color of monks' robes) as his party color. His picture was on the ballot box. Some Burmese thought it mesmerized voters into supporting him.

The elections brought U Nu back, but the administration was weak and ineffectual. The economy suffered, rebellions increased, and the military, the most effective organization in the state, became concerned.

In the two cases in which the military supervised voting (1960 and 1990), the administration ensured the relative honesty of the vote counts. In 1960, campaigning was unrestricted, but in 1990 it was very controlled. Under the planned elections of 2010, which will be held under a military regime, questions regarding the freedom of both campaigning and vote counting are likely to be raised by both the Burmese and international communities. Although various international organizations will ask to monitor the voting and counting (no foreign observers were allowed in the voting on referendum on the constitution in 2008), the government has indicated that this will not be tolerated, as such observers might prompt political problems.

### What caused the coup of 1962?

The military had become restive. They had tasted power under the Caretaker Government and believed they could manage the country. They were appalled by the gross incompetence of the U Nu administration after 1960, when the country's problems, according to the administration, could be symbolically assuaged by the building of 60,000 sand pagodas. They had strongly objected to U Nu's campaign promise of making Buddhism the state religion, as they knew it would offend the Kachin and Karen. In 1961, Buddhism became the state religion, but a separate bill was enacted guaranteeing freedom of religion. U Nu advocated nat (spirit) worship (the thirty-seven principal nats are enshrined in a Pagan-period pagoda). There had even been some talk among the military of a coup before the 1962 military move; one key officer who had quietly advocated it was shipped out as an ambassador.

The ostensible reason for the coup was, however, the preservation of the Union. Various minorities had gathered in Rangoon for a discussion of their options under the 1947 constitution to leave the Union after ten years. The military claimed that the Union must be preserved, and the coup was a defense against the break-up of the state. They believed that U Nu would agree to this move, which would produce "chaos." The prospect of chaos has been and still is both a fear of and an excuse for military action. Others argued that the government had no intention of allowing the Union to dissolve but might have been prepared to offer somewhat more autonomy to the constituent states, and that the minority issue was not the real cause but simply the excuse. The military, some claimed, simply wanted national power.

In any case, on March 2, 1962, the military moved to take over the government, arresting all those who might question their move (the executive officials, legislature, judiciary, etc.); they did so with the loss of only one life, that of the son of the former Shan president of the Union. It was a coup that was designed to perpetuate military control, eventually through a civilianized administration.

### How may we evaluate the civilian, democratic period?

There is no question that the civilian government (1948–1958, 1960–1962) provided more freedoms for the average citizen than any government since that time. Although it used autocratic legislation (some from the colonial period) to control the state and there were political prisoners, there was a significant degree of press freedom. The judiciary was well trained and reasonably independent, occasionally striking down executive detention orders. Although there were arbitrary arrests, they were never as extensive as under military rule. The market was more open than it has been since that time. The government, in spite of limited capacity, was more concerned about popular welfare than any subsequent administration.

These positive factors must be weighed against the problems that the state faced. Insecurity was rife, not only through rebellions but through a deterioration in law and order throughout the country. Local leaders had autocratic powers. Factionalism was apparent and dangerously destructive of state authority, control, and the delivery of goods and services. Corruption was evident and virtually uncontrolled. Personalized power and factionalism were rampant. Institutions were generally weak. The minorities were struggling to administer their areas with inadequate resources under strictures on their cultures and education. Coherent and responsible leadership was lacking, and political jockeying affected the distribution of services from rural credit to imports and exports.

On balance, it would be inappropriate to use the Burmese civilian period as a model for any future government. A new type of relationship is required for the minorities. An independent judiciary is essential for any effective state. Legal and social restraints on corruption are required, as is greater transparency in decision making. A free press is critical to effective oversight of any administration. Strengthening of participatory institutions is necessary; personalism needs control. Thus, a return to the civilian period as a model is not warranted, although lessons from it could provide useful material for any new Burmese administration.

# 5

# THE MILITARY COUP, THE SOCIALIST PERIOD (1962– 1988), AND THE PERPETUATION OF MILITARY RULE

The military coup of March 2, 1962, in retrospect, seemed designed to accomplish four goals: ensure that the Union of Burma would not be dismantled through minority secession, free Burma from what the military regarded as incompetent and corrupt civilian rule, strengthen the socialist base of the economy (thus eliminating foreign dominance), and provide the foundation for the perpetuation of military hegemony over the state either directly or indirectly through a civilian front government control. In the space of a generation, none of these objectives could be considered to have been achieved in any credible sense. Ethnic tensions increased and rebellions mushroomed, socialism as administered in Burma was eventually an admitted failure, the establishment of civilianized control through the BSPP was not effective, and it took a third supportive "coup" (September 18, 1988) to keep the military in power.

### What were the effects of the coup?

The immediate effects of the 1962 coup were to dismantle all elements of institutional and personal power that could invalidate or threaten military control. Military rule was run by the Revolutionary Council—a junta of seventeen officers, at the apex of which was General Ne Win. He was commander of the armed forces, a position he held since 1949 when a Karen leader, loyal to the Union, was forced to step down during the Karen insurrection. All key leaders were arrested, including those in the judiciary who might have declared the coup illegal. It became evident that considerable planning had taken place before the coup, for the pamphlet "The Burmese Way to Socialism" was published on April 30, 1962, and the Burma Socialist Programme Party (BSPP) was formally established on July 4 of that year.

The reaction of the volatile student community was important to the coup. They had been in the forefront of nationalistic and anticolonial demonstrations, but the various student unions came out in favor of the coup. This was vacation period (the hot season in Burma), and when the students returned to class in May, they found unacceptable new restrictions on their hostels. On July 7 some 2,000 students demonstrated and the military fired on them, killing perhaps over 100, although the government only admitted that 15 had died. This shock was compounded on the following day when the military blew up the Rangoon University Student Union building that had been the site of anticolonial student demonstrations for a generation.

This symbolic act at the beginning of the BSPP era in 1962 was to reverberate at its close. General Sein Lwin, who later became known as the "butcher of Rangoon" because of his suppression of demonstrations, was said to be the officer who opened fire on the students. He was hated because of that, as well as for suppressing the student demonstrations that took place in 1974 related to the burial site of former UN Secretary General U Thant, who had been secretary to and a close confidant of U Nu. Sein Lwin was appointed by the BSPP as president in July 1988. This infuriated the students and contributed to the popular uprising. He lasted in that role about three weeks. Dr. Maung Maung, who succeeded him as president until the coup of September 18, 1988, offered to rebuild the destroyed student union building in an attempt to placate student antipathy to the government and as an oblique apology for the regime's past excesses. It didn't work.

## What was the "Burmese Way to Socialism"?

The Burmese Way to Socialism, set forth in a document published on April 30, 1962, was an admixture of socialism, Buddhist doctrine, and humanism. As one eminent Burmese said, "Because it was socialist it was good, but because it was Burmese it was better." This was not a communist document, thus confusing some in the Soviet Union who could not deny its strength as titularly socialist but were concerned that it denied Marxist historical inevitability. It stressed the intellectual links between Buddhist philosophical concepts and socialist egalitarianism (as had U Nu earlier, when he remarked that capitalism and greed were not Buddhist virtues). It specifically brought forth the Buddhist belief in the inevitability of change and it was subject to the same temporal laws.

The document began: "The Revolutionary Council of the Union of Burma does not believe that man will be set free from social evils as long as pernicious economic systems exist in which man exploits man and lives on the fat of such appropriation." It called for the complete ownership of all forms of production, including agriculture, by the state and cooperatives, but it gave no timetable for such actions.

On July 4, 1962, the regime published the constitution of the BSPP (also called the Lanzin Party) for the "transitional period of its construction." This was a cadre party, and until it morphed into a mass party in 1971, it was composed of twenty-four members, of whom thirteen were on the Revolutionary Council.

The philosophical basis of its rule was *The System of Correlation of Man and His Environment*. Published on January 17, 1963, this was an eclectic mixture of abstruse ideas incorporating Buddhist, socialist, and diverse strains into a potpourri that was difficult to comprehend. It also denied a Marxist historical perspective, maintaining that "man is the master and captain of history." The vulgar materialism of the left and right were to be eschewed, and it stated that even the party's ideology was relative—in a good Buddhist context, change was inevitable. Both documents were taught in required courses that civil servants had to take at the government political institute and in the school and university system. This was an example of the orthodoxy that has been required in Burma/Myanmar since the coup of 1962, when all imported books and journals were subject to censorship and the local media strictly controlled (the local English-language newspaper was called *The Working Peoples' Daily*, the name finally changed under the present government to *The New Light of Myanmar*).

### How did the BSPP operate?

The BSPP was at its inception a cadre party with very few members, all of whom were military officers. It claimed to have an "outward garb" of the military, but was "revolutionary in essence." There were less than two dozen full members for a number of years. After three years, it had 99,638 "candidate" members and 167,447 "sympathizers." By 1966, 29 percent of candidate members were from the armed forces.

It was only in June and July 1971 that the first party congress was held. At that time, membership totaled 73,369, of whom 58 percent were military; 24.4 percent of the 260,857 candidate members were also in the armed forces. This meeting reaffirmed the socialist cast of the economic system but changed its emphasis and orientation. In the early stages, the BSPP seemed to adhere to a stolid Marxist approach emphasizing the urban, industrial proletariat. This approach, however, was ineffective. The category was far too small in such a rurally based economy where two-thirds of the population was agricultural. The congress changed this approach and determined that policy emphasis should be placed on Burma's national endowment—agriculture, forestry, and resource extraction, especially (on-shore) oil production. The BSPP recognized that state diplomatic relations were good, but international economic relations were not. The result was to rejoin the World Bank, join the Asian Development Bank, and seek broad bilateral economic assistance. Such support had primarily come from the Japanese following the coup.

The military retained control over the BSPP even after it expanded into a mass organization. To be promoted in the civil service, one essentially had to be a member of the party. The BSPP controlled all mass and professional organizations and essentially prevented the development of any civil society advocacy groups beyond those associated with religion, especially Buddhism.

## What was the impact of the socialist policies?

Following the coup of 1962, the military purged the bureaucracy of the elite, older Burma Civil Service personnel who were adept at running the governmental ministries. They were replaced with military officers who were energetic, loyal, and in many cases intelligent, even if they were placed in positions of authority over organizations and problems they were not experienced to handle. The military command structure permeated decision making, so when orders were given that even common sense would have indicated could not succeed, they had to be obeyed and somehow tortuously justified. To disagree meant essentially dismissal and often jail.

Following the 1963 purge of Brigadier Aung Gyi, a moderate and presumptive heir to General Ne Win who wanted to emphasize agriculture, the administration took a sharp turn to the left toward rigid socialism. An estimated 15,000 businesses and industries were nationalized, run by a bureaucracy that was incompetent to manage a far more simple economy. Political parties were banned in 1964. The country was effectively cut off from the outside world, and conditions at the center deteriorated while on the periphery rebellions spread. In 1967, General Ne Win is said to have remarked to his senior staff that Burma, the largest rice exporter in the world before World War II, could not feed itself.

Many industries, known as the "state economic enterprises" (the public sector) were established, but as the 1970s and 1980s progressed, the costs of intermediate goods and spare parts increased while the price of exports declined. The state had to borrow, the cost of living rose, and salaries remained abysmal.

### How were foreign relations under the BSPP?

The isolation imposed first by the Revolutionary Council, and later by the constitution of 1974, was selective and (over time) modified. Burma's diplomatic relations reflected its intent to remain neutral in the Cold War. If there were a tilt, it was toward China. Burma felt that the nonaligned movement was too close to the Soviet camp. When it was to meet in 1979 in Havana, Burma pulled out in deference to China, which at that time was on its antihegemonic (i.e., anti-Soviet) crusade. Myanmar rejoined the movement in 1992.

The dire economic conditions of the 1960s forced the BSPP at its first congress to reconsider its economic relations. The government regarded its diplomatic relations as good, but they believed economic relations were poor. The state determined to seek economic assistance, and the reintroduction of much foreign aid followed.

General relations continued to deteriorate, however. Tourists were blatantly discouraged; visas were for twenty-four hours early in that period, and later for only a week. Travel outside Rangoon, Pagan, and Mandalay was considered unsafe. In any case, the communications infrastructure was inadequate. The Burmese had few international contacts. Some shortwave radios existed, but television was lacking, and all books and magazines entering the country were controlled. The state censored all local media.

Foreign investment until 1988 was forbidden except for one West German firm, Fritz-Werner, which produced small arms and weapons for the military and was partly owned by the German government. Socialism prevailed, but as the official economy dried up, the unofficial economy mushroomed. The black market became the source of consumer goods, and in some cases black market bazaars operated openly and were taxed by municipalities. Official jobs were the essential source of sustained income, even at very low levels, and entrepreneurship was prevalent only among those who either exercised their acumen in the black market or left the country.

The government was not completely isolated. After the brutal suppression of demonstrations that broke out among students in 1974, first because of economic conditions and then over the burial site of U Thant, the government sought the means to solve both political and economic needs. It became determined to disperse students from congregating in Rangoon and Mandalay, where they created political problems. They emphasized "distance education," in which students did not need to gather to attend classes. They also decided to form community colleges (junior colleges) in the states and divisions. These would filter out the better students, who could go on the full universities, but the others would remain behind and be given vocational training for local employment. Teams were quietly sent to the United States to explore the experience there. The system was not effective.

Perhaps the only benefit from this period of privation was that a lack of industries, trade, and tourism delayed the detrimental environmental and social effects that so many developing societies have faced, and that Myanmar later began to encounter.

### How did the 1974 constitution come about and what was its impact?

The country had been ruled since 1962 by the decrees of the Revolutionary Council, which of course was completely military (this was also true during the 1988–2010 State Law and Order Restoration Council [SLORC]/State Peace and Development Council [SPDC] period). There was no legislature, and the judiciary was effectively abolished in March 1962. General Ne Win decided or was convinced that military rule should be regularized under a new constitution, since the old constitution of 1947 had been set aside following the 1962 coup. A group of eminent Burmese, including many civilian politicians, were asked in 1969 what kind of government should be established for the Union—a unitary state with power at the center, or a type of federal state, with dispersed power foci. After considerable internal debate, the group suggested a federal system. Since at least 1962, General Ne Win had publicly deplored federalism as the first step toward secession. A unitary state with power at the center was the chosen method of governance.

Drafting a new constitution started on September 25, 1971, and it took several years to complete. Over time, the government submitted three drafts to the country in informal educational sessions led by senior officials. A referendum was held December 15–31, 1973, the constitution was approved, and elections followed in 1974, after which, on March 2—fourteen years to the day after the 1962 coup—the new constitution came into force. Although there seemed no doubt that the government would get the approval it wanted for the referendum, and no doubt worked assiduously to ensure that happened, the results were not uniform. Many of the minority areas had substantial negative votes on it, but the Burman areas prevailed. The almost Stalinist approval figures that were achieved in 2008 (92.48 percent) on another military-sponsored constitutional referendum were in sharp contrast to that of 1973.

The constitution seemed derived from an Eastern European model. The state would be a socialist state, the name changed to the Socialist Republic of the Union of Burma. It would be a single-party state run by the BSPP, and no other parties were legal. It had a unicameral legislature with a tiered series of elections from the local level to a State Council of twenty-eight, the chair of which became the president. The government would nominate candidates for a legislature, and there would be no opposition. Although there were various rights stipulated, they were always subject to law and state control. The courts were under the legislature, and judges had no tenure. In effect, Burma became a socialist authoritarian (but not communist) state.

## How did the indigenous minorities fare under the 1974 unitary state?

The unitary state under the 1974 constitution codified the military control that had existed since 1962, but did it under the auspices of the military-directed BSPP. General Ne Win had ignored the recommendations by the advisory group in 1969 for some sort of federal structure, thus causing the ethnic insurrections to spread over broader areas after 1962. Under the BSPP, all state control mechanisms over minority peoples remained in force.

The isolation of the Burman majority in this period was contrasted with the informal contacts that some of the minorities had with their ethnic and/or religious colleagues beyond the state's perimeters. Karen, Mon, Shan, Chin, Kachin, and Rohingya peoples had a modicum (and sometimes much more) of contact with their transborder brethren, and thus with the outside world. Religious contacts, support, and activities of both foreign Christian and Muslim groups intensified these relationships. The result, as one might expect, was the increased isolation of the Burmans and the growing suspicion, present since independence, that some of the minorities, with the support of Christian states in the West, were conspiring to see the break-up of the Socialist Republic of the Union of Burma.

State troops, assigned to the periphery where most of the minorities lived, often felt they were in hostile and culturally unfamiliar territory. The minorities often felt the military was almost a foreign occupying force, which in some instances it culturally was. The government was not in a position to provide schools or medical facilities or even the means to improve agriculture. Minority dissatisfaction grew. The government had yet to build a nation out of a state.

### How were monks registered?

Every government in Burma since independence has been concerned about the dangers of the distribution of too much autonomous power. This has been evident not only in the political sphere but in religion and economics, the latter closely allied to citizenship issues. The socialist orientation of all governments (and the *dirigiste* orientation of the later SLORC/SPDC) has been motivated by the concept of getting the economy out of the hands of various foreigners and back under Burmese (meaning Burman) control. The *sangha*, as a critical social and nationalist force, and also sometimes a refuge for the unscrupulous, has been a target of control both for religious purposes (to purify the *sangha* has been a proclivity of the kings, U Nu, and the military) as well as to ensure the regime's power and legitimacy.

In spite of U Nu's true religiosity and search for state, regime, and personal legitimacy through Buddhist activities, he recognized that the amorphous autonomy of the *sangha* offered various dangers. A common criminal could shave his head, put on a saffron robe, and be considered sacrosanct. A communist insurgent could do the same. Monasteries could become refuges of rebels. Developing a system of control over the *sangha* was always a goal, one that was especially important to the military given the monks' history of antigovernment activity during the colonial period, and as the only national organization of both size and influence that might challenge the *tatmadaw*. In a historical sense, the military was acting within the patterns of the monarchs, for they had purified the *sangha* and texts, tried to eliminate heterodox and inappropriate Buddhist sects, and built pagodas to acquire personal and regime merit and legitimacy. In the civilian period, U Nu in 1956 had convened the Sixth Buddhist Synod in the 2,500 years of Buddhism and built the Peace Pagoda in Rangoon.

In 1980, the state finally placed controls on the *sangha*. In 1979, the military formed the Sangha Maha Nayaka—the centralized Supreme Sangha Council of 33 monks—and a group of 1,219 monk representatives of the *sangha* as a whole, as well as local councils at all levels. The hierarchy of the monkhood was established, and all monks were registered with the state by 1980. The educational activities of the *sangha* were controlled and monitored. The state also placed the monastic educational system, which went though university level, under scrutiny and reviewed the number of sects and their teachings. Committees of various monasteries underwent reform, and retired, trusted military officers placed in these organizations. This control was extensive but not absolute, for at the individual monastic level considerable autonomy existed, depending on the orientation of the abbot of that establishment. After 1988, the SLORC/SPDC tightened control over the *sangha* and its various sects. The Saffron Revolution of 2007, however, demonstrated the volatility of the *sangha* even with a Buddhist hierarchy tightly under government command.

### How was citizenship defined?

Citizenship in the Union of Burma was less disputed under the constitution of 1947 than under the military. Under the BSPP regime, the military completed the final exclusion of Indian and Chinese foreigners from any possibility of assuming official power.

On October 15, 1982, the military passed the Citizenship Act, establishing a three-tiered system of citizenship. Full citizens were those who were Burman or a member of one of the indigenous ethnic/linguistic groups or those who could prove they were descendants of residents who had lived in what was Burma in 1823 (before the start of the first Anglo-Burmese War,

1824–1826). They could be elected to office and assume government posts. One did not lose this class of citizenship by marrying a foreigner. The associate citizens, such as Indians and Chinese, were those who were born in the country after that time. The third group was composed of naturalized citizens. There was to be no dual citizenship, and associate citizenship could be revoked if someone were disloyal to the state "by act or speech or otherwise," or because of moral turpitude or disclosure of state secrets. Only full citizens could run for office or qualify for certain economic and governmental positions and, after the fifth BSPP congress, become members of the party. Those in the two lesser categories could not be given bureaucratic or military positions, could not vote, and were denied higher education. The indigenous Muslim Rohingyas near the Bangladesh border, however, were never considered as any type of citizen and were excluded from any list of ethnic groups. They have become the most deprived group in that state.

However deplorable and discriminatory such laws were (and Dr. Maung Maung, its author, had a doctorate in law from the Netherlands), in a sense they were the logical extension of the effort since independence of moving the economy under Burmese control. In the civilian period, only citizens could get certain types of import and export licenses. After the coup of 1962, the military expelled some 200,000 Indians (those from the subcontinent) back to that region with only their movable baggage. The new legislation, then, was the culmination of long-standing xenophobia.

### What was the role of General/President/Chairman Ne Win?

General (*bogyoke*, supreme commander) Ne Win (1910–2002; his original name was Shu Maung and he was from a Sino-Burman family) has been the most important influence on contemporary Burma. As second in command of the Burma army on independence in 1948, he became commander in 1949 and has since played an unprecedented role in the plight of the state, virtually until his death in 2002. A dropout from the University of Rangoon in the 1930s, he was one of the thirty comrades trained by the Japanese to revolt against the British. He claimed a close association with Aung San that may have been more hyperbole than reality. During the civilian government, he was minister of defense and on occasion deputy prime minister. The coup of 1958 that brought in the Caretaker Government, if not initiated personally by him, was carried out in his name. After the coup of 1962 he was variously not only head of the military but also chairman of the Revolutionary Council and the BSPP and, after 1974, president; in both roles he was head of state. (In 1976, an attempted coup against him failed.) He resigned as president in 1981, but retained his function as chair of the BSSP until his resignation in July 1988. Even after leaving all offices, he is said to have a decisive influence on major decisions, including, for example, approving the removal of General Saw Maung as chairman of the SLORC (and thus also head of state) in 1992 and perhaps renaming of the junta the SPDC in 1997. As he grew older, his influence faded, and his son-in-law and grandsons were accused of fomenting a coup in 2000, a charge that has kept them in jail and his daughter under house arrest until 2008, but which still is questionable. Ne Win died in December 2002 at the age of ninety-two. He was unceremoniously buried.

Ne Win's influence is important not only for the roles he played but because of his disastrous policies or those carried out in his name. He was highly mercurial, and his whims became commands, policy, and law. He could not be contradicted. He changed the currency into multiples of nine, his lucky number, which was astrologically assured to enable him to live to be ninety. He changed traffic from the left to the right side of the road (on the advice of an astrologer) to ensure his success. In his later years, he built a pagoda even though he was against making Buddhism the state religion. He recruited leaders whom he could control, forming his own entourage, often those who had served under him in the Fourth Burma Rifles, which he commanded. As head of the army, all the officers who were promoted owed their success to him. He changed those considered to be his political heirs at will, ensuring there was no one who could threaten his position. He was never an intellectual or even well educated, but he had a sense of political acumen that enabled him to rule officially for twenty-six years and unofficially for much longer.

One future question is: how generic is the Ne Win style of administration? Some believe that Senior General Than Shwe is exhibiting all the same traits of Ne Win, and one issue is whether this type of leadership (and the actions of those that follow the present leader) is virtually inherent in the political culture of Burma/Myanmar and reminiscent of the power of the Burmese kings; whether this is some singular aberration; whether this is inherent in the Burmese military command structure; or whether the actions of the leadership are fostered by their followers. This is a critical, unaddressed issue for the political future of Myanmar over the near term. Any answer proffered should not be interpreted as casting the political future of the state in stone, for attitudes among leaders and the population change, and an analysis today may not apply in the next generation.

### What happened to the economy in the 1980s?

The Burmese economy continued to be dependent on its export of primary products, such as rice and teak. It extracted from the peasant surplus rice beyond consumption, seed, and modest religious donations. The remainder could only be sold to the government at below-market rates. All legal exports were under government control. Burmese industry was light and of mediocre quality. As the 1980s progressed, prices for Burmese exports essentially stagnated; agricultural production could not expand without foreign fertilizer and pesticides that were lacking. The prices of necessary imports—intermediate goods on which Burmese industry depended, spare parts, and consumer goods, however, increased. Smuggling certain types of goods out—such as jade, gems, and even rice in border areas—proliferated, and smuggling consumer goods in, such as textiles and medicines, was widespread and deprived the government of income. Inflation, increased from 1986, causing growing hardships.

On September 1, 1987, the state announced the greatest economic liberalization since 1962: farmers could sell their grains, most importantly rice, on the open market as they wished. This was greeted as a major reform. However, less than a week later (September 5) the government announced the most stringent demonetization (not a devaluation of the currency but the declaration that certain bank notes were no longer legal tender and could not be redeemed) in modern history. (The British did this to Japanese currency issued during World War II, and this had dire effects on the population.) To destroy black marketers, the state claimed, all currency bills over about US$2.50 in value (said to be about two-thirds of the value of bills in circulation) were declared illegal, and there was no possible conversion to the new currency. This was the third demonetization since 1962 (others were in 1964 and in November 1985), but in the others documented assets could be converted; in this case, this option was impossible.

The impact was immediate. No one wanted to hold Burmese currency, because they feared further demonetizations (the constitution of 2008, significantly, has an article against demonetization). Peasants refused to sell their only asset (rice), because no one wanted to hold currency. This raised the urban price of rice, in effect a surrogate indicator of stability. Urban dwellers bought anything that would retain value, such as building supplies and appliances, just to avoid disaster. Many of these items were smuggled in from China, which had begun its economic liberalization program. Because demonetizations had always occurred on Saturday, merchants brought in bags of cash to the banks on Fridays, bribing officials to register these funds as deposited even if uncounted (and thus not affected by any possible future demonetization), and then withdrew the bag of money on Monday to begin business.

In an unrelated act, in December 1987, the United Nations declared that Burma was a "least developed nation," a designation that allowed them to receive highly subsidized loans. Although the country did not meet the objective criteria for such a designation because its literacy rate was too high, it had lobbied to attain that dubious status. When it did so, it never announced it to its people, who only learned of it when a few read the annual Report to the Hluttaw (parliament) on the budget on April 1, 1988. Many Burmese felt disgraced by the fall from the expectation a generation earlier that Burma would be the richest nation in Southeast Asia.

As this sad process unfolded internally, China had embarked on its expansion of private sector production and exports. At the same time, the Burma Communist Party, controlling a large segment of the China border, was collapsing through internal factionalism. The result was the pouring in of low-priced consumer products of higher quality and lower prices than Burma could produce, for the demand for commodities had grown. The overland trade was finally legalized in mid-1988, but by then Burmese industry had effectively been destroyed. All of these factors contributed to the failed people's revolution of spring 1988.

### What were the causes of the 1988 People's Revolution and the coup that followed?

Economic and political frustration had built up over time. Rice prices had risen following the September 1987 demonetization, and widespread dissatisfaction was evident. Following the coup of 1962, a large number of University of Rangoon students had been killed by the military. In 1974, demonstrations over economic conditions as well as over the military's slighted burial of U Thant, Burma's greatest public figure who had been secretary general of the United Nations (had he been in Burma at the time of the coup he would have been arrested because he had been U Nu's secretary), were considered both a national insult to a hero and a surrogate demonstration against BSPP rule. This prompted extensive demonstrations in Rangoon that resulted in many (unknown number of) deaths.

The spark in 1988, however, was apolitical. Students from the Rangoon Institute of Technology got into an argument in a tea shop on March 12; eventually the riot police (*lon htein*) intervened, and some students were killed. This led to more student demonstrations, some of the public joined in, and more were killed. Universities were closed; on March 18 the police took some demonstrators away in a police van, and forty-one died of suffocation, reminiscent of the "Black Hole of Calcutta" during the eighteenth century. Ne Win was out of the country at the time and was deeply disturbed to learn of this on his return.

The government was breaking down, and on July 23 at an emergency meeting of the BSPP, Ne Win suggested that the constitution be changed to allow a multiparty political system. He had even raised the question a year earlier to no effect. This the BSPP rejected. Ne Win, his motives variously interpreted as disgust or attempting to avoid blame, resigned from the chairmanship of the BSPP, taking with him the head of state, General San Yu, his acolyte. He was replaced on July 26 by General Sein Lwin, popularly known as the "butcher of Rangoon," because he had ordered the violence against the students. He lasted only twenty-three days as president.

A popular uprising occurred that was widespread not only in Rangoon and Mandalay but nationwide. It reached its apex on August 8, 1988 (8-8-88 was supposed to be astrologically auspicious for the opposition), and was brutally suppressed. Sein Lwin was forced out, and replaced on August 19 by Dr. Maung Maung, the only civilian trusted by Ne Win (and his biographer). He advocated a new election, but the trust in the present government had been eliminated, and people wanted a neutral interim government. U Nu, who still considered himself the last legitimate prime minister, tried ineffectively on August 9 to form a parallel government, the League of Democracy and Peace.

Purportedly, on August 23, at a secret meeting of the military leadership at Ne Win's home, the decision was made to deal with the situation. First, the students were to be neutralized, and their leadership executed if necessary. Then people were encouraged to run riot, criminals were to be released, and "chaos" created, so that the people would welcome a return to military rule and a coup would be justified. Violence spread, shops and factories were looted, and some who were considered government spies were summarily killed by the populace.

On September 12, a U.S. fleet of five ships, including the aircraft carrier *Coral Sea*, appeared off the coast, whether within or outside Burma's territorial waters is disputed. Although the rationale for their presence was said to be the evacuation of U.S. personnel, the Burmese feared an invasion. China mobilized its troops on the Burma border, and a rumor circulated that if the United States took action, China would occupy the Shan State. (The fear of the U.S. Navy was also apparent in 2007 after the Saffron Revolution, following Cyclone Nargis in 2008, and perhaps in the movement of the capital to Naypyitaw as well.)

The revolution almost succeeded when some elements of the military joined in the demonstrations, and the takeover of the Ministry of Defense was only thwarted by a speech by Brigadier (Ret.) Aung Gyi on September 12, urging calm.

The military believed that chaos had erupted, and on September 18, 1988, the armed forces launched their third coup, this time not to replace the BSPP with a civilian administration but to shore up military control. Retribution against the demonstrators was quick and brutal. In the course of the demonstrations, the coup, and its aftermath, thousands died; early opposition estimates were as high as 10,000, the government claimed only 440. Now, although figures are still unknown, the numbers usually quoted are about 3,000.

The military has continuously justified its actions against civilians by the fear of what they consider chaos—the disintegration of public order. Their fights against the insurgents in the 1950s and 1960s, the coups of 1958 and 1962, as well as that of 1988 are all justified in these terms. Some say that in 1988 the military created the chaos so that they might be praised for ending it. Other observers might conclude that it was not chaos they feared but the attrition or destruction of the military's role in society.

Although the failed people's revolution was prompted by internal economic problems and dissatisfaction with the government, the context of the times in East Asia perhaps puts it in comparative perspective. In 1986, President Ferdinand Marcos was forced to flee the Philippines because of the "people power" revolution. In 1987, the authoritarian government of South Korean President Chun Doo Hwan was forced to liberalize after massive public demonstrations, ending autocratic, military-oriented rule that had been in place since 1961. Burma was next in 1988, followed by the failed public uprising in Beijing at Tiananmen Square in 1989. None of these events were caused by any of the others, but together they indicated that times were changing in East Asia and that governments were forced to be more responsive to popular concerns even when the authorities could not be dislodged.

# 6

# THE SLORC/SPDC ERA
# (1988–PRESENT):
# CONTINUATION OF
# MILITARY POWER

The September 18, 1988, military transfer of power, in a sense a "coup by consent," that produced the State Law and Order Restoration Council (SLORC) was designed to continue military control by alternative means. As war, according to Carl von Clausewitz, is nothing but the continuation of state policy by other means, this coup may be considered governance by other methods. The previous military government that had become civilianized through the Burma Socialist Programme Party (BSPP) had economically failed. Politically it was disintegrating; it had to be resuscitated in some manner. Otherwise, military control would have ended, and the "chaos" (in the *tatmadaw*'s view) would fragment the Union of Burma. To the *tatmadaw*, chaos was descending on the society, and the military considered itself the only savior of the integrity of the state. To many civilians, however, this was the Rangoon spring, when censorship and control were effectively absent as government control broke down. This was part of a pattern of popular protests that profoundly affected East Asia—People Power in the Philippines in 1986, mass demonstrations leading to political liberalization in South Korea in 1987, Burma in 1988, and Tiananmen Square in China in 1989. The popular uprising in Burma was thus part of a wave, one that effectively crested in Seoul and crashed in Rangoon.

*What was the SLORC and how did it change into the SPDC?*

Each time the military has taken over control in Burma/ Myanmar, it has done so through the formation of a small coterie of military officers, even though one general may have been in command. So in 1958, the Caretaker Government was run by a small group of officers (in that period, there was only one general—Ne Win—a few brigadiers, and a considerable body of colonels). Following the 1962 coup, a military Revolutionary Council ran the state, and the BSPP, led by Ne Win, was formed. Even though it was a very small group at the beginning, it gradually expanded into a mass party almost a decade later. Then, in 1988, the military formed the SLORC of nineteen officers.

General Ne Win, ensconced in his mansion on Inya Lake in Rangoon, had retired from the BSPP in July 1988, but the coup could not have occurred and the new leader could not have assumed power without his blessing. General Saw Maung, a former sergeant in Ne Win's Fourth Burma Rifles, was the chair of the SLORC. Although the name SLORC indicated the intent of the military to rectify the chaos they saw as engulfing the state in the summer of 1988, to the outside world the name seemed to be the designation of an evil group from a poor TV spy drama. (A literal translation of the phrase from the original language might be "The Council to Build a Calm and Peaceful Nation.")

There were five key members—the chairman, Saw Maung; deputy chairman, Than Shwe; secretary-1, Khin Nyunt, Maung Aye, and later secretary-2, Tin Oo). The others were mainly regional military commanders. Power lay with the SLORC, and not with the cabinet. Most ministers were also military officers. The cabinet was the face to the external world and the administrative office charged with enforcing the junta's policies. Individual cabinet members could have influence insofar as they had the ear of the top junta members, but they were clearly subordinate to the junta.

In 1992, General Saw Maung was eased from his position as SLORC chair, reportedly for erratic behavior. He considered himself as the reincarnation of one of the great Burmese kings, Kyanzittha of the Pagan Dynasty. He is said to have dressed himself in royal regalia and performed various rituals associated with royalty. Ne Win eventually gave the informal authorization for his removal, and he was replaced by (Senior) General Than Shwe, who remains in command in 2009.

In 1997, when order (if not law) had been restored, the SLORC morphed itself into the State Peace and Development Council (SPDC), indicating by its new designation a change in function. (The name change may have been suggested by a U.S. public relations firm hired by the Burmese.) The junta was revised, and only the four core generals from the SLORC (Than Shwe, Maung Aye, Khin Nyunt, and Tin Oo, who was killed in a helicopter crash in 2001) were retained. The remaining members were also from the regional commanders, who were occasionally rotated.

### Who were the leaders of the military in this period, and how were they trained?

The older members of the military who were in the entourage of General Ne Win have been rapidly aging and fading away. Senior General Saw Maung, SLORC chair (1988–1992) and a sergeant in Ne Win's Fourth Burma Rifles, has died. Senior General Than Shwe was born in 1933, Deputy Senior General Maung Aye in 1937. General Thura Shwe Man is the youngest of the highest echelon (b. 1947). Although a few of the older officers are around and retired, a younger group has begun to come into power.

There are three avenues for advancement in the military. The most prestigious is through the Defense Services Academy, which is a four-year college-level course. This course had an annual intake of about 250. Total enrollment was about 1,500, but that has been increased through an intake of about 1,000. A total of 19,749 were trained since 1955, of whom 17,367 were army. Another avenue is through the Defense Services Officer Training School, which promotes from within the ranks, but most cadets now have college degrees. (In all, 16,251 have been commissioned.) A third route is an apprentice officer program (*teza*), which enrolls cadets after high school. To date, 4,958 men have been commissioned. Personal loyalties, and thus factions, are partly dependent on which school one attended.

The military has developed a number of other specialized schools. The Defense Services Academy of Medicine was founded in 1993 (1,525 commissioned), an Institute of Technology in 1994 (2,558 commissioned), and an Institute of Nursing in 2000 (1,034 commissioned). Applicants to all institutions have exceeded the number of places available. At a higher-ranking level, there is a Command and General Staff College, as well as a National Defense University for colonels and brigadiers. In 1998, it began awarding master's degrees. As of this writing, 350 completed the one-year program, with 292 degrees awarded.

Of the division commanders from 1988 to 2007, 107 graduated from the Defense Services Academy, 45 from the Officers Training School, and 12 from the *teza* program. Overseas training has been less extensive than in the civilian period, but between 1990 and 1999, 942 officers were sent abroad for training, of whom 615 went to China, 53 to India, and 34 to Pakistan. Singapore is reported to have trained some as well, as has Russia. (There were 1,500 trainees, including those in nuclear physics, aviation, and other military skills.) In the civilian period, trainees were sent to the United Kingdom, the United States, and Australia.

Although technical and military subjects are stressed, in the BSPP period, all officers were trained in the doctrines of the BSPP (see previous chapter). Under the SLORC/SPDC, such training focuses on the military itself as the ideological nucleus. This is in line with the general approach to the *tatmadaw* as the core of society. U Nu stressed Buddhism, the BSPP focused on the secular approach through socialism, and the present regime centers on the military itself.

The military has been struck by charges that the officers were poorly educated, and they have required that regional military commanders (there are a total of thirteen military regions including a new one, for Naypyitaw) have master's degrees. Aside from the SPDC members, the regional commanders are the most powerful of the officer corps. Generally, it is probably accurate to characterize the military leadership as highly nationalistic and insular, with limited foreign experience.

The military teaches that there have been eight stages in the development of their ideology since 1941. The first three (1941–1955) involve pre-ideological and an ideological gestation period; stages four through six (1956–1959) are the formation of an ideology of the defense services; stage seven (1962–1988) is the Burmese Way to Socialism, the change from a "praetorian army" to a "revolutionary army"; and finally, stage eight (1988–) contains the principles of the *tatmadaw*—the perpetuation of national sovereignty, national unity, etc., under military leadership.

The expansion of military training facilities may be part of a concerted plan to staff a future government with retired military specialists whose loyalty to the *tatmadaw* is unquestioned. Because civilian institutions of higher education have been closed for extended periods because of the fear of demonstrations, the military institutions have provided greater continuity through these difficult times.

### What political and economic policies were instituted shortly after the coup?

Burma began to change even before the coup of September 18, 1988. In the last days of the BSPP at the end of July, the waning party legally opened border trade with China. It also moved to encourage the private sector. On November 30, 1988, the new government issued a major foreign investment law that they claimed was "the best in the world," which protected foreign investors from nationalization, a justified fear based on Burmese history. The private sector was encouraged (at least on paper), and socialist policies were abandoned although there was very little movement to reduce the extensive state economic enterprises (the public sector industries), for if this were to happen, unemployment—already endemic—would rise. That fall, the government encouraged contracts with foreign firms to explore the oil resources of central Burma, and ten contracts were signed with a variety of international firms, each of which provided a signing bonus to the government, which was pitifully short of foreign exchange. After the visit of Thai army commander General Chavalit Yangchaiyut in December 1988, the first high-level external arrival, a variety of concessions were given to the Thai for hardwood extraction and maritime fisheries. The timber extraction contracts were highly significant—Thailand had recently banned all internal logging because the resulting deforestation had led to hundreds of deaths from landslides near the Burma border; these contracts were thus exploiting Burma in lieu of Thailand. Some years later, the Chinese also banned logging and moved into Myanmar to repeat the ecological damage.

Following the coup, the military moved to arrest as many people as they could find that were involved in the demonstrations. The repression was severe, and thousands were arrested and subjected to incarceration for varying periods, and many tried in camera (without a jury). There was no appeal in this process. Some 10,000 people, mainly students, fled across the borders, mostly to Thailand and to rebel areas, where some joined resistance groups. Schools and universities were closed for long periods.

At the same time, and perhaps because of the repression that shocked the public, the military promised that there would be multiparty elections. President Maung Maung said they would take place within three months of September 11, 1988. Many did not believe that the junta would carry this forward, but it seemed evident, even shortly after the coup, that the *tatmadaw* would honor its commitment. In private conversations, however, military officials implied that it had no intention of giving up effective power over the state, and an elective process (for what positions and when the elected group would assert its authority remain contested) was one that need not diminish their control. On September 27, 1988, the Political Parties Registration Law was promulgated, and 235 parties eventually registered. This was the basis for the elections of May 1990.

### How did the political opposition develop and what was the National League for Democracy?

There was widespread dissatisfaction with the BSPP regime and its thoroughly inadequate economic performance. Together with pent-up general and local political frustration, which became manifest in the popular uprising against the military, and the announcement that multiparty elections would be held, the National League for Democracy (NLD) was formed (as were 234 other parties over the period prior to May 1990 when the elections were actually held). The NLD was an amalgam of disparate individuals coalescing under the banner of democracy and under the leadership of former military officers under the BSPP but more immediately under the flag of antipathy to continuing military control. General (Ret.) Tin U, Brigadier (Ret.) Aung Gyi, Colonel (Ret.) Kyi Maung, and others joined together with people from all levels. Aung San Suu Kyi, who was junior in age and who had held no Burmese post, became the secretary of the NLD. Friction arose early, as the some on the left wing, accused of being communists, joined. Aung Gyi wanted them expelled and when Suu Kyi, the most articulate and respected member (because of the heritage of her father, Aung San), refused to do so, he and his colleagues walked out and founded a new party, the Union National Democracy Party.

Opposition also developed in other circles. U Nu, last civilian prime minister in 1962, believed he was the last legitimate leader and had wanted to form an interim government, but he was denied that chance. At the same time, local leaders around the country, many associated with ethnic groups, formed parties in opposition to the junta. It was in effect a period—as the Chinese said in another context—of 100 flowers blooming, and 100 schools of thought contending.

### What was the role of Aung San Suu Kyi and what has happened to her?

Aung San Suu Kyi (b. June 19, 1945) has become the icon of Burma/Myanmar and the international symbol of tethered democracy. Without her image, the excesses of the regime, which are less than the horrors in parts of Africa or Asia (Cambodia, China, North Korea, for example), would be barely internationally noted.

She is the only daughter of the founder of Burmese independence in 1948, who was assassinated by a rival Burmese politician on July 19, 1947. (There is also one son, who has eschewed politics and has lived in the United States.) That anniversary, Martyrs Day, is still remembered in Myanmar. Aung San Suu Kyi (her name incorporates that of her father in a most unorthodox Burmese manner) was in Burma in 1988 by accident. She grew up partly in India, where her mother was ambassador, and was schooled in England, where she married an English scholar on central Asia and had two sons. She returned to Burma to care for her sick mother in 1988 and was caught up in the opposition to military rule. She joined the NLD as secretary but soon became its primary spokesperson and intellectual force. The NLD attracted opponents of the military from all segments of the Burman population, from the left to the moderate right.

In July 1989, she was arrested for the most heinous crime—attempting to destroy military unity, essential for continued military dominance—and was sentenced to house arrest, where, off and on, she remained until 2009. She has been in various stages of isolation for about thirteen years during that time. When she has been occasionally released, she has tested the limits of military endurance through statements and attempted travel. On two occasions she has been in some physical danger from progovernment mobs, but at least some of the higher echelons of the military understood that it was in their interests to keep her safe and out of commission, because if anything untoward were to happen to her, even if from natural causes, the military would be held responsible, and it could give rise to revolution. "The lady," as she is known in Myanmar in official circles and the media (when she is mentioned) is the appellation used for her, because even to speak her name evokes the memory of the national founder, Aung San, and indirectly provides her some legitimacy. There are persistent rumors than Senior General Than Shwe will not hear her name mentioned in his presence.

Through outside pressure, the United Nations has been able to have two quiet interlocutors (Special Envoys Tan Sri Razali Ismail and Ibrahim Gambari) try to mediate between the junta and Aung San Suu Kyi, and the junta in 2007 assigned the minister of labor as an intermediary, although sustained progress has not been apparent at this writing (June 2009). At various periods, there seems to have been some peripheral movements in improving relations, but these have rapidly dispersed. There is fear among some of the junta that her full release or any public activities by her could disrupt the 2010 elections.

The views of Aung San Suu Kyi, as reflected in her writings and in the platform of the NLD, are in line with democratic concepts in most such states: representative government, civilian control of the military, better education (including scholarships), improved access to health, and some form of federal structure for the minorities. In her writings, however, she noted that democracy would come slowly to Myanmar. Yet the NLD is a Burman party, even though the Shan variant won the second largest number of seats in the 1990 election.

The West has basically supported her even more than it did the NLD. It may be argued that the views of Aung San Suu Kyi (or at least her past or purported views when she has been held incognito) shape or strongly influence U.S. policy and are vigorously supported by an effective democracy and human rights lobby and a large contingent of Burmese expatriates. An obscure amendment to some U.S. economic assistance legislation even stipulates that the NLD leadership must approve the UN development assistance program in Myanmar. To criticize her or the tactics of the NLD that she supports and that support her is regarded as heresy in the opposition community.

At this publication, she is sixty-four years old and could, under normal circumstances play an important role in Myanmar political life. She has occasionally called for dialogue, compromise, and discussion, which the junta has denied, and she has been specific in indicating that the military would play an important role in any government she might influence. The senior general has indicated the regime would be willing to have such dialogue if she rescinded her call for sanctions and was more flexible. But whether the aging leadership of the SPDC might agree to some form of coalition, and whether she would accept such a role given her long-held views of the inheritance of the mantle of her father, are not answerable at this stage. Some in the *tatmadaw* accuse her of arrogance, as she is said to believe herself the equal of Than Shwe.

### What were the May 1990 elections about and what were the internal and external results?

Even before the coup, the junta promised that there would be multiparty democratic elections. Certainly, one must assume they did this to placate a restive population. The opposition did not believe it would conduct them fairly and called for a neutral interim government, which the military rejected.

The first question that must be asked is: What were these elections to be for? Was it for a new parliament that would immediately take over government, as the NLD and public external observers seem to have expected, or for some sort of constitutional convention that would draft a new constitution, after which a government would be formed? This lack of clarity has resulted in high tensions.

The junta had publicly stated almost a year before the elections that those elected could not form a new government until there was a new constitution. On several occasions at press conferences, this was reiterated by Saw Maung and Khin Nyunt. Aung San Suu Kyi personally indicated on July 5, 1989, just prior to her house arrest, that "Whoever is elected will have to draw up a constitution that will have to be adopted before the transfer of power." Yet this condition had not been sufficiently stressed, and there seems to have been no direct contact between the military and politicians on what the rules of the game were to be. In that sense, the government bears the responsibility for the opaqueness of the process.

As preparations for the election progressed, the military did not discourage the formation of parties. Eventually, 235 of them were registered with the government. Some were said to have ulterior motives: they were anxious to get a telephone (in short supply and very expensive), as well as a ration of gasoline, which could be sold on the black market. Clearly, however, this was considered some sort of countrywide landmark, and people wanted to participate.

By the time the election of May 27, 1990, took place, 2,209 candidates from 93 parties and 87 independents competed for 479 seats. Aung San Suu Kyi was under house arrest at that time and could not stand for election. She had campaigned earlier and was almost shot, although cooler military heads prevailed. Although there were severe restrictions on campaigning, the parties emphasized local interests, including those of the ethnic nationalities. The BSPP was reincarnated into the National Unity Party, with many of the same ideological tenets as their former organization. Some Burmese observers expected them to do well because they inherited the resources of the BSPP. The military, however, was not said to be anxious for their victory.

The vote resulted in a 72.59 percent turnout, the highest in Burmese history. The NLD received 59.87 percent of the vote—392 seats or about 80 percent of the positions. The Shan NLD came in second with twenty-three seats (with 1.68 percent of the vote), and the National Unity Party won only ten seats, although they received 25.12 percent of the votes. This was both a remarkable and unexpected victory and no doubt shocked those in the military, who obviously had not been in touch with popular sentiment.

The NLD, flush with their remarkable victory, finally demanded on July 29 at what became known as the Gandhi (Hall) Declaration that the military turn over power to them by September 30, after which they would write an interim constitution and then a more permanent one after the transfer of power. The junta was not prepared to do this. Of great concern to the military was an off-hand remark by an NLD leader that there would be no Nuremberg trials. Although this was phrased in the negative, it heightened anxiety among the military leadership. Certainly, many in the population wanted to see justice done for past illegal actions. (Significantly, a provision of the 2008 approved constitution stipulates that no person can be held legally accountable for any official acts committed before that constitution has come into force.) In any case, the NLD and the outside world assumed that the NLD had a mandate to govern, and the United States still holds that position.

As the stalemate went on, all positions hardened. The military adamantly refused to certify the results of the elections, claiming they were looking into anomalies and irregularities (and the commission to do so was a geriatric rubber stamp of the government). The NLD claimed they had the right to govern. The Western international community backed the NLD. For many years, the U.S. State Department, in its semi-annual reports to Congress on Burma, called for the Burmese authorities to honor the results of the 1990 elections before discussions could take place. This was interpreted to mean that the *tatmadaw* had to give up power before normalization of relations could occur. This was patently something it would not do.

Some elected members of the NLD, believing that they represented the elected body as a whole because they had a wide majority of the seats, secretly formed the National Coalition Government of the Union of Burma (NCGUB), as a parallel government or government in exile, and moved to a rebel area, and then Thailand, after which they went to the United States to lobby for their cause.

It seems likely the junta thought that if they encouraged broad participation in the elections the votes would be so widely split that the military could remain in control. What became apparent was that the votes were generally fairly counted even if campaigning was heavily restricted. The military-sponsored elections of 1960 and 1990 produced results abhorred by the military authorities. In the first instance, they allowed those elected to take their seats, and in the second they did not. In the third military-sponsored election of 2010, the distribution of power has been predetermined. Even if the military allows open campaigning and a fair count of the ballots, the outcome of the locus of power in Burmese society will not change.

### What were the SLORC/SPDC's international relations, and how did Asian and Western nations react to the coup and the regime?

The generals who came to power in the SLORC were largely insulated from the outside world. All had been trained in Burma, and most had fought against Burma's various insurrections. The leader was General Saw Maung (he was ousted in 1992 for becoming mentally erratic, but only after the regime consulted with General Ne Win). His education had basically ceased in the eighth grade. He had been a sergeant in the Fourth Burma Rifles (originally commanded by Ne Win), and thus was part of the Ne Win entourage. The second in command was General Than Shwe (at that time army commander). General Maung Aye was charged with handing economic affairs. International relations were given to General Khin Nyunt, who was secretary-1 and also the head of military intelligence. He controlled an extensive network of officers but never commanded troops in the field, and thus he was at a disadvantage in not having a large and loyal military following. He was said to be a protégé of General Ne Win and consulted with him after Ne Win's official retirement in 1988. He was also said to be close to China.

General Khin Nyunt was promoted to prime minister in August 2003 and finally ousted in October 2004 because of corruption among the intelligence corps along the China border. This may have been an excuse, as through his intelligence functions Khin Nyunt had material that might be damaging to other junta and senior officials and was said to be vying for power with General Maung Aye.

It was Khin Nyunt who negotiated the cease-fires with a multitude of ethnic insurgent groups, and he received credit for that process. He also initiated the informal contacts between the junta and Aung San Suu Kyi through Ambassador Razali, the special envoy of the UN secretary general. General Khin Nyunt focused on foreign affairs and through that official role both had more access to international opinion and activities and was more accessible to foreign visitors. It was likely he who was interested in getting Myanmar to join the Association of Southeast Asian Nations (ASEAN; in July 1997). Some observers described him as a "soft-liner" compared to the "hard-liners" among the junta, but it is more likely he recognized that Myanmar was hurt by poor international relations and wanted to do something about it. He had to work within regime confines that were highly restraining.

While carefully cultivating the "national sovereignty" that the leadership believes is one of its highest priorities, Myanmar has moved to cement relations with China, its major supplier of military equipment, development assistance, and infrastructure construction. Innumerable high-level national and provincial delegations continuously visit Myanmar. Because it does not want to be dependent solely on China, it has improved relations with India, and has bought military and nuclear equipment from Russia. It seems likely that it would wish to improve relations with the West, but national pride seems to prevent the government from being perceived as retreating from its international, nationalistic position and submitting to Western demands. Although Thailand in 1992 called for "constructive engagement" with Myanmar that would lead to eventual political change, this was interpreted elsewhere as simply a euphemism for economic exploitation.

Myanmar joined a number of other regional groupings: the Greater Mekong Sub-Region Economic Cooperation Organization in 1992, BIMSTEC (Bangladesh, India, Myanmar, Sri Lanka, Thailand Economic Cooperation) in 1997, and the Irrawaddy, Chao Phraya, Mekong Economic Strategy Group (ACMEC) in 2003. In August 1999, Myanmar attended the Conference on Regional Cooperation and Development in Kunming that also included China, India, and Bangladesh. Known as the Kunming Initiative, it was designed to discuss ways to improve communications among all the countries; in essence, the revival of the southern Silk Road between Assam and Yunnan.

The personification of democratic ideals in Aung San Suu Kyi, resulting in her being awarded the Nobel Peace Prize in 1991, also increased her visibility and role (and through her, that of Myanmar), thus making her an icon throughout much of the world. The excesses of military rule, although deplorable, would probably have not received such broad and continuous condemnation without Aung San Suu Kyi as the representation of liberty. The junta claims discrimination, believing that the issues of democracy and human rights in other Asian countries, such as China and Vietnam, with worse records in some areas such as religious freedom, have received far less attention than those in Myanmar.

### What is the state of social services in Myanmar?

Perusal of the state's statistics on its role in expanding health and educational institutions would lead a naive observer to conclude that progress was evident in Myanmar. Yet these are essentially inflated figures that mask the brutal reality of decay and neglect for most of the population.

Enrollment in education at all levels has expanded, yet the quality has declined. The government claims those enrolled in primary education are at the ninetieth percentile level, but UNICEF notes that perhaps 50 percent of students do not finish primary school. Classes are overcrowded and teachers underpaid, with the result that "tuition" schools have privately been established, often by the very teachers who teach in public school, to educate the children after normal school hours (and provide the teachers some modest livable income) and for which the parents of students pay. Essentially, teachers teach extracurricularly the material that the state has paid them to teach publicly.

Only a small percentage of students go on to middle school and high school (ten years is the total primary and secondary years of instruction, excluding kindergarten). College- and university-level institutions and enrollments have proliferated (undergraduates are relegated to a campus on the outskirts of Yangon). Yet the bulk of students are in "distance learning," which keeps them from congregating on campuses and thus potentially causing trouble for the government. The state has formed colleges in each state and division (sometimes with more than one branch). According to those who teach at university or college level, corruption is rife in grades and attendance, and students are not motivated because jobs are scarce. In addition, at the slightest hint of a possible demonstration, schools are closed, often for long periods, which results in chaotic admissions and examination scheduling. The government spends 1.3 percent of gross domestic product (GDP) on education, a very low percentage in international comparisons.

Health services are in disarray. Health expenditures are even lower than in education—only 0.5 percent of GDP, one of the lowest in the world. Primary care is usually not available, and those doctors serving the state in rural areas have to moonlight to get by. Medicines are unavailable except to the rich or connected, and most doctors serve for a period in the military, which has its own medical school. Civilian doctors must serve three years in the military to receive a license. Medicine is a desired career for both men and women, and in the civilian period, medical standards, reinforced through external examiners, were so high that graduates were automatically allowed to practice in the United Kingdom. This has all changed. Malaria (700,000 cases annually) and tuberculosis (130,000 per year) are rampant. HIV/AIDS is common and far more significant that the government admits. There were estimated to be some 350,000 cases in Myanmar in 2005. The United States quietly and informally scuttled a plan called the Global Fund to provide US$90 million over five years to assist in alleviating the problems of tuberculosis, malaria, and HIV/AIDS on the grounds that monitoring could not be assured. In response, six donors (Australia, the European Commission, the Netherlands, Norway, Sweden, and the United Kingdom) established a five-year fund of US$100 million over the same period to provide assistance to deal with the problem of these three diseases, or 3DF, as the program became known.

Infant mortality is said to be 75 per 1,000 live births, and on a national average an additional 105 children die before the age of five years. In eastern Myanmar, where conditions are worse, the infant mortality is 221 per 1,000, compared to 106 in central Myanmar and only 21 in Thailand. The life expectancy of the Burmese is just over sixty years, the lowest in ASEAN.

For a country that was never supposed to have a famine (in contrast to India and China), malnutrition is now common, and some 35 percent of infants suffer from this to some degree. Some 73 percent of income is allocated to purchase basic foods, especially rice, and so the incessant inflation undercuts living standards for the poor. The UN Human Development Report of 2000 ranked Myanmar as 124 (out of 174 countries) in terms of this development. Cyclone Nargis obviously and drastically lowered living standards. The pervasive corruption, so necessary for survival, has negatively affected the equitable distribution of relief in Nargis-affected areas.

There is thus a socioeconomic crisis that the government has denied, and when the UNDP resident representative brought this to the attention of the cabinet in November 2007 and went public with his views, his visa was not renewed. Although the junta may believe there is a strategic and military security crisis, actual conditions indicate that the security crisis is instead a human security crisis. Food supplies for half the population are not secured, and more broadly the dire state of internal affairs indicates a profound human security crisis—including food, health, education, livelihood, and personal tranquility.

One unanswered question in contemporary Myanmar is the relevance of concepts of the traditional Buddhist virtues of the state (ruler) to treat its people with compassion and that of individual karma, or one's present status as retribution for activities in previous existences. Thus, if one suffers, is it due to one's bad practices in a previous incarnation or the lack of interest or inability of the state to supply social services to the population? The degree to which Buddhist karmic concepts of individual responsibility, in conflict with modern beliefs in state responsibility, affects present attitudes in Myanmar is unknown. Karmic concepts were evident in the past, as is apparent from earlier field research a half-century ago, but how much it has changed in rural areas is unclear. It has evidently changed among the educated urban population and seems to have disappeared as a political explanation in another Buddhist country, Thailand.

### What is the status of the private sector in Myanmar?

When the government announced in July 1988 that the rigid socialist doctrine of the BSPP would be rescinded, this passed effectively unnoticed outside the country because of the political turmoil of that time. Yet this was the most significant and positive change in Burma since 1962. It had been brought about by quiet pressure from the Japanese in March 1988, when the Burmese deputy prime minister was told in Tokyo that economic reforms were essential or the Japanese aid program, comprising over half of all foreign assistance, would have to be reconsidered.

Ironically, the movement away from socialism occurred in the waning days of the BSPP, and by November 1988 a new foreign investment law was promulgated. Outside investors were very interested in Myanmar, especially its on-shore oil reserves. Ten foreign firms quickly bid to secure exploration rights in central Myanmar.

This was followed by a broad infusion of foreign investment and the opening of indigenous banks to provide capital to local investors. This surge of interest concentrated at first on mineral exploration, especially oil and gas. Subsequently, the low-wage, literate, and controlled labor market proved attractive to foreign investors who sought sites for the establishment of textile and garment factories, often to circumvent quotas on their own countries. Many investors had joint ventures with government ministries or organizations. Most of these investors were from Asia, with the exception of the largest one, an amalgam of French, U.S., and Thai companies brought together to exploit natural gas found offshore and to build a pipeline to Thailand. By the end of 2008, the Burmese authorities cumulatively listed 422 foreign investment projects totaling some US$15 billion over the previous twenty years, although unauthorized Chinese investment in small business activities would likely push the total higher.

One attraction of Myanmar to foreign investment has been a forcibly controlled labor force, where strikes are prevented and demonstrations curtailed. A literate, productive, docile, and inexpensive labor force has attracted labor-intensive industries, and workers have responded because of the lack of alternative employment. *Corvée* labor has been used by the state, much against ILO regulations, resulting in past threats to exclude Myanmar from that group.

Human rights advocates effectively lobbied to shame some foreign investors from working in Myanmar, claiming that they were effectively supporting the military. Aung San Suu Kyi was against foreign investment, tourism, and even humanitarian assistance for a period, although her views on humanitarian support changed. Criticism of the regime grew, and in 1997 the United States imposed sanctions on all new investment beyond those initiated after the coup of 1988 that stopped military and economic assistance. Restrictions were also imposed by the European Union. The United States followed with further, more stringent sanctions in 2003, prompting many foreign businesses to refuse to invest or to pull out. The United States passed additional sanctions in 2008. One of the probable motivations behind Myanmar joining ASEAN in July 1997 was the prospect of greater investment from those states; ironically, the month that Myanmar joined was the month the Asian financial crisis of 1997 started in Thailand, and this effectively prevented the investment that Myanmar had sought.

By the late 2000s, new foreign investment had dropped. In monetary terms, foreign investment has been heavily concentrated in the extractive industries—oil, gas, minerals, timber. Foreign investment in Vietnam, which opened to the outside business community at about the same time, was booming. Although the Vietnam internal market is about 50 percent larger than the Burmese one, that seems to be an unlikely explanation. Obviously, part of this has to do with sanctions and the opprobrium effectively directed against that government. Other causes are also at work.

Myanmar is rated as one of the most corrupt countries in the world, according to Transparency International, which places it at the bottom along with Somalia. To do any business, whether one is a foreigner or a citizen, one needs if not a Burmese partner then at least a Burmese protector. Rent-seeking and corruption are endemic in a society where wages are low and inflation is high, and a system of patron–client relationships is critical in such a political culture. Yet the established patron of today may become the outcast of tomorrow. Furthermore, law is essentially irrelevant—whereas "policy" is important: today's policies may also be tomorrow's crimes. Further, seemingly on a whim or at least without consultation, regulations change. Businesses need predictability, and this is sorely lacking in contemporary Myanmar society. Rarely does the military allow the repatriation of profits, which are usually invested in Burmese raw materials for export.

The indigenous Burman private sector, deprived of capital and subject to the whims of political leadership, flounders. Yet one type of individual succeeds. This is the Chinese entrepreneur, sometimes a legal resident or a Sino-Burman, or sometimes an illegal migrant who has acquired Burmese identity papers. These individuals have access to capital through traditional clan and linguistic associations and are not dependent on the formal banking system. They transfer funds internally and externally through secure but informal mechanisms. If present trends are not reversed, they will become the new Burmese middle class, and the specter of ethnic foreigners holding the reins of the Burmese economy could exact xenophobic reactions.

### What is the status and role of the military in Myanmar?

As one Burma/Myanmar specialist put it, the military in Myanmar is a state within a state. The *tatmadaw*'s view of their position in society confirms this. General Saw Maung said, "It is in accord with the 'law of nature' that the indigenous people [have] love and respect for the *tatmadaw*." As the military has asserted, "Only if the Armed Force is strong, will the Nation be strong." The *tatmadaw* is, according to its slogans, the "mother and father" of the people. Their earlier exhortation was "don't look over the shoulder of your mother at your aunt" (don't rely on foreigners). It is virtually a self-contained community of some 400,000 (figures vary) active-duty members, and when families are included, it totals some 2 million people, or some 4 percent of the population. A large (but unknown) number relate economically to the military in a type of dependency. If one considers the retired military and their families, who also play important roles in Burmese society, the number is greatly magnified. All in all, not an inconsiderable percentage of the population is in some manner dependent on the present military role and rule.

Until 1988, the army was reasonably well administered, and corruption was not a major problem. The expansion of the military since that time (the *tatmadaw* totaled 198,681 in 1988), however, has led to looser control and the recruitment of less desirable elements. Organizationally, there are said to be 504 battalions of 826 men each, up from 168 battalions in 1988. There are ten light infantry divisions. The provision of more sophisticated arms from China (estimated at more than US$3 billion) and elsewhere will require high budgetary maintenance allocations and greater training requirements.

The military's role in the power structure and administration has been explained a number of times. But the ancillary functions and its influence are less well understood. The government has built up institutions run by or under the influence of the military in all fields. Military training institutions are producing not only officers for the present administration but also a future elite cadre who will staff ostensibly civilian institutions. The *tatmadaw* also runs its own schools for dependents, and the best health care in that disease-prone state is in military-run hospitals. Businesses and manufacturing are frequently run directly by military conglomerates, which also have extensive joint ventures with foreign firms. Every substantial enterprise needs someone in the military establishment to ensure that the economic gears turn smoothly. There also said to be monasteries that the military favor that are under their influence. The military encourages private contributions to such institutions as well as other good works. They then donate such material under military auspices in an attempt to garner the karmic credit that such giving provides.

These are the direct or quasi-direct elements of the state within a state. The ancillary elements of this substate, if you will, are the tentacles that reach out administratively into civilian life. These include the Union Solidarity and Development Association (USDA; the membership of which has been reported at over 24.6 million, perhaps two-thirds of the adult population) explicitly established to serve military needs, the cooperative movement, the Maternal and Child Welfare Association, the firefighters association, and the Myanmar War Veterans' Association (which operates twenty-six businesses worth over K.9.6 billion). A significant number of other groups all serve the *tatmadaw*'s political purpose of control, whatever other functions they may perform. The USDA may be the intellectual descendant of the National Solidarity Associations that the military formed in the Caretaker period (1958–1960). One may assume that the membership in many of these groups is not completely voluntary—not physically coerced but socially and often professionally necessary. Social pressures and administrative requirements regarding membership come into play when acceptance or advancement is at stake.

Many families in opposition to military rule want their sons to join the *tatmadaw*, as it is the prime avenue to social mobility and economic success. At the local level, the military situation has become more complex. Local units have been encouraged to fend for themselves by growing their own food, which often leads to confiscating land for this purpose. As the military has built its own exclusive structure of controlled and supporting institutions, it is more than likely that the inclusiveness of this control, and the arrogance that seems to have gone with it, has resulted in broad resentment among those who have not been so favored.

### How does the narcotics trade affect the society and international relations?

In some circles, Myanmar has been called a narco-state, one in which the incomes from narcotics production, distribution, and sales are critical factors in regime continuance. This pejorative characterization is not justified by facts. No government, including that of the United States, has charged that the Burmese administration directly receives funds from the narcotics trade.

This, however, is only a partial description. Opium production and its transformation into heroin have been important factors in contemporary Burma/Myanmar. A large number of ethnic minorities in the hill areas of northern Myanmar have relied on its production. The name Golden Triangle refers to the opium-growing areas where Burma/Myanmar, Thailand, and Laos come together. That local officials, including local military, engage in its production or tax its distribution is clear. The government freely admits that the drug lords have been able to cease their activities and retire in comfort in the country and use their funds for more legitimate economic projects (and thus more wealth). The United States calls this money laundering; the Burmese call it development projects. The government passed a money-laundering law, with strong encouragement from the United States, but implementation seems to have been lacking.

We need not go back to the opium war between Britain and China in the nineteenth century to understand the nature of the opium problem. The British encouraged (or at least legally tolerated) the growing of opium in the Shan State. Shan leaders taxed its use. It was finally declared illegal during the military Caretaker Government. The Kuomintang troops in Burma fostered its expansion. Opium production swelled from some estimated 250 tons per year to over ten times that amount in 1989 (although alternative estimates abound), producing heroin essentially to feed the Western markets. It was the cash crop for hundreds of thousands of hill dwellers who otherwise existed on subsistence agriculture. These farm families did not grow wealthy; most remained poor. The middle men and dealers were the beneficiaries. The sale of opium and its ultimate product, heroin, provided the means by which to fund ethnic armies and, following the cessation of Chinese support, the Burma Communist Party.

The Shwedagon Pagoda in Yangon. (Photo © Mark Van Overmeire, courtesy of Shutterstock)

Than Shwe salutes during the 63rd Armed Forces Day in administrative capital Naypyitaw on March 27, 2008. (KHIN MAUNG WIN/AFP/Getty Images)

Damage from Cyclone Nargis on Haing Gyi Island, in the Irrawaddy division of southwest Myanmar, May 7, 2008. (AFP/AFP/Getty Images)

U Nu, or Thakin Nu (1907-1995), the Burmese prime minister, during most of the civilian period. (Photo by Central Press/Getty Images)

General Ne Win (1911–2002), Military Commander, Prime Minister, President, Chair BSPP, head of states. (Photo by Keystone/Getty Images)

Aung San Suu Kyi meets with Thein Sein in his office in Naypitaw,
August 2011 (anonymous/AP)

Thein Sein in Seoul, October 2012 (Kim Hong-Ji/Reuters)

Barack Obama and Hillary Clinton tour the Shwedagon Pagoda, November 2012 (Carolyn Kaster/AP)

Barack Obama meets with Thein Sein in Yangon, November 2012 (Peter
Souza/White House web site)

As in many parts of the world, the United States provided assistance to the government to eliminate the crop. The United States supplied helicopters (twenty-seven helicopters and twenty-eight other planes), pilot training, and other equipment, and surveillance increased. Because insurgent armies could shoot down the helicopters, their use was confined to areas in which the military had ground forces and could prevent this. Much of the production was beyond their military capacity to control, however; the effects were limited in that period. The United States cut off assistance for aerial spraying of the poppy fields after the coup of 1988.

Perhaps because of international opprobrium, the junta, under Khin Nyunt's leadership, began a program of eradication of the opium crop. ASEAN as a whole had a target of 2015 as a drug-free region. This effort was at first treated with skepticism in international circles, but eventually the United Nations indicated that such production had become minimal compared to the previous decade (130,000 hectares under production in 1998, compared to 27,000 in 2007). In 2002, the United States and the junta met quietly to discuss steps to take Myanmar off the international narcotics list, but a number of congressional members sought to continue to isolate the regime, preventing this. There has been one negative effect: the loss of income for these hill dwellers has made them some of the most deprived people in the state. In the 1975–1985 period, 75 percent of all heroin imports into the United States came from Burma; in 2007, this figure was less than 2 percent. In that year, Afghanistan produced 93 percent of the world's opium, and Myanmar only 5 percent. These encouraging statistics may well prove ephemeral, as other crops providing alternative incomes are not easily cultivated or marketable in those remote areas, and a return to poppy production is likely.

If opium production is down, drug production is not. Methamphetamines, chemically produced drugs with no agricultural base, are produced in Myanmar among the Wa and transported into Thailand, through which the chemical components are imported back into Myanmar, and where it has became an important political issue. The Wa are the most heavily armed of the ethnic groups with which the government has verbal cease-fire agreements. They cannot be controlled by the *tatmadaw*. Even entry to their areas by any Burmese military personnel requires their approval. Prime Minister Taksin Shinawatra in Thailand in 2003 ordered a war against these drug dealers that resulted in nonjudicial government executions of over 2,800 dealers and others and causing a quiet confrontation with the United States and human rights groups over evident violations of human rights. An estimated 700,000 to 1 million tablets of methamphetamine enter Thailand every year from Myanmar, and they have become a scourge of Thai youth. Some 4 percent of the Thai population is said to use this drug. To protect this trade, the United Wa Army on the Myanmar side of the border has had skirmishes with the Shan State Army South, armed by the Thai and supported by the United States. These minority armies have become surrogates for the Burmese and Thai governments in that border region.

### What are the roles and influence of minority religions (Islam, Christianity) in Myanmar?

Minority religions have important negative and positive influences in society. The positive influences of solace and group solidarity result among peoples on the periphery, especially non-Buddhist groups. Three minorities have been especially prone to Christian conversions, and it is significant that few Buddhists are converted. Most conversions take place among animist populations. Foreign influences have become important, but under the constitution of 2008 no religious group in Myanmar will be able to receive or expend funds from foreign sources.

The most Christianized ethnic groups are the Chin and Kachin. The 1983 census notes that among the Chin in western Myanmar along the India border, about 70 percent were

Christian; some now say the figure is closer to 90 percent. Observers believe that perhaps 90–95 percent of the Kachin in northern Myanmar are now Christians. The Karen have been noted as prime converts to Christianity since the early nineteenth century when the American Baptist Mission went into Burma. Although accurate figures are lacking, some say about one-third of the Karen people are Christian, one-third Buddhist, and one-third animist.

Although foreign missionaries are no longer allowed residence in the country (most of those resident in 1962 were allowed to remain but could not return once they left), there are strong ties with external churches. They have maintained liaisons, churches in Burman areas are accessible, and seminaries still exist to train local pastors and priests. There have been charges of church burnings and oppression, especially in the east where Karen insurgents, many of whom are Christian, operate. The Chin State has also been the scene of harassment and forced labor to build Buddhist pagodas.

The charges by some foreign organizations that there has been a national concerted effort to wipe out or threaten Christians cannot be substantiated. There are, however, serious impediments to Christians rising in the military and the bureaucracy. There are evidently glass ceilings that prevent Christians from assuming senior positions, such as colonels or higher officers in the *tatmadaw*. Local military commanders have considerable latitude to act against minority religious groups, so occasionally incidents no doubt occur. Members of unregistered and informal Chin churches in Burman cities have been subject to harassment.

Muslim problems are more severe. Although mosques operate freely in major cities, there are severe prejudices that provoke outbursts. Muslim–Buddhist riots are an irregular but not uncommon occurrence in various towns and are usually based on some perceived insult by a Muslim to Buddhism or to a Burman woman. Some charge that such riots are engineered by the military to direct antagonisms away from the government to helpless scapegoats. Beliefs persist even at the cabinet level that Muslims attempt to convert Burman women, and, if successful, Islamic organizations provide rewards depending on the social level of the converted person.

The most severe issue related to Islam is the plight of the Rohingyas on the Bangladesh border. This group is effectively stateless. They are not recognized by the government (and have not been so since the Panglong Agreement in 1947) as a minority group or a national "race." The government has claimed that they are, in fact, Bengalis. They have no rights and cannot even legally leave their area in the townships along the border. Some tens of thousands have fled by sea to Malaysia, a supposedly a friendly Muslim state, but their status has been ambiguous. Thailand has turned some back out to sea. In 1978, Burmese police and troops made a sweep through that region and prompted more than 200,000 to flee into Bangladesh. Most were repatriated under UN auspices. A similar flight occurred in 1991–1992, and again there was UN repatriation (although some 10,000–15,000 still remain in exile). In January 2009, the government again denied that they were one of the state's national "races."

The military claims that these people are in effect illegal immigrants, and therefore they have no right to citizenship. The migrations along that portion of the Burma/Myanmar littoral from the early nineteenth century onward are complex. The fusion of India and Burma in the colonial period, and the exodus during World War II and in the current period, made matters even more murky. Burmese authorities have also charged that there is terrorist training among Muslims on the Bangladesh side of the border; through their military intelligence service they have monitored such activities. The Rohingya situation is far more severe regarding human rights violations than among any other minority. In August 2008, however, the government announced it would issue identity cards to some 37,000 Rohingya as a first stage in their registration, although whether this would give them improved status is questionable.

In acts that seem designed to demonstrate Burmese sovereignty over some of the border regions inhabited by both Christians and Muslims, the government has been building pagodas. They have been constructed in the Kachin State on the China border in a Christian area, and in the Rakhine State on the Bangladesh border in a completely Muslim area. General Than Shwe is said to believe that the most dangerous of the Burmese frontier regions is the one with Bangladesh. In historical terms, he is correct.

### What is and has been the status of women in Burma/Myanmar?

The role of Aung San Suu Kyi as the icon of democracy in Burma/Myanmar has led the expatriate Burmese opposition to make her birthday (June 19) an international women's day. They have also protested the perceived subjugation of women under the present Myanmar government, especially exemplified by the house arrest and denigration of Aung San Suu Kyi. This has been compounded by charges of systemic rape of minority women by the Burman troops.

This movement is somewhat ironic, for among the major cultures of South and East Asia, the status of Burmese women has historically been higher. They traditionally married under their own volition. There was no foot binding in Burma as there was China, nor the practice of suttee (widow suicide) as in India. Burmese women had equal inheritance rights with their male siblings and retained control over their dowries. If there were a divorce, the wife would keep the dowry; this kept divorce rates low. Early English observers felt that the status of Burmese women was higher than that in Europe at the time, and one British observer in the early nineteenth century believed that Burmese women were more literate than English women. Burmese women not only control most family affairs but also have important economic roles; most trading in the bazaars is by women. In modern times, females equal males in the educational system, and women have been prominent in the professions, especially in education and medicine.

In 1959, the military Caretaker Government passed a universal military draft law on an Israeli model that included women. It has never been implemented. There are women in the military, but not in combat roles and not at the decision-making level. There are, however, many women in the higher echelons of the civil service, and some at the director general level, although not in the cabinet. During the BSPP period, abortions for medical reasons needed approval by the husband and the party.

Although rape in wartime and periods of conflict has been prominent, there is no evidence that this has been a state-sponsored policy, as some have charged. Few have been charged or convicted of such crimes by the government, which amounts to avoidance of the issue. The charge that rape has been an effort to dilute the minority population by genetically "Burmanizing" them seems unfounded. Yet in one sense women are treated as inferior: to enter Buddhist nirvana, they must first be reincarnated as a male. Burmese nuns, numbering over 40,000, have far lower status than monks. As one scholar wrote, "Military rule, however, has reinforced the authoritarian, hierarchical, and chauvinistic values that underpinned male-dominated power structures."

### What is the status of the cease-fires with minority insurrections in Myanmar?

The SLORC/SPDC, in a tactically clever maneuver, began the process of negotiating cease-fires with a broad spectrum of the minority organizations that revolted against central authority. This process was led by General Khin Nyunt, at that time secretary-1 of the SLORC and in charge of military intelligence. When he was ousted in October 2004, the SPDC said that the cease-fires were a product of the junta as a whole, and that they would continue and be respected. At this writing, there are about twenty-five such cease-fires, almost all of which are verbal agreements. Seventeen have been recognized, and those minority troops control special regions where they are effectively local government. There are approximately twelve groups still in some form of rebellion. Splinter groups form and reform, so the situation is dynamic. The remaining military forces in revolt have dropped to only several tens of thousands distributed among all insurgents.

These cease-fire groups have widely divergent relations with the central government and different degrees of autonomy or control. Three degrees of authority exist: those that have near devolution of authority (and thus are essentially autonomous), those effectively under military occupation, and those where a fragile form of coexistence exists. The most autonomous are the Wa and the Kokang, both on the China border. Here, the local authorities are in command, and it is said that Burmese army troops cannot go into Wa territory without permission of the Wa and in some cases without surrendering their weapons. The second group includes those in which a military occupation is the reality: the Rakhine State in the west, and in the east in parts of the Kayah and Karen States. The coexistence groups are in the north among the Kachin, and also on the eastern frontier and include the PaO, Mon State Army areas, and the Buddhist Karen region.

The general agreements were that these groups would retain their arms but not engage in any action against the government; within the territories they controlled, they could continue to engage in their normal economic activities, with the exception of opium production (see that question in this chapter). The agreement originally was that these groups would turn in their weapons before a referendum on the new constitution. This has not happened.

The fear that pervades minority–majority relations means that such groups will have little incentive to comply with this regulation except in some meaningless, formalistic manner. They might turn in some outmoded arms in some symbolic ceremony, while retaining their essential weapons in hidden caches. Minorities fear not only the *tatmadaw* but also other potential adversaries of the same ethnicity. When Khin Nyunt was prime minister, it seemed apparent that he was prepared to offer some compromise on the questions of arms, such as enfolding some of these groups into militias or national guards or some Burmese equivalent (this occurred under the BSPP). This seems to be a necessary step if the fighting is not to erupt again. Under the new constitution of 2008, various militias are allowed, but there can only be one national *tatmadaw*.

Before the scheduled elections of 2010, the government is said to demand cease-fire groups be reconstituted into border patrols or forces with a significant admixture of Burman troops (10 percent). Whether the minorities will comply with this order is unclear at the time of this writing.

In addition to allowing some of the cease-fire organizations to retain the territory they administer, the government has offered to some groups economic incentives to enable them to increase their wealth and services to their own people and to tie them to the central government. Investments in a jade mine by the PaO minority has brought them considerable wealth that they have invested in other, countrywide ventures.

The Burman–minority relationships cannot be easily characterized, for they vary in the degree of intrusion and repression. In many cases, the *tatmadaw* and government, and through the government its agents such as the USDA, are seen as predatory. They have confiscated land, forced villagers to grow food for the troops, coerced the building of Buddhist structures and other forms of construction, set up checkpoints to extort funds, and increased license fees for many activities. For decades the state has enforced a system known as the "four cuts," which has been widely condemned. This is the denial to insurgents of food, finances, recruiting, and intelligence in village areas. This system was also used in the BSPP period and seems derived from the British attempts to wipe out the communist insurrection in Malaya in the 1950s and by the U.S. counterinsurgency programs in Vietnam.

The complexities of the various stages of the rebellions and the cease-fires as well as their causes preclude simple, standard approaches to mediation that may have occurred in other countries. These are old animosities and fears, dating back to independence in many cases. Some have had international dimensions and links, but most are related to deeply rooted decades-old social and humanitarian issues. Some of the insurgents and former insurgent groups have developed what have been called "alternative systems of profit, power and even protection"—that is, vested interests in maintaining control over certain areas and peoples. This makes solutions even more difficult.

The BSPP had founded in Sagaing Division an institute for minority education, perhaps formed along a Chinese model, to train minorities in the official ideology. In 1991, the SLORC changed this into a University for the Development of the National Races.

Many of these cease-fire groups participated in the National Convention that produced the new constitution. The dilemma for these organizations now, and for others as well, is whether they should participate in the planned 2010 elections. To do so undercuts whatever status and validity may still accrue to the 1990 elections, but to eschew them means to be cut out of even a modest role in a new government. In minority areas, by early 2009 various groups were considering organizing political parties on either ethnic or regional bases. Yet the various exiled ethnic organizations have each produced drafts of constitutions they deem acceptable. They have done so abroad, because to do so internally was considered an offense by the military. All of them, to one degree or another, call for a federalism that the military abhors. Whether these cease-fire groups—a few of which will be given townships where they will have some local governing authority—will be satisfied with the situation remains uncertain.

## What are relations with the United States?

As Myanmar enters its third decade of military rule following the coup of September 18, 1988, relations with the United States have sunk to their lowest ebb since that date. Prospects for the near term are not optimistic, although some alternative approaches have surfaced in 2009 under President Barack Obama. The United States has enacted four stages of sanctions against the regime.

Although the previous government run by the military through the BSPP was an autocratic, single-party socialist state without any fig leaf of democratic governance, since 1979 the United States had an economic assistance program centered on basic human needs (today called humanitarian assistance). This was prompted by the poverty of the people. It also had a military assistance program to provide helicopters and equipment that was designed to help reduce opium production, which was at that time the primary source of the U.S. heroin supply. It started in June 1974 and by 1983 the cost totaled some $47 million. The violence with which the people's revolution of 1988 was repressed, together with the coup and subsequent retaliation against its opponents or sympathizers, prompted an immediate U.S. reaction.

Whether U.S. legislation legally required the cut-off of economic aid following the coup is unclear, as the law indicates that all foreign assistance monies, except humanitarian assistance, have to cease if a coup overthrows a democratically elected government, which the BSPP obviously was not. The United States also halted military assistance. In effect, these comprised the first wave of sanctions against the SLORC. For a period, the U.S. ambassador consciously decided not to meet with the authorities because it might confer a degree of legitimacy on their actions. When he finally did, there was agreement that there would be no publicity.

Following the elections of May 1990, and intensified by the awarding of the Nobel Peace Prize to Aung San Suu Kyi in 1991, the U.S. antipathy toward the junta increased and hardened.

It also became more personalized around the figure of Aung San Suu Kyi. Further sanctions were enacted in 1997. These restricted visas for certain Myanmar military officials and their families and prohibited new American businesses from investing there. Some in Congress pushed for divestiture of previously established businesses, but the State Department's views prevailed, and the action was limited only to those firms that had not invested prior to the act's passage.

The third stage came following the Depayin incident in central Myanmar in May 2003 when an NLD caravan, including Aung San Suu Kyi, was attacked and an unknown number of people were killed. This was the most strict of Myanmar sanctions, preventing the use of U.S. banking facilities (including interbank transfers that went through New York), and further restricting travel to the United States of higher ranking military and their families, as well as senior civilian employees of the government. The minuscule Myanmar assets in the United States were frozen. All users of U.S. banks needed to have individual U.S. Treasury waivers, for example, to pay for programs or international nongovernmental personnel. All Burmese imports into the United States were stopped, including textile imports that annually amounted to some US$350 million. The law was shortly amended to allow the import of educational materials, art, and handicrafts. Diplomatic relations, however, continued, although the representation by both sides was reduced over time to the chargé d'affairs level.

The fourth stage (Public Law 110-286), which occurred in 2008, was prompted by the Saffron Revolution of 2007. It restricted the importation of jade and rubies of Burmese origin even if processed in some third country. Also, U.S. executive orders prohibited any U.S. citizen from aiding third-party foreign investment in that country, purchasing shares in a third-country business if its products are primarily for Burma, and required U.S. representatives to vote against any multilateral financial assistance for which Myanmar was the recipient.

The United States had carried out an extensive International Military Education and Training (IMET) program in Burma. In the period 1950–1962, 972 officers were trained in the United States, and during 1980–1988, 255 graduated—more than in any other country. The restart of program corresponded with the restart of USAID program. During 1974–1980, the United States sponsored an antinarcotics program that provided helicopters and pilot training. In the period 1980–1988, 415 officers were trained abroad, of whom 255 went to the United States (61.4 percent). During the civilian era, 1948–1962, 1,852 officers were trained overseas, of whom 1,227 went to the United States (66.3 percent). Contrary to the European Union, which withdrew all military attachés, the United States wisely kept that position open in the embassy, thus providing a modest but desirable avenue of professional contact between the two militaries. The 1978 International Security Act stipulated that the United States could not provide IMET in countries "engaged in a consistent pattern of human rights violations"—which certainly should have excluded Burma under the BSPP—but this provision was ignored. The claim was that although such training did not improve human rights, it set standards that were important.

In the semiannual State Department reports to the Congress on Burma, the U.S. government has most often called for the recognition of the results of the May 1990 election, swept by the NLD, in effect calling for the resignation of the junta. This was in fact a call for regime change, and the Burmese government interpreted it as such. The futility of such a demand on a foreign state by the United States should have been obvious. The United States lobbied hard for ASEAN to deny entry to Myanmar in July 1997, and the United States, contrary to international practice, has refused to call that country Myanmar, instead using the older term Burma. High-level U.S. officials did not travel to Myanmar, but in June 2007 the Chinese arranged a meeting between a deputy assistant secretary of state with three Burmese ministers in Beijing. There were no apparent positive results of that meeting. In March 2009, an office director from the State Department met with the Burmese foreign minister at Naypyitaw, signaling interest on both sides for exploring improved relationships.

Perhaps to improve his standing in the SPDC or because he felt better relations with the United States would be useful, in 2002 General Khin Nyunt took an initiative that eventually proved unsuccessful and may have contributed to his downfall. In February 2002, the State Department did not refer to the May 1990 elections but rather to the need to improve human rights and governance, to which the United States would positively respond. The change in the U.S. position was one factor in the release of Aung San Suu Kyi on May 6 of that year. This was followed by the visit to Washington, D.C., of the highest-ranking Burmese military official since the imposition of sanctions to discuss conditions for the removal of Myanmar from the list of countries engaged in narcotics activity. (This was possible because of changes in the legislation prompted by the political need to ensure Mexico did not fall into that category.) It was only after the congressional elections of November 2002, which the Republican Party won, that the assistant secretary of state for Asia and the Pacific, at a Washington conference on Burma/Myanmar on November 21–22, reverted back to the hard line of the May 1990 elections, thereby vitiating any potential progress for improving relations between the United States and Myanmar at that time.

The goals of U.S. policy toward Burma—regime change and the seating of a civilian government—have not been reached in two decades. Instead, it has produced a nationalistic reaction and the fear of invasion that, however unrealistic to the outside world, is palpable in Myanmar among the *tatmadaw*. Spurred by an effective lobby of democracy and human rights groups and expatriate Burmese, the United States essentially has allowed its policy toward Myanmar to be made by Aung San Suu Kyi, or by what others claim to be her current views, since she is unavailable and under house arrest.

Two aspects of U.S. legislation create unanswered legal questions. In the Foreign Affairs and Reform and Restructuring Act of 1998, a provision (Section 1106) states that any U.S. assistance to the UN Development Program cannot be given to the government but only through nongovernmental organizations and only after "consultation with the leadership of the National League for Democracy and the leadership of the National Coalition Government of the Union of Burma." Because the NCGUB is a "parallel" government (or government in exile), questions of the legality of such legislation arise. In the Burmese Freedom and Democracy Act of 2003 (the third tranche of sanctions), Section 2 (14) states: "The policy of the United States, as articulated by the President on April 24, 2003, is to officially recognize the NLD as the legitimate representative of the Burmese people as determined by the 1990 election." The 2008 legislation stipulates that the U.S. policy is to "identify individuals responsible for the repression of peaceful political activity in Burma and hold them accountable for their actions." This is in opposition to the 2008 Burmese constitutional provision legally absolving officials from prosecution for past actions.

The U.S. government has officially decried both the proposed constitution of 2008 and the referendum that will bring it into effect following the 2010 elections. One practical result of this attitude has been the Burmese refusal to allow U.S. ships and helicopters to deliver relief supplies directly to the victims of Cyclone Nargis, causing great external consternation about the callousness of the SPDC. This refusal, and the initial reluctance (or neglect) by the Burmese government to provide assistance to the victims of the cyclone, led the French foreign minister to propose employment of the United Nations Responsibility to Protect (R2P) provision that would allow foreign assistance to a state even when it denied such action. This was originally passed in 1995 to be used in cases of war. Wisely, this was not implemented. The Burmese feared a U.S. invasion, and the cyclone relief effort seemed a plausible excuse to carry it out, since the United States had been calling for regime change for almost two decades. Had the United States insisted on a military intervention for solely humanitarian purposes, it seems likely that there could have been a Burmese military response that could have escalated into some form of skirmishes or limited warfare.

In January 2007, the United States brought to the UN Security Council a resolution calling for censuring Burma/Myanmar as a threat to regional peace and security. This was vetoed by both China and Russia, which claimed that the Economic and Social Council of the United Nations should handle the problem of Burma/Myanmar. They opposed Security Council involvement because none of Myanmar's neighboring countries had indicated that such a threat existed. That a veto was anticipated indicated that the U.S. attempt to place Burma/Myanmar on the agenda was more to satisfy internal U.S. pressure groups than to effect change. The 2007 Congressional Gold Medal was awarded to Aung San Suu Kyi. In 2008, the United States agreed to admit a large number of Karen refugees from the camps in Thailand along the Myanmar border.

The White House under President George W. Bush increased worldwide attention and pressure on the regime. On January 18, 2005, the presumptive secretary of state referred to Burma/Myanmar as an "outpost of tyranny." In May 2007, President Bush called Burma "a continuing unusual and extraordinary threat to the national security and foreign policy of the United States." First Lady Laura Bush met with dissidents, issued a number of public statements against the junta, and even held an unprecedented press conference on the subject. Both President Bush and his wife met with dissidents and others in Thailand shortly before the 2008 U.S. elections.

Even though some members of the administration had recognized that the sanctions policy had not achieved its objective and was not likely to do so, publicly condemning Burma/Myanmar remained politically popular and no doubt was also motivated by personal conviction. In the waning days of the

Bush administration in the fall of 2008, the administration nominated an ambassador-level appointment to coordinate Burma policy (as stipulated in the 2008 sanctions legislation), but this person could not be confirmed before the Obama administration came into power. Myanmar will continue, in the words of an Obama administration official, to be a "boutique issue," but U.S. policy, according to Secretary of State Hillary Clinton, is under review in 2009.

### What are relations with China and what is the status of the Chinese in Myanmar?

Although we can only speculate on Chinese motivation for the close relationship with the Myanmar authorities, strategic and economic issues seem paramount. Chinese influence in Myanmar is potentially helpful in any rivalry that might again develop with India, although Sino-Indian relations now are quite cordial. As China expands its regional influence and develops a blue-water navy, Myanmar provides access to the Bay of Bengal and supplements other available port facilities for the Chinese in the Indian Ocean in Pakistan, Bangladesh, and Sri Lanka—called a "string of [Chinese] pearls." Although the southern reaches of Myanmar are at the extreme western end of the Straits of Malacca, the free use of these straits are critical strategic concerns to China, Japan, Korea, and the United States. Some Chinese sources consider continued access to the straits to be a critical policy objective, and a close relationship with Myanmar is a potential advantage. Eighty percent of imported Chinese oil passes through these straits. To the extent that pipelines for oil and gas cross Myanmar and relieve Chinese dependence on the vulnerable Straits of Malacca, this is clearly in China's strategic interests.

Access to energy sources is both a strategic and economic concern. Diversification of the supply of oil, natural gas, and hydroelectric power is an issue in which Myanmar looms large. The exploitation of offshore natural gas fields in Myanmar is important, as is the ability to transport that gas, as well as Middle Eastern crude oil, to China avoiding the Straits of Malacca, which is a strategic plus for China. China is helping construct some thirty dams, most of which will supply electricity to Yunnan Province as well as power and irrigation water to parts of Myanmar.

Under the SLORC/SPDC, China has become the single most important economic and military support of the Myanmar government. Its military assistance is estimated at more than US$3 billion, and its economic assistance is in the hundreds of millions of U.S. dollars. It has and continues to build extensive infrastructure: roads, railroads, ports, dams, and irrigation facilities. The trade relationship is close, officially estimated at US$1.577 billion but likely to be much higher. There are perhaps some 300,000 legal Chinese registered with the Myanmar government, but unofficial estimates of Chinese illegal migration into Myanmar are as many as 2 million. Chinese goods now dominate many of Myanmar's markets, and Mandalay, the seat of Burman culture, is said to be 20 percent Yunnanese, whereas the population of Lashio, the most important city north of Mandalay, is estimated to be 50 percent Chinese. China has negotiated to buy a significant share of the offshore Rakhine gas, which will be sent to Yunnan via pipeline. China also plans to build a second pipeline for Middle Eastern crude oil across Myanmar to Kunming.

Constantly, delegations from both the central government in Beijing and from individual provinces like Yunnan visit and meet with Myanmar officials, and those from Myanmar travel frequently to China.

The continued development of Chinese interests in Myanmar depends on the stability of that Burmese government. There is evidence from the carefully crafted Chinese remarks (designed not to insult the Burmese) on the need for positive changes in Myanmar that they recognize as in their own (Chinese) national interests. Although much of the Western world believes Chinese influence is paramount there, the Chinese claim that their ability to effect change is limited. They also seem to want the Burmese to have better relations with the United States. In addition, they are said to have convinced the Burmese to speed up a visa for UN special envoy Gambari.

The Chinese have also been heavily involved in exploiting Myanmar's natural resources, especially timber, and they have dealt with both the government and minority cease-fire groups. There are many problems; their gold mining operations in the Kachin State, for example, have led to extensive pollution of the rivers. The Chinese seem to have brought Chinese workers, thereby providing even less benefit to local communities. Individual Chinese provinces, especially Yunnan, have their own supplementary interests in Myanmar, and they pursue them with considerable vigor.

Chinese penetration of Myanmar has unique aspects, but it is also related to their broader strategy in Southeast Asia. To date, it has been quite effective, both toward ASEAN as an organization and toward the individual countries of the region.

### What is India's policy toward Myanmar and how did it change?

The Western world has questioned India about its policies toward Myanmar. There is considerable sympathy for the Burmese democracy movement in India (itself the world's largest democracy), both in government circles and among segments of the knowledgeable public. There are probably Indians once resident in Burma who might like to go back there and who believe that a nonmilitary regime could be more receptive to their presence. But geopolitical issues take precedence.

Following the Burmese coup of 1988, India—led by Rajiv Gandhi, who emphasized India's regional influence in Sri Lanka, the Maldives, and Nepal—was extremely critical of the military junta. All India Radio (AIR) was known as the most vocal adversary of the military, and the station even hired U Nu's daughter to be in its Burmese language service. There was, in addition, a long history of Burmese military antagonism to India, demonstrated most forcibly by the *tatmadaw*'s expulsion of some 200,000 people from the subcontinent following the military coup of 1962.

As India saw Chinese penetration and influence grow in Myanmar, in the 1990s India sought to discuss its concerns about growing Chinese influence there with the United States, but Washington was not interested in such discussions. The Indian foreign minister went to Myanmar, and programs began in which India attempted to counter Chinese influence. This relationship has grown, and although it cannot now compete with the Chinese presence, it is significant. In October 2004, Than Shwe became the first Burmese head of state ever to visit Delhi.

India has several motivations, primary among them the attempt to limit Chinese influence in the Bay of Bengal. New Delhi has considered the Indian Ocean and the Bay of Bengal as their primary waters. Chinese access to the bay is of great concern to them. India has also competed with China for access to the rich offshore natural gas reserves of the Rakhine coast in Myanmar but has lost out to China. New Delhi wants Burmese cooperation in the elimination of Burmese-based sanctuaries for Indian Naga rebels, as well as those among the Mizo, Kuki, Bengali, Assamese, and Manipur groups in India's poor and volatile northeast. In addition, India hopes that its support to the development of the Burmese port of Sittwe (near the Bangladesh border) will enable them to anchor an economic development program through western Myanmar (the Chin State) to Manipur and the Northeast that would help alleviate the poverty of that region and cut down on separatist sentiments in that area. It has allocated US$120 million to upgrade the Sittwe port and construct the Tamu-Kalewa-Kalemyo road, among other programs. The target for increased trade was US$1 billion by 2006/2007, but it only reached US$733 million, less than half of that with China.

## What was Japan's relationship with Burma/Myanmar?

During the influential tenure of General Ne Win, Japan had the closest association with Burma of any industrialized foreign state. This relationship was at first personal and started through Ne Win's Japanese training (along with Aung San) as part of Burma's "Thirty Comrades" just prior to December 1941 and the U.S.–U.K. entry into World War II in the Pacific. (Aung San had first intended to contact the Chinese communists but was intercepted by the Japanese.) Institutional and foreign assistance relationships grew from this association, but they remained in large part personal in nature. Until the coup of 1988, the Japanese ambassador was the only foreign ambassador with relatively easy access to Ne Win, who was quite friendly with the ambassador and his wife. If Prime Minister Mahathir bin Mohamad of Malaysia had an explicit national "look east" policy focused on Japan, Ne Win had a personal, more inchoate one.

Ne Win seemed quite taken with Japan, and during the Caretaker Government even brought up the possibility of importing Japanese farmers to teach the Burmese how to be more productive. This never occurred. Quiet Japanese pressures for economic reform in March 1988 led to Myanmar opening its private sector. At that time, Japan and Burma had a "special relationship," but it was based on warm friendships that had developed among the older Burmese military and the Japanese during World War II. These continued until the turn of the century.

Japan's assistance to Burma started with World War II reparations in 1955. Japanese aid until 1988 has been calculated at US$2.2 billion and comprised over half of all foreign assistance to that country at that time and about two-thirds of all bilateral assistance. Japanese aid kept Burma afloat during those difficult years. During the BSPP era, imports from Japan were about 40 percent of all imports (Chinese imports were about 5 percent), but under the SLORC/SPDC the pattern was reversed; Japanese imports after 2002 were about 5 percent, whereas Chinese imports were 35 percent.

Under Japanese law, Burma had to be re-recognized following the coup of 1988. Japanese conglomerates, which were losing money with the stoppage of the Japanese aid program and the cessation of economic assistance, petitioned the embassy in Rangoon to restart the program. In addition, to avoid the embarrassment of having the Burmese sit next to the Palestine Liberation Organization at Emperor Hirohito's funeral as an "unrecognized state," Japan re-recognized Burma on February 17, 1989.

Under the SLORC/SPDC, Japan's assistance has annually averaged some US$86.6 million from 1988 to 1995, and US$36.7 million 1996 to 2005. Such assistance has not been for loans but for humanitarian assistance and debt relief. Japan's definition of humanitarian assistance, however, is quite different from what in the United States was once called "basic human needs" (health, education, nutrition, agriculture). It has expanded to include infrastructure, such as recent repairs to the Rangoon airport and the Baluchaung hydroelectric project (a stellar example of a successful Japanese aid project from the 1950s).

Still, Japanese influence in Myanmar has waned; access is lacking, and the esteem in which the Burmese held Japan has diminished. Two factors are probably responsible. The first is that Japan's personal relationship with Ne Win disappeared. The second is that the United States has pressured Japan to stop aid as part of their sanctions approach to Myanmar. The result was the provision of humanitarian assistance only. In addition, in 1992 Japan also signed on to the official development assistance charter, which advocated increased emphasis on human rights and democracy. Some Japanese blame their government for the loss of influence in Myanmar, a loss that has serious strategic implications. This criticism, however, fails to consider the personalized nature of the Japan–Burma attachment through Ne Win.

Japan's strategists see the increasing influence of China in Myanmar as inimical to their security interests because of China's direct access to gas and oil through Myanmar. As the Burmese move toward their 2010 elections, Japan will be under increasing internal strategic and economic pressure to recognize that some political progress has taken place and that Japanese assistance should increase.

### What has been the role of civil society and quasi-governmental groups?

This author once wrote that the BSPP killed civil society and prevented the functioning of any significant advocacy groups outside of its purview. In a somewhat ironic change, the SLORC/SPDC in 1988 (in the Law Relating to Forming Organizations) allowed the mushrooming of many types of indigenous nongovernmental organizations (NGOs), although not advocacy groups they could not control or were deemed a potential threat. There are estimated in the country to be some 214,000 community-based organizations, such as those that service a local need such as parent-teachers' associations, day care centers, and so on. A wide variety of religious-based organizations (almost half of such groups) of all the major faiths have been established, even if they are not exactly flourishing. In addition, some 270 apolitical indigenous NGOs operate at a various levels, providing services the government does not want to give, ignores, or is incompetent to provide. As long as they are not seen as threatening the power base or engaging in efforts that undercut the state, they seem to function. Their effectiveness in any geographic region depends on their relationship with the local military command. In some areas, these local NGOs are the link that provides cultural continuity between past ethnic, linguistic, and cultural norms and needs, such as language instruction, that have effectively been undercut by the state in their Burmanization ("Myanmaification") process.

Somewhat under fifty international NGOs also provided services before Cyclone Nargis, but since January 2006, they had been under more stringent and controlling operational requirements (travel, government liaison, banking, etc.) and government surveillance. The strictness with which these regulations are enforced varies by locale and organization. After Nargis, however, regulations were relaxed, and they expanded their roles and increased their local staffs, providing needed relief in stricken areas.

Civil society organizations, those nonprofit groups variously distanced from government and providing space between it and the family, might be the basis for a degree of pluralism in a unitary state. Thus, insofar as they have local influence, they mitigate centralized control and could form the basis for more representative authority and eventually more democratic governance.

The military government, having seen the ineffectual nature of the BSPP, has essentially replaced it with overarching GONGOs (government-owned or -operated nongovernmental organizations), the most important of which is the USDA. This is a mass organization, comprising 24.6 million members—about half the total population, and because many children are too young to join, perhaps two-thirds of the total adult population. It explicitly was designed to service military needs; its patron is the senior general. It carries out business, engages in paramilitary activities, and sponsors educational programs ranging from Buddhism to computers. It has been used for government-sponsored rallies and occasional violence against demonstrators or the opposition. It often operates from government buildings and gets government contracts to earn income (e.g., bus routes). There are considerable social and economic pressures to join, and some economic advantages to doing so. It is not explicitly a political party, because civil servants and military cannot join political parties, but it effectively functions as one like the BSPP. It is the most important mass organization in the country. Other government groups include the Myanmar

Maternal and Child Welfare Organization, chaired by the wives of the leadership, fire fighters, veterans, and members of other organizations that mobilize hundreds of thousands of citizens toward professional and state-sponsored goals.

In its early incarnation, the USDA seems to have been modeled after GOLKAR, the Indonesian "functional groups" organization that supported President Suharto. That changed from a civil organization into a political party. The USDA may go a different route after the failure of the BSPP and form separate but effectively affiliated parties that would do the government's bidding in the 2010 elections. Rumors exist of the USDA being behind the formation of two or three such parties (variously named the National Prosperity Party and a National Security and Development Party) and that they hope to garner some 26 percent of the seats, which—along with the active-duty military holding an additional 25 percent—would give the military a clear majority. Whatever its future function, it has been a mass mobilization organization to service the state's perceived needs and will continue to be significant in the campaign period.

### What is the status of human rights in Myanmar?

However one may wish to define human rights—political, economic, social, or cultural—Myanmar authorities have deprived their citizenry of any of these fundamental rights. Since the coup of 1988, Myanmar has been ruled essentially by martial law. There is no independent judiciary, and "policy," which in the Burmese context means the proclivities of the regime at any point, supercedes whatever vestiges of law that may exist. The rules regulating any public activity are stringent. The regime has denied to all its peoples political representation and has censored all media. It has not provided an effective educational system. It has vastly underfunded health services, making it the second worst in the world after Sierra Leone. It has strongly limited the expression of minority cultures. Access to the market, except for petty trading in the bazaars, is subject to discriminatory practices. Public gatherings of more than five people are illegal without state-authorized permits.

Trials are usually secret, sentences perversely long (and extendable at the state's command), and prison conditions deplorable. Torture is widespread and arbitrary. There have been, however, few judicially authorized executions in contrast to many authoritarian states. Although the government denies that there are any political prisoners, external observers estimate there are over 2,100. The government claims they are incarcerated for other activities. Surveillance of suspect civilians is widespread and extends to their families, who are often harassed. Sometimes, to score an international point, some prisoners are released, but others are rejailed. One foreign diplomat described the process as the releasing little caged birds at Buddhist temples to gain merit, only to have them recaptured and recaged for further use. It is evident that in 2008–2009, potential leaders who might disrupt the 2010 elections were being held to prevent state-defined "chaos" from occurring.

The rights situation is worse in areas bordering fighting. People are often conscripted to be porters for the military, and "free fire zones" are created—anyone found in that area is suspect. Many villages have been burned. There are said to be many child soldiers in the Myanmar army, although the number of them is in question. In proportional terms, however, the percentage is probably higher among some minority troops, who have been in rebellion for a generation or two.

Reputable international organizations, including the International Red Cross, Amnesty International, Human Rights Watch, the International Labor Organization, as well as official organs such as the U.S. State Department, have issued reports on the sorry state of human rights.

The junta has claimed, however (and will continue to claim), that Myanmar is on the road to democracy. Although the newly approved constitution of 2008 affirms a variety of rights, they are always subject to laws or issues that the junta stresses, such as national unity, morality, order, and other state policy directives.

## Why was General/Prime Minister Khin Nyunt removed from power, and what did this mean?

General Khin Nyunt was removed from office in October 2004. He was a pivotal figure in the junta since 1988. One of three members who were present at the creation of the junta and who remained in power until 2004 (Than Shwe, Maung Aye, and Khin Nyunt—Saw Maung has died), General Khin Nyunt was said to be a protégé of Ne Win. He never commanded troops in the field, in contrast to most of his peers, but he had been in charge of military intelligence, which gave him access to not only what was going on throughout the society but also the high command's public and private affairs. He was secretary-1 under the SLORC and SPDC, the third highest position in the state. He was also in charge of international affairs and thus had more contact with the outside world, in contrast to Generals Saw Maung (until 1992), Than Shwe, and Maung Aye. Khin Nyunt was reportedly close to China. Although the division of the junta into hard-liners and soft-liners may be somewhat misleading, it was evident that he was more concerned with what the outside world thought and was more interested in joining ASEAN than his colleagues were. It was he who negotiated the cease-fires with the ethnic rebellions and was responsible for the external contact between the United Nations and Aung San Suu Kyi (even if he did not initiate it). It is unclear how much of this was his idea, but on his arrest the junta was careful to state that the work he was carrying out was SPDC policy, not that of any individual. Yet his failure to improve relations with the United States may have contributed to his downfall.

In August 2003 he became prime minister and was in charge of the "roadmap toward discipline-flourishing democracy."

This staged set of efforts involved completing the drafting of the new constitution, a referendum on that constitution, new general elections in 2010, and the installation of a new government thereafter.

Khin Nyunt's arrest supposedly came about because of corruption in the military intelligence unit along the China border at Muse. Whatever may have occurred—and it is widely believed that corruption flourishes along that border because of the lucrative smuggling trade—it is said that he had too much information on too many high-ranking people in the military. When he became prime minister, he was asked to resign from military intelligence, but he refused to do so. Because he never commanded troops, he had no mass military loyalty base, as such loyalty is personal rather than institutional. As long as Ne Win had his faculties, it seems unlikely that any of Khin Nyunt's adversaries or competitors could touch him. At the same time, since he did not command troops, he was incapable of launching a countercoup. His 2002 efforts to assuage the United States on narcotics issues failed through U.S. recalcitrance to deal with him following the Republican victory in the November 2002 U.S. elections, which may have undercut his credibility further with the senior general.

Because power is personalized, leading to entourages, when one person at the apex of any organization is purged, that person's entourage has to go as well. This led to mass arrests of military security personnel and decimated that institution. When Ne Win arrested General Tin Oo's (head, military intelligence) in 1983, it eliminated the capacity of the government to prevent the intended assassination by North Korean agents of visiting South Korean President Chun Doo Hwan; Khin Nyunt's arrest and the depopulation of military intelligence may have led to lethal and unprecedented bombings in Rangoon and Mandalay in 2005 that killed a number of people. Khin Nyunt was tried in secret, found guilty, and sentenced to forty-four years in jail, but is instead under house arrest.

The impact of the fall of Khin Nyunt goes far beyond the demise of military intelligence (its functions related to the civilian population had been taken over by the Special Branch of the police), but the Office of the Chief of Military Intelligence is now gradually taking back some civilian responsibilities. A window to the outside world has been shut, for the foreign ministry staff has no real policy power. Khin Nyunt seemed more pragmatic and more immune to exaggerations of power than some of his associates. If foreigners could not directly influence him, he listened to them and sometimes had real exchanges of opinion with him. Since his arrest, foreign contacts with the military junta and civilian hierarchy have been far more limited.

### Why was the capital moved from Rangoon to Naypyitaw?

Naypyitaw, an area not far from the central Burmese town of Pyinmana on the Rangoon-Mandalay road and railroad some 240 miles north of Rangoon, is not the jungle site described in the foreign media but is located in scrub land near rice paddies. The capital Naypyitaw (literally, the site of the royal country; under the Japanese, the pseudo-independent state's capital was "Rangoon Naypyitaw") is to be designated as a special bureaucratic enclave, akin to Washington, D.C., and separate from the states and divisions that make up the administrative structure of local governance in Myanmar. It will have its own capital military command. Numerous reasons have been given for the secretive move. They range from the practical to the astrological. Foreign embassies are supposed to follow by picking building sites in that area in 2009 (since delayed), although the United States and Thailand have just constructed new embassies in Rangoon.

On July 12, 2006, the government announced that Naypyitaw would become the new capital of the state. The term *Naypyitaw* was used in precolonial Burma to designate the royal capital or palace site. On November 12, 2006, a ceremony was held for the start of construction of a new pagoda there. Called Uppat-tasanti (the title of a Buddhist sutra, meaning development and stability, but invoked in the face of foreign invasions), it is supposed to rival the Shwedagon in size but stands one foot lower. The invitation card to the ceremony stated that the site was the Rajahtaninaypyitaw, or "the royal capital where the king resides." (One of the streets is named "The King's Friends.") The pagoda was inaugurated by the lifting of the *hti* (umbrella) in March 2009. In 2006, the costs of Naypyitaw construction were estimated at 2.4 percent of GDP. Some believe 80,000 migrant laborers worked on its construction at a monthly cost of some K.46 billion per month (approximately US$46 million at free market rates).

There are a variety of explanations, both classical and contemporary, for the move. The capital of the country has been moved many times before under the Burmese kings. A particular site was chosen because it was auspicious, and in time the site became the center of power because the king and the throne were there. Indeed, it is evident that the timing of the move was based on astrological calculations. Some believe the cause was *yadaya*, an action taken on the advice of an astrologer to ward off potential evil. Others maintain there were numerological reasons for the move. Some now say that because Cyclone Nargis in 2008 did not touch Naypyitaw but did hit Rangoon, this demonstrates the mystical efficacy of the move. In addition, Naypyitaw lies on the fringe of the dry zone, which has been the traditional site of Burman power. The move may also be related to the nationalistic effort to "decol-onize" Myanmar and eliminate the hated humiliating colonial heritage of Rangoon as the capital. Others claim that the site, near the PaO ethnic region, was chosen because Senior General Than Shwe's wife is a PaO.

There may be strategic and political reasons for the move as well. Naypyitaw is far inland from Rangoon and is less susceptible to U.S. or foreign invasions (the military had also moved its Western Command headquarters from Sittwe, on the sea, somewhat inland to An for the same reason, and in December 2008 announced the move of its major air force base at Mingaladon, a suburb of Rangoon, to central Myanmar at Meiktila). Its location would allow time for a protracted guerrilla war of attrition or until China might come to its aid. Others say because it is located on the edge of minority areas, this gives the central government greater control over the minority groups in that region. Naypyitaw was constructed out of scrub land with few inhabitants. It is essentially a company town and is easily controlled by the military. Thus, it is not subject to the vagaries of popular unrest as are Rangoon and the other major cities of the country. The military has complained that the government in Rangoon is subject to information leaks to the populace, and this would be less possible upcountry. The *tatmadaw* is also concerned about foreign spying in Rangoon.

Naypyitaw is divided into two new major physical sections: a civilian section housing all the ministries, employee housing, and the new Pyithu Hluttaw (legislature), and a military section; it also encompasses the neighboring town of Pyinmana and its outskirts. The civilian facilities are spread out over a vast area, with considerable distances between ministerial buildings that all look the same. Equal housing is provided to all ministers; staffs are housed in apartments that are color-coded by ministry and whose space increases as the rank of the occupant rises. There are markets, schools, a hospital, pagodas, a golf course, a zoo, and other facilities. A newly refurbished and expanded airport connects the capital to Rangoon and other cities, and the roads into Naypyitaw from the airport are sometimes six-lane divided highways. A major new limited-access divided highway connects Rangoon and Naypyitaw; it eventually will connect Mandalay. In some places, underground sprinkler systems at roundabouts keep the grass green in the hot season. There are a number of hotels. The concept is grandiose, but the isolation means increased expenditures for travel by those who need to do business with the government.

How all this construction (which evidently totaled in the hundreds of millions of U.S. dollars) was budgeted is unclear. Some say that import licenses for luxury automobiles were sold off to construction companies, others claim that the government sold buildings and land in Rangoon. Whether the construction, which continues apace, has or will be paid for is less important than other practical and even ideological elements of the move. The considerable resources required for the construction have obviously undercut the government's interest or capacity in improving the exceedingly low level of social services provided to the general population. Furthermore, this isolation also increases the capacity of the junta to ignore the reality of the sorry state of the country as a whole and further isolates them—and through them the state—from the external world. They may feel this is positive, rather than negative, but the megalomania that such isolation may produce, combined with a exceedingly hierarchical command structure, could further aggravate the isolation of the top leadership and the unwillingness of the administration to deal with the real problems facing that country.

## What is the role of Buddhism in Myanmar today and what is its relation to political legitimacy?

Buddhism is the primordial value of Burmans and some other groups, and it is the religion of about 89 percent of the population. It is associated with many rites of passage in Burman society, and many social and cultural customs are predicated on it. It, and the members of the *sangha* who practice it, have the highest social prestige; from village through university level it permeates education. It is an avenue of social mobility and prestige. As a means to rally support, it is paramount. It is also a singularly important element of political legitimacy.

The monarchs relied on Buddhism, as we have seen. Buddhism was also integral to the rise of Burmese nationalism and anticolonial activism. U Nu could win an election in 1960 because of his association with Buddhism and a platform of making it the state religion. The military understood that this prompted rebellions among some Christian minority groups, and after the coup of 1962 stressed the secular concept of socialism as the state's rallying cry, even while ensuring that Buddhist rites and authority (subject to state control) were respected.

The SLORC/SPDC has engaged in a concerted campaign to use Buddhism for political legitimacy. There are continuous stories in all the media related to the good Buddhist works of the *tatmadaw*. Offerings to and the feeding of monks are frequent activities. Pagodas have been built and many repaired, including the renowned Shwedagon in 1999. Some sarcastically say that Myanmar's color television is only green and yellow— the military and the monks. The state has raised funds for good Buddhist works, and private funds donated through state and military organizations get the karmic merit, which is the basis of such giving. When monks (on two occasions) turned over their begging bowls and refused to accept offerings of food from the military, the military considered them to be virtually treasonous acts of defiance. In 1990, monks in Mandalay demonstrated, and the military raided various monasteries and arrested some 400 monks, claiming in justification they were simply purifying the *sangha* as King Anawrahta had done in the eleventh century.

The monks demonstrated in 2007, marching peacefully through the streets of Rangoon while protected by youth. This was a defiant act, demonstrating to the populace that the administration had not cared for the people, whose meager livelihood deteriorated even further because of the abrupt rise in prices associated with the removal of subsidies on gas and oil. When these religious and nascent but quiescent political marches were infiltrated by political opponents of the regime and political slogans against the junta were seen and heard, the military violently cracked down on both the monks and the general population involved. At least thirty-one persons were killed and many injured.

The images of these brutal actions against the most revered figures in the society were seen on international television and, even more important, by many Burmese through satellite television. The population was horrified, and it became evident that however much the junta had tried to build up its image of religiosity (because of personal beliefs or for political legitimacy purposes or both), they had lost the authority they so assiduously cultivated. In March 2009, Senior General Than Shwe dedicated the Uppatasanti pagoda at Naypyitaw. Only a foot shorter then the magnificent Shwedagon pagoda in Yangon, it was an act of merit that enhances the legitimacy of the new capital, the regime, and personally the senior general and his wife. But if one were to point a single act that undermined the prestige of the *tatmadaw*'s leaders, it was the violent suppression of the Saffron Revolution.

### What happened in the Saffron Revolution of 2007?

The violent suppression of the Saffron Revolution, which as noted was neither saffron nor a revolution, was the watershed that has probably destroyed the legitimacy of the junta because it struck at the primordial Buddhist values of the Burman population. Named after the traditional color of the Buddhist monk's robes (which are no longer saffron but a dull reddish brown) and named in line with the orange, rose, and other multicolored democracy revolutions in other countries, the demonstrations by Buddhist monks was significant in itself, but it was also significant in that this violent suppression was seen live on television by many urban Burmese, those tens of thousands who have satellite television dishes. For the first time in Burmese history, violent suppression by the state was not simply a matter of rumor but was palpably visible. The violence was further spread through videos posted on the Internet. Even the military, whose leadership is devoutly Buddhist, may have been conflicted by the actions the junta authorized.

The immediate spark was economic—the August 15 government-mandated abrupt rise in the price of gasoline and energy. The causes, however, are far more profound and reflect the pent-up frustration so evident throughout the country that occasionally boils over (as in 1974, 1988). When the military raised the price of energy overnight without warning, its immediate effect was on the poor. Buses raised fares the poor could not afford. Around the world such changes, often advocated by the International Monetary Fund and the World Bank, have led to demonstrations and riots. Buddhist monks had noted that people could no longer donate the usual amount of food to the monasteries because of economic deprivation, and some were bringing children to temples and asking the monks to feed them because the families could no longer do so. Monks in Pakokku in central Myanmar demonstrated on September 5 and were roughed up by the military, who refused to apologize.

The demonstrations then moved to Rangoon, where thousands of young monks marched quietly through the streets without political slogans (some even by Aung San Suu Kyi's house on September 22, a remarkable event), flanked by students and youth who were to protect them. As the demonstrations grew with some 50,000 marching on September 24, they became more political, and even the flying peacock flag of the NLD was seen. The junta stepped in and violently beat the monks and demonstrators on September 26 and followed up by raiding local monasteries, closing a few of them, and making night raids on the homes of those they believed were supporters of the demonstrations. While the United Nations says that 31 persons died, some foreign accounts say 100 died. A Japanese photographer was shot dead, creating tensions between the two states. On October 11, the UN Security Council issued a presidential statement call for restraint and the early release of political prisoners. ASEAN issued a statement that it was "appalled" by the use of automatic weapons against the *sangha*.

The military was bent on denying the public outcry. It is unlikely that many of the military themselves believed the state's explanation that those monks demonstrating were "bogus," incited by the imperialists (the United States) and their perfidious minions, together with the opposition. Because foreign observers have limited access to the military hierarchy, they can only surmise through indirect or surrogate evidence that the crackdown and later the cyclone led to any significant cracks, splits, or fissures in the junta and its associates. Differences in personalities and programs have been evident for some time, but as we have seen, such issues do not necessarily result in open, public splits. The military may recognize that open fissures in the *tatmadaw* could lead to chaos (which the military always invokes as one of its constant fears) and/or the end of military rule.

What seems evident is that all the good will and political legitimacy that the military has sought through its public Buddhist works and its continuous emphasis on Buddhism was destroyed in this crackdown.

### What were the internal and external effects of Cyclone Nargis in 2008?

Cyclone Nargis was the single most devastating disaster to strike Burma/Myanmar in recorded history. It is common for cyclones in the annual monsoon season (May through September or so) to sweep up the Bay of Bengal from the south and inundate the Bengal area of India and Bangladesh. Such torrential rains frequently affect Burma/Myanmar, and along the Rakhine coast the annual rainfall can approach 200–300 inches per year, about three times that of Rangoon and almost ten times that of the dry zone of central part of the state, as the Arakan Yoma mountains stop most of the precipitation.

Nargis was unprecedented, however. Stories circulate that the government issued warnings, but these were said to be less than adequate in two respects: they did not emphasize the severity of the storm, and many of the affected areas are so remote that no warning reached them. Although the figures are imprecise, some 138,000 people were killed. The mangrove swamps that offer some protection against cyclones had been severely diminished to make way for shrimp and other aquatic farming, so villages were exposed to the full force of the storm, in much the same way that New Orleans suffered more in Hurricane Katrina because it had lost its wetlands protection. The absurdity of the government's response was apparent when it officially indicated the exact number of ducks, chickens, and water buffalo that had been killed but could not count the number of people. It is estimated that damage has amounted to US$2.4 billion at the free market exchange rate, and was 27 percent of GDP in 2007.

Regardless of the accuracy of the rumor that the junta in Naypyitaw, out of the path of the storm, delayed responding because they do not like to hear bad news, or the additional rumor that the informants did not want to interrupt Maung Aye's golf game, these are indicative of the cynicism with which the actions of members of the junta are treated. However, these are but subsidiary elements in the junta's reaction to the events.

We should remember that the cyclone of May 2 preceded the planned referendum on the constitution on May 10. The government had explicitly denied foreign requests for referendum observers, even turning down suggestions that the United Nations play that role. They did not want any foreigners watching the referendum. It is highly probable that the date of May 10 was chosen by the government because astrologers considered it was auspicious for their cause; thus, canceling that date was exceedingly difficult. To solve this dilemma, the date was allowed to stand for most of the country, except in the delta where the cyclone hit. That new date there was May 24. Aside from whether this was a credible delay, it is significant that the government denied visas for foreigners to go into the affected areas until May 24, thus effectively preventing them from observing the referendum.

As worldwide offers to provide assistance poured in, the United States had its ships off the coast and was prepared to fly in helicopters with relief supplies to the most remote areas. The junta adamantly refused the offer, although supplies (estimated at some US$75 million) eventually were allowed to land in Rangoon. The United States was extremely upset by this apparent lack of concern by the military for its own people, and American newspapers complained about the callousness of the government. The most important issue from the junta's vantage point was likely to have been something completely different. For two decades the United States has advocated regime change and the overthrow of military rule in Myanmar, and there is no question that the junta believed that this would be the best excuse for an invasion—an invasion that some dissidents inside and externally have called for (although the NLD has never done so). The absurdity of the United States starting another war was not apparent to the Burmese, who have been ever fearful of a U.S. invasion since 1988.

The Burmese government's response was in sharp contrast to that of the unaffected Burmese people, who organized their own relief teams and response. They carried out assistance and equated themselves with great worldwide appreciation. The Burmese government response was also in sharp contrast to the reaction of the Chinese leadership to the massive earthquake in Sechuan Province at about the same time. The Chinese leadership showed up at devastated sites and comforted the affected, while two weeks after the cyclone Than Shwe was shown inspecting a carefully constructed tent village in what was a photo opportunity, not a realistic appraisal of the situation. (Officials later privately admitted this was a mistake.) Autonomous social workers and helpers were often detained because they were operating free from government control.

Important as well was the inherent nationalism of the junta's response that the Burmese do not need the outside world. Even at such a dire time, it would have been most unlikely for the junta to allow unrestricted access to its territory. When it later tried (unsuccessfully) to raise some US$11 billion for relief, it stipulated that relief was to be managed by the

Burmese themselves. They certainly would resist and deplore the suggestion by the French foreign minister that the United Nations should invoke the R2P, which would authorize foreign intervention without the approval of the state concerned (a provision that was passed in 1995 in cases of conflict). The junta would have been perceived it as evidence of invasion by foreign powers, to which the Burmese might well have responded with military force, thus escalating tensions into confrontation.

Cyclone Nargis exhibited the systemic problems of the military's administration: its fear of foreign intervention and civilian leadership; nationalism; the propaganda elements of administration; and the low priority it placed on the welfare of its people. The coordinated response was eventually led by ASEAN with assistance from the United Nations. But the Burmese clearly did not want to be seen as beggars in the international community.

### What happened in the referendum on the constitution in 2008 and what are its provisions?

The constitution has been in preparation since 1993. The junta carefully chose a special group, the participants in the National Convention, to draft the major provisions of that document. It began meeting January 9, 1993. The discussions at all stages were strictly controlled and heavily scripted. Very few of those who won in the 1990 elections were included in the Convention, and indeed the purpose of the Convention was not only to begin the process of writing a constitution but to erase the results of the May 1990 election that the military disastrously lost and the NLD had so dramatically won. The military's primary provision from the inception of the process was that the military would play the primary role in the society. This was never in doubt. Early, the military published the 104 principles on which the constitution was to be written. Most important was the planned primary role of the military under any new government (reflected in the constitution in Chapter I,6 (f)):

"enabling the Defense services to be able to participate in the National political leadership of the State."

At one point in 1995, the NLD delegates walked out of the conference, claiming it was too restrictive, and they were never allowed back, although at a later stage some wanted to return. Over time, the National Convention was convened and recessed on several occasions. Some claimed that the longer the military delayed this first step on the road to "discipline-flourishing democracy," the longer it would take to hold new national elections.

The Saffron Revolution may have speeded up the process. Some speculate that the military became concerned about the repression of the Buddhist *sangha* and the danger to its rule and brought the process to a quick end after interminable delays. The reasons may include the provision in the constitution that no one can be held legally responsible under a penal law for any excesses prior to its approval (Chapter I, Section 43; Chapter XIV, Paragraph 445). Thus, the regime's leaders get a free pass, at least as long as they stay in the country.

The date chosen for the referendum was May 10, 2008, and it seems more than likely that this was considered astrologically auspicious by the leadership. Events of this magnitude in Myanmar are often so timed. When the cyclone hit on May 2, the military had a dilemma. To postpone the referendum would be to court inauspiciousness, so to speak, but the devastation was so extensive that something had to be done. Thus, the referendum was to take place as planned in central and upper Myanmar, while it was postponed until May 24 in the stricken areas in the delta. Even that date was improbable, yet it was almost impossible to carry out any voting in that region. But the date loomed as important because until the referendum was completed, foreigners were not given visas to provide relief supplies there. The government has adamantly refused to have foreigners, even those from the United Nations, observe the referendum.

If the National Convention was heavily scripted, the referendum was even more so. Reminiscent of Stalinist election figures, the military claimed that 98.12 percent of those eligible voted and that 92.48 percent of the people approved of it, although there were widespread charges that many had their votes submitted in advance and without their approval. The provisions of the constitution were not widely circulated in advance of the referendum. Elections are scheduled for some-time in 2010, following which the new constitution will come into effect.

The preamble of the constitution begins:

Myanmar is a Nation with magnificent historical tradi-tions. We, the National people, having been living in unity and oneness, setting up an independent sovereign State and standing tall with pride. Due to colonial intrusion, the Nation lost her sovereign power in 1885. The National people launched anti-colonialist struggles and National liberation struggles, with unity in strength, sacrificing lives and hence the Nation became an independent sovereign State again on 4th January 1948.

The provisions of the constitution ensure military control at all levels. There will be one bicameral National Assembly, and other legislative bodies at the state/region and township levels. The People's Assembly (*Pyithu Hluttaw*) will have 440 seats, of which 110 will go to active-duty military nominated by the minister of defense. The Upper House (*Amyotha Hluttaw*), for nationalities, will have 224 seats, of which 56 will be held by the military. Thus, active-duty military personnel (nominated by the minister of defense) will have a quarter of the seats at the national level, at the state/regional level (Paragraph 161 (d)), and at the self-administered ethnic zones and division level (Paragraph 276 (i)).

The head of state, the president, indirectly elected by the assembly for not more than two terms of five years each, must have military knowledge and be resident in the country for twenty consecutive years (except when abroad with official approval). Such a person and his or her family can owe no allegiance to any foreign power. There will be three vice presidents also chosen by the assembly (one of whom will be from the military group), and from among whom the president would be elected. Military budgets and promotions cannot be subject to civilian control. "The Defense services has the right independently and to adjudicate all affairs of the armed forces" (Chapter 1, 20 (b)). A state of emergency can be declared by the National Defense Security Council, composed of the president, vice presidents, the commander-in-chief of the armed forces and his deputy, the minister and deputy minister of defense, the two speakers of the houses, and the ministers of home affairs and border regions (all chosen by the minister of defense). The commander-in-chief of the armed forces thus will have exceptional powers, and while appointed by the president, can effectively overrule a president when, under an emergency decree, power is transferred by the president to the commander, who at that time "exercises state sovereignty" (Chapter 1, Section 40).

Provisions exist for the protection of various rights (religion, assembly, press, etc.) including those of the minorities, but as is common in many societies, these are not absolute but subject to public order, morality, and the like. Women are to have equal rights and salaries (Chapter VIII, 35a). Freedom of religious practice is stipulated, but religious groups cannot engage in any economic, financial, or political activities. No foreign support to any such group is allowed. Buddhism, although not the state religion, is given special status.

No area of the state will ever have the right of secession (Chapter I, Section 10), as did the Shan and Kayah States under the 1947 constitution. There will be six small ethnic enclaves (self-administered zones for the Kokang, Palaung, Naga, Danu, PaO, and a self-administered division for the Wa) that will have local government. The constitution can be amended, but only by a 75 percent vote, which precludes any amendments not approved by the military. There is a stipulation that there will be no demonetizations, a reflection of the disastrous results of that in 1987, and no nationalization of enterprises (Chapter I, Section 36). There are provisions for environmental protection, and a Constitutional Tribunal to determine the legality of legislation. The judicial system is supposed to be independent; the civil service should be free of politics. No foreign troops will be deployed on national soil, and there will be no aggression (Chapter I, Section 42).

The constitution provides, in effect, a clean slate for any offenses by government personnel that might have been previously committed: "No proceeding shall be instituted against the said Councils [SLORC, SPDC] or any member thereof or any member of the Government, in respect of any act done in the execution of their respective duties" (Chapter XIV, Paragraph 445). The president is not "answerable" to any court or the Hluttaw "for the exercise of the powers and functions of his office" or acts associated thereof, except impeachment (Chapter V, 215).

There will be, in effect, a multiparty system, but political parties may be abolished if they receive or expend assets from foreign organizations, including religious ones (Chapter X). The system will be somewhat on the lines of that under Suharto in Indonesia. Every citizen has the right to vote and be elected, but whether this applies to associate citizens and naturalized citizens (under 1982 legislation) is unclear.

How the various local and regional governments will interact with the thirteen military districts and their commanders is unclear, as these relationships have not been mentioned within the constitution.

The Burmese will say to the outside world that they have made good on their promise to bring democracy to Myanmar, whereas many Western states will question that conclusion. The military will claim, with a certain justification, that it has provided more local authority to some of the minorities than heretofore, and in some sense that will be true. But it will be far less than the federalist structure that most of the major minorities had wanted, and military control will still exist at local levels. It seems likely that ASEAN and the United Nations will claim that some progress has taken place and that the rights specified in the constitution should be protected.

The elections that follow in 2010 present a dilemma for those in opposition. Some say that a 75 percent elected body is better than the present conditions, where there is no voice in the administration and the military government rules by decree. Others claim that if the opposition groups agree to the election, they are in effect invalidating the results of the May 1990 election, which, of course, the military hopes will happen. Who will have the right to vote? The members of the *sangha* will not be allowed to vote. Aung San Suu Kyi cannot be president, but could she run for the assembly? Would she if she could? These are issues that at this writing are still unclear.

As one foreign academician wrote, under the new constitution the role of the military in Myanmar will change from "ruler-military" to "parent-guardian military," but there should be no doubt as to where essential power lies.

# 7

# THE NATURE OF BURMESE POLITICS

The generalizations that follow—as difficult to form as they are necessary if we are to gauge and anticipate the country's prospects—should not be interpreted as either rigid or deterministic. They lie along a spectrum, one in the eyes of this writer, and are tendencies that if properly and judiciously considered should enable us to look toward the future more realistically and anticipate the changes that will inevitably occur. As we have seen in other societies, development predictions are difficult, and political and other cultural attributes morph over time. Broad characterizations of the political culture of peoples, societies, and even regimes can lead to miscalculations and erroneous policies, so as important as such generalizations may be, caution is in order. How much the analysis that follows simply reflects tendencies reinforced by this or any military command system rather than one inherent in Burman society is an issue that only the future will reveal.

Whatever our assumptions about specific events, we should broadly estimate the social forces that affect politics even as we should recognize that these tendencies will shift over time, in accordance with good Buddhist teachings on the impermanence of all things. One broad assumption is necessary if we are to consider the future over the next half-decade and beyond: the 2010 elections will be carried out and a new government formed in line with the provisions of the constitution approved in 2008. That is the most likely scenario. The possibility that some untoward events might take place that would prevent the election from occurring and that some elements internally would be able to form a new government, perhaps of mixed military-civilian character, is remote and seems highly unlikely at this writing. This could occur, however, either through the evolution of military leadership or in the streets. In any case, change *will* occur minimally through a generational shift, and it is important that this change be anticipated and planned for. External observers need to be in a position to understand the challenges with which any new government must cope.

Whatever the administration that finds itself in power, it will be faced by a series of dire internal problems (outlined in chapter 1) it must deal with, and it will likely do so within the context of how power is viewed throughout that society (in both the military and civilian sectors) and the consequences of such concepts of authority. It will also have to cope with an external environment likely to become more complex and diverse, requiring considerable diplomatic skills both on the part of the Burmese and among foreign observers. How much the 2008 constitution might affect the generalized notions that follow is unknown; it might mitigate or exacerbate some of the traits.

### How do politics in Burma/Myanmar function, and what are its implications?

History matters, and culture is important. They are not residual categories of analysis, as some social scientists might claim, but are central to understanding societies. Traditional concepts of the state in Burma and the status of its leadership derive from an Indian model of the god-king and the capital and palace as Mount Meru, the center of the universe. However remote, abstruse, and even unconscious these concepts may seem, they remain relevant today, if only in symbolic form. Naypyitaw may not be the center of the universe, but the way it has been fashioned bespeaks its symbolic importance and almost regal quality. The head of state remains inextricably linked to Buddhism, if not as defender of the faith (e.g., the Thai monarch) then as a devout adherent whose legitimacy is in part dependent on this relationship. This is constantly reaffirmed in the Burmese media but is now questionable after the suppression of the monks in the fall of 2007. The building of the massive Uppatasanti Pagoda (only one foot lower than the Shwedagon in Yangon) at Naypyitaw, dedicated in March 2009, serves to legitimate the regime, the capital, its leader, and his family. Political atavism is said to be a characteristic of Burmese politics; past patterns of governance persist today. Widespread belief in reincarnation may contribute to such atavism.

The ruler (and the military) claim to rule with *metta*, or Buddhist loving kindness, and thus such acts are not to be disparaged: their motivations are pure, and their edicts thus must be obeyed.

Power is unconsciously conceived as finite, not infinite as in "modern" administrative theory. *Ana* (coercive power) is conceptually different from *awza* (the power or influence of moral authority, charisma), although they may occur in a single individual (e.g., Aung San). The military is said to have the former but lacks the latter, which Aung San Suu Kyi is said to possess.

There is an unwillingness to share power since, because it is finite, to do so diminishes the authority of the leader. Power is thus a zero-sum game. Advocating power-sharing political systems becomes difficult at best. The status of the leadership and the finite nature of power thus leads to its personalization. Loyalty is to the individual with power (this particular king, chairman, leader, etc.), not to the institution. This has been evident from the Pagan Dynasty and since then throughout all the kings and in the republic. This has also been apparent under U Nu, Ne Win, and now Than Shwe. The authority of the leader is reinforced in the popular mind because in traditional Buddhist terms he has come to power through his good karma; although present peccadilloes or offenses may result in dire reincarnation consequences, in some sense he deserves the position he holds. It is unclear how much this belief has eroded in modern, urbanized settings, such as urbanized but still devoutly Buddhist Thailand. The centrality of personal relationships diminishes the effectiveness of institutional relationships, the institutions themselves, and the continuity of institutional policies/priorities. Thus, personalized "policy" is more important than law.

Personalization of power leads to loyalty (but not necessarily competence) as the prime requisite of hierarchical relationships outside the *sangha* and mistrust of those outside of the relationship (who must be loyal to someone else, which partly explains why the military generally distrusts civilians). There is thus a lack of institutional trust (social capital) except as reflected through this personalized channel, and even that can be ephemeral. One exception where there is social capital is at the level of the village or local Buddhist monastery and those who support it.

Power is dependent on developing entourages through personal loyalties, which encourages factionalism. This entourage system has been called the patron–client relationship or clientelism. (In Burmese, it is called *saya-tapyit*, or teacher–pupil relationship.) Because military members have been in leadership positions for almost half a century, such power entourages are usually dominated by the military, and there is a profound distrust within the military of civilian leaders and civilian-controlled institutions at all levels. Many nonmilitary organizations are likely to be controlled by retired military, and retired military people will be prominent in the proposed legislature.

These entourages tend to become unstable over time as some make attempts to vie for leadership. This instability or insecurity is apparent in the society at large—at personal, institutional, and even at national levels (fears of invasion, subversion, cultural hegemony, etc.), and results in national paranoia (with some historical justification), suspicion, and a lack of confidence in planning for the future. This may be traced to karmic considerations, historical roots, and/or personal upbringing, although this is speculation, and too little is known about causes.

There is a strong hierarchical system within Burmese society that tends to enhance the authority of the leader and his or her power. This has been reinforced by a military command system and is further solidified by the concept of *a-na-de*, or unwillingness to embarrass the leadership (or any social superior) by bringing bad news, or causing someone to be uncomfortable. Thus, statistics and data are manipulated by underlings to please the apex of the hierarchy. This pervades the system from the bottom, and planning is characterized by often unrealistic quotas or targets that are often falsely reported as having been fulfilled. This extends to unsubstantiated but internationally reported economic statistics, providing an atmosphere in which the leadership may not recognize deleterious conditions beneath them as they are fed specific but spurious data (e.g., economic growth rates officially were 12.4 percent in 2007 but were estimated at 0.6 percent by foreign economists). There is, thus, what has been called "mutually strategic ignorance," in which both the apex and the base of the power ladder are intentionally kept ill-informed of existential conditions; this makes planning exceedingly difficult.

The role of the state has been preeminent historically (including during the colonial period) and is likely to continue because of the powerful position of any political leader. Thus, not only will governance tend to be centralized, but (as historically and under the previous military government) a market economy is likely to be subject to severe restrictions and state influence.

Succession remains at the whim of the leader and is subject to change. Even under proposed constitutional provisions, personal influence will likely be the critical factor within such administrative strictures. Succession plans, if they exist, are kept secret to ensure that the power of the leader remains undiminished and potential adversaries are kept off-balance. The leader neither shares plans nor consults easily because this would diminish his or her power and perceived authority. Thus, what the leader may think, plan, or advocate at any time may be obscure even to his or her closest associates.

Any alternative center of power is viewed as a new, potentially destabilizing influence in the zero-sum game and is considered with suspicion. There are thus strong forces working against institutional pluralism (an autonomous legislature or judicial system), regional political autonomy, and the development of civil society, although nonthreatening fragments of civil society may emerge at local levels. Even state-sponsored groups in local communities, however, may develop particularized interests that create modest, localized centers of apolitical pluralism.

Information is an aspect of power and is not to be lightly shared. It should be controlled (e.g., via the media). If shared, there is a tendency to manipulate timing and data for power purposes (e.g., production figures, statistics on money supply, inflation, budgets, company reports, etc.). Decisions that are reached at the apex may be publicly implemented without warning, reinforcing the power of the leader(s) but resulting in frustration for those affected both within and outside the regime entourage.

To ensure power and the cohesiveness of the entourage, orthodoxy of views is generally required on important issues, and dialogue on policies does not seem to be possible once a leader issues authoritative decisions. Even mundane questions may not be brought to the attention of senior leadership unless that supreme leader first raises them.

The effectiveness of entourages requires the distribution of assets (financial, prestige, rewards, lower levels of power) both down the system from the top and, in the case of loyalty and financial assets, up from the bottom. Because official salaries are low and inflation normally high, subsidies at best and usually rent-seeking and corruption are required to generate the funds to make the entourage system work. This system extends into economic and business matters. Efforts to eliminate corruption, however necessary, by exemplary dismissals or arrests are unlikely to affect the systemic problem except for short periods and with only localized results.

Because the leader has great powers symbolically and in practice and conceives of himself in imperial style, he is able—and has the moral authority and, indeed, imperative—to intervene into society at all levels to achieve his—and by direct association and implication—national ends. Because his role is "undifferentiated," there is no effective separation of powers; an independent judiciary or a neutral adjudicative body is difficult to achieve, and thus there are few checks on his authority, although senior Buddhist abbots might play such roles. These interventions, including the formation of economic policies, are based more on personal inclination and the limited experience of the leader. Because he does not necessarily consult with others who might appropriate his position, such policies are subject to constant, unpredictable changes. Thus, enforcement of edicts are based on "policy" (what the leadership determines as desirable at any point) and not on law, which is more constant. This has important implications for foreign or internal investment, which is based on reasonable predictability (e.g., no sudden or seemingly arbitrary changes in foreign trade regulations). This may partly explain the sudden shifts in policies (e.g., the energy subsidy issue in 2007) for which there had been no public preparations.

Although there is and was social mobility (there was no planned succession to the throne or the military leadership and no tenure in the precolonial administration), hierarchy is extremely important and has been reinforced by the military system, and mobility avenues have been channeled and controlled by the military. This has resulted in great frustration and despair among youth. The military controls all avenues of social mobility, of which the most important is the military itself and its educational institutions.

Because of the paucity of available private capital through the banking system, private sector mobility is effectively limited to the military's entourages and the Chinese community, which has its own access to private sources of capital (clan, linguistic groups) as well as knowledge of foreign markets.

The leader (under both civilian—U Nu—and military governments) maintains secret information on all associates and their families to command loyalty and conformity. This is effective because (a) breaking existing laws is required for economic survival; (b) the entourage system requires extralegal funding; (c) policy replaces law and is controlled at the apex of the system, and this what may have been "legal" yesterday may be illegal today; (d) loyalty requires the follower to obey leadership commands even when they contradict legal norms or common sense; and (e) wives often have business interests based on "insider trading" and have been accused of corruption in the past.

When a person falls from an entourage's grace, all those associated with him in the hierarchy of lesser entourages are also purged because loyalty is presumed to be to the leader, not the institution. This happened to General Khin Nyunt in 2004 and General Tin Oo in 1983, both of whom commanded military intelligence.

The personalized system effectively discourages shared responsibility at the top. When such sharing has occurred, splits have followed (the Anti-Fascist People's Freedom League in 1958), and ultimately a single leader has emerged (e.g., Than Shwe).

Fear of conspiracies (even invasions) by foreign powers or elements against the leadership have made Burmese leaders both wary and skeptical about the motivations of foreign governments toward the state and its leaders. This is reinforced by previous foreign attempts to destabilize governments and rulers and support of dissident ethnic/political groups. These nationalistic tendencies are only magnified by derogatory foreign comments about the regime, its goals, and its leaders.

Fear of foreign domination may contribute to the suspicions about Aung San Suu Kyi, who is supported by the Western foreign community.

Given the touted natural resources of the state, there is a belief that if necessary, the state could continue to be effective with limited foreign exposure or economic investment, and such isolation may be desirable because of foreign cultural imperialism. Although widespread, this view is inaccurate because of the increasing infiltration of foreign ideas and concepts, as well as increasing dependence on foreign markets.

Nationalism reinforced by past colonial oppression has become a central factor in political legitimacy and affects all foreign relations and foreign assistance. Foreign public criticism of the regime or its leaders invokes negative and defensive responses. There is a persistent (however erroneous) believe that Burmese (i.e., Burman) culture is under attack from foreigners, and only the military can save both the state and its (Burman) culture. These beliefs are deeply held and are not propaganda, although they are often portrayed as such by foreign media. Ultimately, Burmese governments have always stressed the need to protect national sovereignty.

The state generally considers indigenous minorities, even some that are Buddhist, as less cultured at best (the exception being the Mon) and attempting to escape Burman control, aided and abetted by foreign states and those with non-Buddhist affiliations. The leadership often points to past historic episodes without understanding that changes over half a century have rendered these conditions invalid. Strong internal anti-Muslim prejudice continues to affect state policies and are generally prevalent, although they are most obvious in relation to the Rohingyas of Rakhine (Arakan). There are Christian and Muslim administrative ceilings for state and military positions, which was not the case under the civilian government. This stems in part from beliefs in the superiority of Buddhist culture, in part from group (Burman) solidarity, and in part from foreign support to religious minorities.

The hierarchical system fosters intensive pressures on underlings to please superiors, whether through achieving arbitrary quotas or through unauthorized actions based on vague leadership policies. The system sometimes backfires, resulting in inappropriate or detrimental activities that undercut regime objectives or even the regime itself.

The state often tolerates foreign humanitarian or other support by international nongovernmental organizations for the funding or programs they bring and closely monitors their activities out of suspicion. The degree of such monitoring is partly dependent on the personal whims of local military commanders. Still, some mid-level officials may mitigate inappropriate orders from on high by selective enforcement or interpretation to achieve other, localized state-sponsored, necessary, or personal goals.

At present, the Burmese middle class seems to be composed predominantly of some retired military, Chinese, and Sino-Burmans because of the limitations on local access to capital except though military-approved channels. This presents potentially destabilizing social and ethnic tensions should this trend continue or be exacerbated. More broadly, Burman control over the economy has been a hallmark of economic policies in all governments since independence and is likely to continue.

These characteristics of politics are most evident in the regime's behavior, but they pervade opposition groups, local governments, indigenous governmental and nongovernmental organizations, academic institutions, and businesses.

# 8

# ISSUES IN MYANMAR'S FUTURE

Winston Churchill once characterized Russian policy as "a riddle wrapped in a mystery inside an enigma." We might apply the same analogy to Burma/Myanmar's future for all the diverse reasons previously discussed. As Dante Alighieri wrote in the *Divine Comedy*, soothsayers go to a very low circle of hell. Yet it is imperative to try to delineate the issues that this state will face and must address if it is to deliver to its own peoples, whether civilian or military, the fruits of its own slogans and promises, and if it is to find a respected place in the international community. Some might argue that the junta has had no intention of meeting any of the above targets and that they have been either designed for foreign consumption or internal propaganda. Although some attribute the tenacity of the *tatmadaw* in continuing its rule through various means as an obsession with power and venality, this writer believes that there is an ideological core and a sense of national purpose, misdirected sometimes and often overzealously pursued, that in part motivates many of the *tatmadaw*—whatever excesses they have committed (and they have been many and egregious). Although the military is grammatically singular collectively, there is a degree of plurality that should be internationally recognized, even though outsiders may have difficulty in assessing the various players or groups.

## *What are the current and future strategic interests of foreign powers in Myanmar?*

Myanmar's geographic position between the two major regional powers in East and South Asia make it a pivotal nexus on the Bay of Bengal. This will likely continue and even intensify. Adjacent to both China and India, Myanmar has become an important element in the strategic planning of both states. This concern extends to Thailand. They are not only regional and expanding economic powers, but ones with growing military capacities. Although China may not fear an expansive India, the reverse is not true; India is concerned about growing Chinese influence in general and specifically in Myanmar.

China has engaged in an effective Southeast Asian foreign policy both with each of the countries of the region, but also institutionally with the Association of Southeast Asian Nations (ASEAN). The Chinese consider Southeast Asia, especially the mainland, to be within their traditional sphere of influence. Although the People's Republic has rejected Chinese citizenship for its indigenous and extensive Chinese populations in that area (*jus sanguinis*), a natural confluence of influence and even capital is apparent.

Myanmar is especially important to China for various strategic reasons, the least of which is its potential as a market for Chinese products in that poor land of some 53–58 million people (even though this market will increase). More important, Chinese strategy for defense in any future conflict in all of Asia depends in part on elimination of a great vulnerability— reliance on the Straits of Malacca for its supply of energy. Now, some 80 percent of China's gas and oil imports pass through those straits. Elimination of this bottleneck is important to China, for it could be blocked by any riparian nation or major power, such as the United States, and alternative routes are both more expensive and also subject to blockade. Chinese pipelines (one for natural gas found offshore in Myanmar, and one for Middle Eastern crude oil) from the Bay of Bengal to Yunnan Province would mitigate one of its strategic problems. Chinese access to the Straits of Malacca directly through Myanmar could also inhibit the control of the straits by other powers. Although an earlier concern over possible Chinese military bases in Myanmar has been assuaged, potential Chinese naval use of Burmese ports and facilities has not. The new Burmese constitution, however, prohibits foreign bases on Burmese soil.

Chinese interests in Myanmar also stem from access to the internal energy and natural resources of that state. In addition to the off-shore natural gas that China has bought and will ship into Yunnan through a pipeline, China has constructed and continues to build a large number of dams (thirty at last count) to capture the hydroelectric power from Myanmar's untapped rivers. Chinese mining, including gold and other minerals, as well as exploitation of timber reserves, make Myanmar an important economic asset beyond China's geopolitical interests.

A compliant Myanmar (or one reliant on China) also enhances China's strategic position in relation to India. India is evidently concerned over China's increased role in Myanmar. Delhi feels threatened and surrounded with Pakistan to its west allied with China, China to its north, and a penetrated Myanmar to its east. Chinese access to the Bay of Bengal, considered by India as *mare nostrum* ("our sea"), is of concern, as a major Indian naval base is located at Port Blair in the Andaman Islands, and India tests its missiles in that region.

From a virulent antimilitary policy toward Myanmar beginning in 1988, India shifted to support the junta and provide assistance in the early 1990s in an effort to mitigate Chinese influence. A friendly Myanmar is also of importance to India to help suppress the Naga rebellion and a variety of other rebellions in its remote northeast, as the rebels as well as refugees often sought sanctuary in Myanmar. India has also developed a major plan for the economic development of that poor and restless region where some eleven insurrections of varying intensity have taken place. It will employ a transportation network from the Myanmar port of Sittwe (which the Indians will modernize) north up the Kaladan River to Manipur (known as the Kaladan Multi-Modal Transit Transport Project). India is also hoping to buy Burmese off-shore gas, of which China has contracted for the lion's share.

Japan has informally expressed concern over Chinese capacity to strengthen its defense and economy through these actions. The United States needs free access to the Straits of Malacca to ensure deployment of its forces in the Indian Ocean. Thailand is perpetually concerned about a strong Myanmar, and because Thailand is a non-NATO treaty ally of the United States, Thailand's security is of importance to the United States.

Myanmar does not want to become too dependent on China but needs China for both military support and economic development. Thus, Myanmar has tried to diversity its suppliers by buying MiG-29 fighter aircraft and a nuclear reactor from Russia (US$300–500 million in May 2007). It also has received military supplies from a variety of other states, such as the Ukraine, Israel, Singapore, Pakistan, and North and South Korea. The junta has officially written that the reason the United States wants to see regime change in Myanmar is because Myanmar is the weakest link in the U.S. policy of containing China.

The interest of foreign powers is just one facet of the issue; another is the attitude of the Burmese regime toward foreign governments and individuals. As Senior General Saw Maung said, "The nation should be one in which only Myanmars reside and which Myanmars own. We have to be vigilant against Myanmar, the home of Myanmar nationals, being influenced by anyone. It is important that Myanmar does not become the home of mixed bloods influenced by alien cultures though it is called Myanmar." For any foreign government to consider Myanmar simply as a pawn in regional politics or easily subverted to foreign positions (such as to China) is to mistake the nature of nationalism and the political imperatives within that country.

## What is the future of the military in Myanmar under any new government?

The Burmese *tatmadaw* has played a far greater role in modern Burmese history than the militaries in the contemporary period in the West. The general Western concept that the military should be under civilian control is thus far more difficult to achieve in Myanmar, even though it was a part of the National League for Democracy (NLD) party platform in 1989. Under the constitution approved in 2008, the military in effect will have veto power over any substantive decision on state policy. Military members will hold the ring of power. Under present provisions of that constitution, any amendments would in effect require military approval, which would mean the military would have to vote to diminish its own role. This is most unlikely in foreseeable future. Thus, the *tatmadaw* will have the coercive, executive, and legislative power within the state. It is not likely that judicial control will remain beyond their grasp; the State Law and Order Restoration Council/State Peace and Development Council (SLORC/SPDC) may have replaced the "people's" untrained judges with lawyers, but this does not equate with improving the rule of law. Their influence on the economy will be substantial, and the state will attempt to monitor (if not influence) civil society activities.

Over the next decade or so, it is most likely that the military will play a leading role in the distribution of power in that state. This is a provision of the new constitution, but it would have been likely under any government, even a civilian one. Should some civilian administration take over the state and the military step back from the obvious exercise of power, military influence would still be substantial. It would likely still retain its control of coercive forces, the personal influence of its leaders would be highly important, and there would remain substantial economic institutions under its auspices. The military controls the Myanmar Economic Holdings Corporation (MEHC) and the Myanmar Economic Corporation (MEC) that are, in effect, conglomerates that have been incorporated outside the public sector and employ hundreds of thousands of workers with extensive joint venture and contract operations with foreign firms.

Founded in 1990 under a Special Companies Act, the MEHC, between 1990 and 2007, wholly owns seventy-seven firms with thirty-five firms started since 2007. It has nine subsidiary firms and seven affiliated companies. Its shares are available to military units, active duty and retired military, and veterans' groups, and it has returned a 30 percent profit since 1995 to 1996. The MEC is the "most secretive" business group. Founded in 1997, it has twenty-one factories, including four steel plants, a bank, a cement plant, and an insurance monopoly.

The Ministry of Defense also runs factories that produce matériel outside of military supplies. Acting autonomously of any civilian government, the *tatmadaw* could control the markets on various commodities and goods and have monopolistic potential in industries of their choosing. Both as producers (of goods) and consumers (of a large percentage of the state's budget), their influence under any administration would be extensive.

The military offers a critical avenue of social mobility; even if it were to relinquish other aspects of its command of educational and economic institutions, its influence would still be important. Although strictly controlled, it is likely that the extensive military educational facilities are probably the best in the country. It seems evident that the *tatmadaw* has consciously developed a cadre of trained doctors, engineers, technicians, and administrators who will play pivotal administrative roles in any new administration for a substantial period. The *tatmadaw* in effect has reversed a Western concept. Instead of the military as a source of support for the civilian population, in Myanmar the civilians are seen as a source of support for the military.

Many military officials will be required to retire before the 2010 elections and run for public office both at the national and regional Hluttaw levels. In addition, many retired military officers will likely gain election because they are prominent people in their own districts. A free election in 2010 would probably produce a significant number of military alumni allies of the administration, in addition to the one-quarter of active-duty officers who will be placed in the national Hluttaws by the Ministry of Defense and at state and division level legislatures and one-quarter in the self-administered zones and division.

For the military to retire from effective political control would probably require a long gestation period. That will only occur if two factors are in play. First, the *tatmadaw* must be convinced that there is no possibility of any of the minority areas seceding from the Union (a provision of the 2008 constitution). Second, there must be alternative and desirable avenues of social mobility that will attract youth, who currently still opt for a military career because in fact it is the only avenue to success. This especially means the development of the private sector that can absorb ambitious young people but also autonomous educational and nonprofit institutions. Such changes are likely to take a generation. It has happened in South Korea, Thailand, and Indonesia, but only over extended periods.

### How will the minorities deal with the new government?

Following the institution of a new government after the 2010 elections, the Myanmar administration is likely to counter external criticisms and claim, with a certain degree of justification, that the minorities have more autonomy than they have had in fifty years. This is unlikely to be sufficient from the minorities' vantage points, however. The six minority areas that have local and limited self-government at the township level may be more pleased than heretofore (the Kokang, Wa,

Naga, Padaung, PaO, and Danu ethnic groups), but the major minority groups are unlikely to be satisfied. Since 1962, they have been directly controlled by the center, so some local legislative authority, even with military dominance, might be a respite from rigid command. But many in the major minorities that now have states (Chin, Kachin, Shan, Karen, Kayah, Mon, Rakhine) have wanted some form of federal structure and in some cases virtual autonomy from central control. There will probably be continued dissatisfaction with what some regard as a Burman occupation. For example, the *tatmadaw* has increased its battalion strength in the Chin State from two to fourteen battalions since 1998, and from twenty-four to forty-one battalions in the Kachin State since 1994. (The Kachin Independence Organization has also increased its recruitment.) The *tatmadaw*, through its own regional command structure, will still have ultimate power over these peripheral regions.

Under the new constitution, there will be elected councils at the state/region and township levels. Any real authority at any administrative level thus will require military approval, and it would be exceedingly unrealistic to expect local *tatmadaw* officials to disregard central commands.

Although local elections at the state/region level will be hotly contested, the choice of the chair of that assembly rests with the president of the Union. There are likely to be former military Burmans whom the government would like to see in some of those positions, but whether such choices would be acceptable to cease-fire or other minority groups is unclear.

### What types of economic crises does the country face?

The macroeconomic crises that plagued the state over the past half-century are no longer operative. Myanmar's international reserves were US$3.187 billion in 2008, increased from US$562 million in 2003. The present income from the sale of natural gas from the Yadana and Yetagun fields to Thailand (43 percent of foreign exchange earnings in 2006) and the projected income from the off-shore gas fields in Rakhine, plus that from two Chinese pipelines and perhaps one from India, as well as a variety of exports, will increase these reserves (even at lower energy prices) and with prudent management should resolve any of the regime's immediate economic concerns. The SLORC came to power in 1988 with reserves of some US$30 million. If some call Myanmar a "failed state," it is not failed in its economic present or likely future.

The economic crises that the country faces must be disaggregated. There is now no crisis in macroeconomic terms: the state has a favorable balance of trade (US$2.89 billion in 2008) and international reserves in 2009 of US$3.361 billion. The crisis is thus not with funding but with the knowledge of economic affairs, priorities, and the distribution of the state's considerable present and future resources, even with falling world prices in 2009.

Although many Western states struggle to fund social entitlements as well as other requirements, the Burmese regime has not had that concern. Instead, their priority has been military expenditures. The increases in the size of the military from about 199,861 in 1988 to somewhere in the neighborhood of 400,000 today (with a previous target of half a million, although some say the real total is about 350,000 excluding riot and other police units—desertions and overreporting are said to be high), together with increasingly sophisticated military equipment, spare parts, and more training, will all mean that the already sizable expenditures on the military—officially varying from 25–37 percent of state administrative expenses (2.46 to 3.94 percent of GDP) but more likely to be far in excess of either figure—will continue and perhaps rise. The amounts available for social services will remain limited, even though the United Nations had indicated that there was a humanitarian crisis in the state that predated the Cyclone Nargis tragedy. Already, the official expenditures on education and health are minuscule—1 to 2 percent of the budget. The burden of education and health expenditures has thus quietly been shifted onto the backs of a population already among the poorest in the world, and one suffering from inflationary pressures that go underreported in official circles, even though they were officially calculated at 35 percent in 2007 and at 26.9 percent in 2008.

Various international private institutions have uniformly rated Myanmar low on their international scales. The Fund for Peace considers Myanmar the fourteenth among the twenty most unstable states. The Brookings Institution noted that Myanmar was the seventeenth weakest of 141 countries. The World Press Freedom Index listed Myanmar as 163 of 164 countries in terms of press freedom. The Economist Intelligence Unit rates Myanmar as 163 out of 167 countries in its 2008 Democracy Index.

The present military mistrust of the notable but now aging corps of civilian Burmese economists, some of whom achieved international recognition and have worked for international agencies, has limited the junta's economic policy options. This has been compounded by the great mistrust of foreign advisors. This latter problem is not new; the government in the past has accepted foreigners who would deal with specific technical issues and projects, but since the 1950s the government have felt that policy advisors, at least those publicly recognized, were an infringement of national sovereignty (unless they worked directly under and were paid for by the Union government, as in the civilian period). The military has felt that it had the capacity to plan and execute economic policies and programs, but the reality is that it lacks the basic sophisticated understanding of monetary policy, such as money supply (it no longer makes those figures public, and the central bank is not independent). One foreign economist commented that "monetary policy is incoherent." Economic decisions seem arbitrary: overnight increases in government salaries or the elimination of energy subsidies without careful consideration of their effects. The banking system is in disarray, and other financial institutions are of questionable capability. In 2003, a crisis occurred that was, in effect, a type of pyramid scheme to pay higher interest rates, because official bank interest rates are below inflation levels. The state closed many institutions. Only 3 percent of GDP is raised through taxation.

In November 1988, I listed for the World Bank a series of economic reform measures necessary for improvement in the society. Among them were exchange rate reform, public sector salary reform, financial institutional reform, reform of the private sector and state economic enterprises, regional industrial and economic development diversification, economic planning and technical improvements, establishment of an independent board of audit, enhanced revenue collection, and training in statistical methods. Twenty years later, these needs have not been met.

The restructuring of economic and social policies are necessary for the well-being of the people and even for the military's hold on authority. As other states in the region progress while Myanmar stagnates, invidious comparisons will become more widespread. This could endanger regime survival, and the exodus for better (or indeed any) jobs would likely increase even if fighting ceased. This could cause further regional problems.

It is unclear how much foreign exchange overseas Burmese remit to Myanmar. Whatever official figures that might exist are undoubtedly underestimated, as there are various informal and safe means to transfer funds into the country. Although Myanmar will not be like the Philippines, where such remittances total some US$15 billion annually, such a social safety net could be important for some hundreds of thousands of families remaining in the country. Some estimates indicate that they may amount to more than US$200 million, although other figures range from US$3–4 billion. The world economic crisis of 2008–2009 may cause remittances to drop, thereby further lowering internal income. The government taxes overseas incomes at 10 percent, but anecdotal evidence is that such incomes are normally underreported.

The economic potential and importance of Myanmar should not be overlooked. It is the world's tenth largest exporter of natural gas. Its off-shore and on-shore reserves are estimated as 2.46 trillion cubic meters and off-shore crude oil at 3.2 billion barrels. The Shwe gas field reserves should yield US$37–52 billion over twenty years, of which Myanmar will get US$12–17 billion.

## What are the social crises facing the state?

The political crisis is well known even if a solution acceptable to the international community is distant. But the crisis of youth, the frustration of a lack of a future in the society, the belief that emigration is the only possibility, and the second-class status of civilians, even those with full citizenship, all have resulted in a malaise so deep (yet seemingly unrecognized by the junta) that deliverance from this morass will be exceedingly difficult.

All avenues are under military authority or surveillance. Access to higher education is militarily controlled. All mass interest groups are under state authority. Registration in the *sangha* is required. Private sector mobility is severely limited because of a lack of capital. The most extensive mass organization, the Union Solidarity and Development Association (USDA), is a civilianized military voice. Futures in opposition politics are hazardous to one's health. Despair is evident.

Health and nutritional standards are appalling even by regional criteria. Infant mortality is said to be 79 (per 1,000 births), life expectancy is about sixty years at birth, and Myanmar rates 125 of 174 countries on the UN Human Development Report of 2000. Even where doctors practice in rural areas, medicines often have to be purchased privately at unaffordable prices.

There is increasing landlessness in rural areas as the population has expanded. Landlessness affects 25 to 40 percent of the rural population. Fertilizer is scarce, and farmers only receive one-third of the export price of rice (compared to 50 to 60 percent of the price for Vietnamese farmers). Paddy prices have dropped 50 percent from 2007 to 2008, so farmers are in even more need. Debt has increased with usurious interest rates of 10 to 15 percent a month, sometimes 100 percent daily interest in the bazaars. The state provides only about 30 percent of the agricultural credit required. Because land is state-owned, even those farming cannot use it as collateral. The government denies that these conditions are serious.

Environmental degradation has become rife. The overcutting of hardwoods, especially teak, is well known. Extinction of wildlife is evident. Mangrove forests have been destroyed for shrimp farming, increasing the devastation of Cyclone Nargis and in turn being decreased by it. Pollution stemming from uncontrolled gold and other mining, as well as the construction of major dams for hydroelectric power and irrigation, many of which are sponsored by the Chinese, is rampant. Some of these problems lie in the hands of minority cease-fire groups, but most responsibility must fall on the Myanmar government.

### What are the needs of the state in a transition to a new government?

Whatever government evolves from the 2010 elections—or even whether there is a civilian/military government through negotiations or because of a popular uprising against the present or future government—the needs of the state will be enormous. Yet should change occur, there will be very high expectations for immediate progress that will place inordinate pressures on a new administration of any stripe. The Burmese people will expect deliverance from economic as well as political oppression, and the government, if its policies were acceptable to the external world, would also expect immediate and substantial assistance. If such a new government were democratic (or at least pluralistic), then the disparate local demands may become tumultuous. The honeymoon period for any new government is likely to be quite short.

A massive infusion of funds would be required—a figure of about US$1 billion had been rather arbitrarily mentioned a decade ago, but this is probably a gross underestimation. Yet the absorptive capacity of the state is likely to be extremely limited. Recalculating government budgets based on a realistic, floating, and unitary exchange rate would be required. Examination of the viability of the state economic enterprises (the public sector) would be needed (they have increased from 624 enterprises to 794 between 1988 and 2008). Ensuring the autonomy of the central bank will be necessary. Updated skills in technology and science will be required. In any of these efforts, Burmese would have to be trained in a wide variety of analytical and planning skills that are currently lacking, and most of this would have to be done abroad. Foreign advisors/ consultants would be necessary but subject to political scrutiny and probable criticism. Multilateral donors are more likely to be acceptable. Given the present and likely future role of the military in the society, there is an obvious need to expose the upcoming military elite to international standards of military responsibility through overseas training programs.

Yet the present policies of most donors preclude supplying the depth of training required to manage a sophisticated and increasingly complex economy and society. To wait for change when such needs are obvious is to invite future problems that could undercut any positive political developments that might occur.

### What role is there for multilateral and bilateral donors?

The military might, as it did in 1972, recognize that more multilateral and bilateral assistance was required, and the world's humanitarian concerns might prompt efforts to assist a new government if that new government diminished its repressive measures. But the past is not prelude. The World Bank and the Asian Development Bank now have criteria, lacking earlier, for transparency, good governance, and at least some semblance of popular participation in the political process for assistance to take place beyond humanitarian or relief support. In spite of the U.S. administration's supposed strong democracy stance, the reentry of the U.S. assistance program in 1979 did not consider that as a necessary criterion for its foreign aid program or for its military training under the International Military Education and Training program in spite of legislation to the contrary.

Under the new constitution, it seems likely that Japan would begin new aid programs, although pressures from the United States might cause some anguish in the Foreign Ministry.

It is also questionable whether international nongovernmental organizations would increase their programs in Myanmar unless the new government issues more relaxed guidelines for its operations. In some cases, directives of control from the center are often sporadically or partly implemented in the field. The stringency of control will probably depend on the degree of confidence the new administration has in its own capacities and tenure, as well as the ability of local officials to achieve mandated targets or resolve problems.

### Is democracy a reasonable expectation for Myanmar in the near term? In the future?

Democracy is neither inevitable nor inaccessible in Myanmar. If it were to come, it would not be instantly born fully formed from the head of some Zeus-like person or event. Democracies evolve, often in unbalanced directions, and political cultures also evolve to accommodate and then encourage democratic continuity and deepening. A political system recognized internationally as a democracy is certainly possible over time in that country. But to expect that even a peaceful transfer of power to a real civilian regime would automatically, ipso facto, result in such a system, which seems to be the unsophisticated international mantra of the moment, is more than unrealistic. That is not to claim that there should not be political change, just that evolution is far more likely than revolution in this instance. The range of criteria to define democracy is complex, and elections are just one element of that process.

The new government, still run by the military but under civilianized auspices, will claim that its "discipline-flourishing democracy" is in place with a multiparty system and an elected legislative branch not only at the center but in each of the states and regions and down to township levels. The government will also claim that any criticism of its democracy is a form of Western prejudice and that Myanmar, because of the nefarious imperialistic designs of the United States and its minions, is being discriminated against. Although there was muted Western criticism of Suharto's Indonesian "democracy," the West has been unwilling to accept the Burmese protestations of democratic governance with anything less than a complete elimination of the Burmese military from power. This is highly unlikely to happen. There has been growing international realization, on the other hand, that the military must be part of the solution to any of Myanmar's multitude of problems.

However, if there were to be a major change in the power structure in the country and the military were to relinquish titular control, would there be democracy in Myanmar? Titularly, democracy as defined by some form of representative government administratively might be in place, but the spirit of compromise and the degree of plurality that are at the core of the democratic process would take time to evolve. The opposition is united only by its antagonism to the junta. It would have to develop policies that would satisfy the very diverse demands of many different populations. Furthermore, within the country now there are few who understand democracy, as two generations have been prevented from legally studying or reading about it, let alone experiencing it. One Burmese observer described his country as "politically gelded for fifty years." Another wrote that "since 1962, the Burmese military has occupied the entire political matrix." A few understand the process, most prominently Aung San Suu Kyi, but a new generation has to be inculcated into the mysteries of this particular cult. Now, the electoral cries for democracy may equally be interpreted as calls for the elimination of the military in executive positions.

A strong middle class is usually associated with democratic governance. Yet an indigenous middle class has been weak; most in that category were not Burmans. The strength of a middle class of Burmans will only slowly develop. There is, however, an intellectual class, once active in the civilian era, that could once again emerge if the strictures of control of information and expression were to be loosened. This, too, is likely to be an extended and gradual process.

Because democracy is a process, there are intermediate stages that might be encouraged. The most obvious is some form of political pluralism. Fostering this development is possible through assistance in the development of civil society. The old adage that Burmese do not join organizations except for those with a religious focus has been disproved by survey work and the response to Cyclone Nargis. Even under the present administration, these organizations have grown, and they include (but are not limited to) those localized around a monastery or school. Those at the ward level, and even national ones that are apolitical in nature, although often treated with suspicion and infiltrated, continue. They were given a great impetus by Cyclone Nargis, when they performed admirably to bring relief to those affected areas. For them to have an impact on democratic growth, there needs to be close interplay among networks of such organizations.

Whatever government is in power, the tendency will be for those elements of the Burmese political culture, discussed earlier, to take effect. The short-term prognostication would tend toward considerable trouble, but in the longer term that culture will evolve, and if the educational system can be improved and freed from the rigidities of the SLORC/SPDC, one would expect considerable positive change in that society.

### What role can the major powers play in Myanmar?

The roles of the major powers, especially the United States and the European Union, have generally been counterproductive in terms of improving the sorry state of the people in Myanmar. The imposition of various economic sanctions that have periodically increased has not produced their intended effect—regime change. Rather, the vituperative language of much of the world has prompted a nationalistic response that on many occasions became strident and xenophobic. Although sanctions provide the moral high ground to those imposing them, they have been proven to be ineffectual. Even if sanctions were enforced by all of Myanmar's neighbors—and none of them now do so—it seems likely that the junta would resist and retreat into itself. Yet there is no possibility of regionally approved sanctions—Myanmar is too strategically located and too richly endowed with gas and other products in demand.

The major Western powers will remain suspect in any government elected under a new constitution. Insofar as they might provide economic or humanitarian assistance for projects or activities, these are likely to be accepted as long as they do not formally engage in policy. Myanmar in 2007 received about US$2 per capita in foreign assistance, compared to twenty-five times that amount for Laos. Informal policy discussions on an individual level may be welcome, but whatever changes or reforms occur, they must appear to come from within. Japanese support is likely to become extensive under an elected government. Chinese and Indian assistance is already a given. Some in the *tatmadaw* regret that it indicated a willingness to go along with Western concerns, such as on anti–opium production activities, because the response from the United States especially was not positive. In fact, it undercut those who had proposed making some overtures, exposing them to internal Myanmar criticism.

The Burmese will object to any role by foreigners that appears to be condescending and infringing on what they regard as Burmese sovereignty. The tendency to publicly lecture the Burmese of any persuasion (and indeed most countries) is counterproductive.

### What might be the roles of ASEAN, the UN, and the EU?

Of all the organizations in the foreign community, ASEAN probably stands the best chance of assisting reform in Myanmar, but even that role is likely to be marginal. The political heritage of each of the member states has politically questionable pedigrees. Noninterference into the internal affairs of any of these states is an ASEAN cardinal principle. There has been growing dissatisfaction with Myanmar, especially after the 2003 attack on the NLD in central Myanmar (in 2006 Myanmar forfeited the ASEAN chair) and because of the suppression of the Saffron Revolution in 2007. ASEAN would likely claim that there has been modest political progress should the elections of 2010 go smoothly. Following them, it is quite possible that ASEAN will accept the political progress that the Burmese claim under their new government, and Myanmar may finally chair ASEAN after that time.

In November 2007, the ASEAN states, including Myanmar, signed the ASEAN Charter, which their governments ratified by the end of 2008. The Charter contains a human rights provision but without stipulations of monitoring, enforcement, and penalties. Myanmar has signed that document, but what provisions will be considered and how it might operate are vague at this writing. Because there is an antitrafficking provision in the Burmese constitution, starting to discuss enforcement of that section would not be held to be discriminatory against Myanmar. The problem is widespread within the region.

In spite of previous Burmese respect for the United Nations—indeed, a Burmese citizen, U Thant, was its secretary general—the United Nations has proven to possess only marginal influence. The United Nations initiated ineffective dialogue with Aung San Suu Kyi through two different special envoys of the secretary general, and Secretary General Ban Ki Moon visited Myanmar after Cyclone Nargis. But little significant or lasting results followed, except expected platitudes. Through Chinese and Russian efforts, the UN Security Council has effectively blocked U.S. efforts to censor Myanmar. There have been fourteen General Assembly resolutions on the human rights situation in Myanmar between 1991 and 2008. On July 14, 2008, a group of Burmese dissident organizations led by the National Council of the Union of Burma (NCUB) filed a petition to the UN Credentials Committee to challenge the credentials of the SLORC. On August 1, the National Coalition Government of the Union of Burma (NCGUB) supported that effort to recommend to the UN General Assembly that the credentials of the SPDC to the United Nations be withdrawn because of violations to various human rights provisions. This was, as anticipated, rejected by the United Nations on September 23, 2008. In August 2008, the new UN Human Rights envoy, Tomas Ojae Quintana, visited Myanmar but was not allowed to see Aung San Suu Kyi. In early 2009, the NCUB announced that it intended to form a "government in exile," thus creating factional issues with the NCGUB, which already considers itself in that role.

The European Union adopted its Common Position on Myanmar on October 28, 1996. It called for the expulsion of all military personnel and an embargo on arms, munitions, and military equipment. It suspended all nonhumanitarian aid but allowed assistance to help alleviate poverty and basic human needs. It banned entry visas for SLORC and family members, and suspended high-level bilateral government visits to Burma (ministers and political directors and higher). All provisions were renewable and in force for a six-month period. In 1997, the European Union withdrew the general system of trade preferences for agriculture; previously, those for industry had been withdrawn. There seems to be growing discontent within various EU countries that the approach to Myanmar has not yielded the desired effects, and individual countries have been restudying their approaches. Six donors instituted the "Three Disease" (malaria, tuberculosis, and HIV/AIDS) program that will provide about US$20 million annually to that country for a five-year period after the United States effectively refused to provide assistance to the Global Fund for the same purposes, although in the spring of 2009 there were indications that the United States might reconsider its position. The visit in January 2009 by the ministers of development of Norway and Denmark is an indication of growing frustrations with the effectiveness of present EU policy.

## What might the role of the Burmese diaspora be in a new government?

Had political change occurred in Myanmar within a relatively short period after 1988, the return of the educated Burmese who fled the country would have been fairly easy, and they probably would have assumed significant positions in any new administration. Before 1962, Burma was one of the few countries in Asia from which there was no brain drain. At low incomes but in a culturally comfortable atmosphere, most Burmese preferred to stay home even after receiving doctoral degrees from Western institutions that offered them employment.

Now, the situation has evolved. There are two elements of the educated diaspora. The first is the NCGUB, which claims to be the legitimate government because it is composed of NLD members who were elected in 1988 and were in a majority in that (disputed) body. They fled the country and have been operating in Washington, D.C., with representation in New York and Brussels. Under the 2010 election, they would have no role and could not return unless they publicly gave up their claims to govern. Their return under any situation in which the NLD were not free (unless they publicly recanted) is highly unlikely.

Another element of the diaspora, composed of an educated elite, probably would be split, with a small percentage returning but the bulk staying abroad for several reasons: there are few jobs in Myanmar, they may fear for themselves if the military still exerted major influence (which is more than likely), they have families abroad and often children in school, and they have become embedded in their local communities. They may be articulate about the problems and have ideas about solutions, but many would remain overseas. Those who did go back may not obtain the level of social recognition and positions of influence that they may expect and feel they deserve.

Unless a new government were to improve conditions in the minority regions and significant development were to take place along with peace, the perhaps two million workers in Thailand might be reluctant to return, as would the 150,000 or so Karen, Kayah, and Mon in UN-supervised refugee camps in Thailand along the Myanmar frontier. The United States in 2008 began to admit thousands of Karen from these camps (18,139 as of 2008), which have become a way station for emigration to the United States. In fact, because Burmese are prepared to work overseas to support their impoverished families at home, there may even be a further outpouring of laborers seeking even the most marginal of jobs in other countries. The world financial crisis of 2008–2009, however, may force economic migrants back and overseas remittances to diminish.

# CODA

*This Coda was written in the summer of 2009. See chapter 9 for a reassessment.*

The prognosis for early socioeconomic progress in Myanmar is not sanguine, and that for politics is marginal. In spite of *tatmadaw* protestations to the contrary, there will be little incentive for it to significantly reform the basic economic and social ills to which the state is and will be heir. Inaction on reform in those sectors, however, is not simply maintaining the status quo. In effect, it is retrogression—delaying understanding the plight of its own people, the inevitable requirement to restructure the government's priorities for the common good, and positively mobilizing the whole population in creating something that has been lacking: the ethos of a nation. The use of nationalism to mobilize the garrison state against mythic or perceived foreign enemies cannot replace a positive multiethnic message credible to the whole people.

Although the junta claims that political progress is now self-evident, having progressed through their roadmap toward "discipline-flourishing democracy," this is only half accurate. The year 2010 will produce a new national parliament and a variety of regional and local ones. It is accurate to say that the people have some voice. But it is a somewhat sotto voce, in contrast to that of the *tatmadaw*, which will still hold the prima donna role.

Each government in Burma has attempted to legitimate itself and mobilize the society toward its self-defined ends. It sought internal legitimacy through Buddhism in the civilian period. To counter the divisive religious focus in minority circles, secular socialism became not only the ideological structure of the economy but also the basis of legitimacy. Since 1988, however, legitimacy has been centered on the military itself, and history has been rewritten and reinterpreted to confirm that end. The appeal, insofar as it succeeds, will probably positively affect only the present and future military, and not the population as a whole and especially not minority groups. The military's stress on its own present and unique contribution will not create the cohesion toward which it claims it strives nor allow it to achieve its central goal—national unity. Indeed, there is inherent tension between the military's conception of its role and the national unity it espouses.

In spite of its emphasis on the construction of infrastructure—which is of some present and potential importance but which has been both underreported and underappreciated in international circles—the administration has exhibited a lack of understanding of the critical social needs of the society and the malaise pervading the country. By concentrating on building, which it evidently believes gives the regime legitimacy, it has ignored the reasons for such construction—the early betterment of people's lives.

The tragedies are multiple, and the political stasis with the opposition is only a part of them, but foreign observers concentrate on this aspect. The people, of course, suffer most, and among those most affected are the minorities, who have been subject to discrimination at best and exploitation and persecution in some areas. The vilification of the junta by foreign governments, groups, and media has increased the already heightened sense of insecurity, sometimes verging on panic, and resultant xenophobia among the *tatmadaw* leaders.

Many influential foreigners have argued that ending the political confrontation must precede any changes in the economic or social arenas. Of course, this view reflects that of the political opposition. Whether change must be sequential or in parallel is an issue in many societies, and whether, for example, economic change might precede political development is, in part, an argument of the junta, which claims that economic progress under its leadership will allow political transformation over time through its imposed constitution with its elected legislatures.

Either approach would seem to be insufficient. Quick transformational political change is unlikely, and even economic evolution is glacial. Ideally, a conscious effort by all parties to recognize the limitations of their self-imposed concepts of power would seem to be the nexus of any real reformation. This is as unlikely as it is desirable. The attrition of traditional views of authority and their evolution into more consensus-building and modernized concepts will occur slowly and to the dissatisfaction of large numbers of Burmese who hope for more immediate and positive changes.

However understandable the high moral tone voiced by foreigners toward a repressive regime may be, this unending vituperative chorus has served to solidify the military leadership in a bunker-like mentality against foreigners, even those who simply wish to assist the impoverished. Even then, according to the authorities, they must have ulterior motives. As the junta has proclaimed, "Foreigners cannot love us." This is a product not only of the colonial experience but also of neighbors who have conspired against the government and the antipathy continuously voiced against the regime.

The perpetuation of military control will result not only from the new constitution but also from the formation of a new class—the sons of the military who have and will join the *tatmadaw* and/or wield political and economic influence. Their access to the power and spoils of the system will limit the capacity of the civilian elite to attain positions of authority and access to the benefits of (eventual) economic development.

There is, thus, likely to be restrictions on all forms of mobility under the projected system.

The near term will focus on the 2010 elections and their aftermath. Even before those elections, and even with U.S. disapproval of the politics of Myanmar, the United States is considering signing the ASEAN Treaty of Amity and Cooperation, an act long overdue that has been a significant deterrent to effective U.S. policy throughout the region. The Obama administration will likely appoint someone to a new coordinating ambassadorial position to deal with U.S. policy toward Myanmar, but whether the direct talks stipulated in the legislation of 2008 will take place within Myanmar at an appropriately high level may well depend on the status of Aung San Suu Kyi and her release. The United Nations and the International Crisis Group have advocated restarting economic developmental assistance to reinvigorate its dialogue with Myanmar, but this will be resisted by the United States. The Burmese, in response to these efforts, may simply say that they are well along their own road toward "discipline-flourishing democracy," which will be in place after the 2010 elections. The United States has already dismissed that argument. Improving relations may require acts of compromise by all parties—actions that are not immediately apparent.

The normal academic dualism describing countries as either weak or strong states does not seem applicable in the case of Myanmar. The state may be considered weak under normal criteria if its government cannot or will not deliver goods, services, and security to its people. Such a definition neglects the reality of the military presently as the national core, having controlled or eliminated any potentially contending institutions. Myanmar is a strong state in terms of its ability to mobilize coercive forces against any internal threat to its continuance, and in the absence of any significant alternative decision-making institutions. It has become an economically stronger state, although it has not used its new financial resources for the common good. It is, however, weaker in that its leadership seems overly fearful of foreign machinations, and because of that behaves as if it is under political, economic, and cultural siege internally and externally. This affects its capacity to respond to foreign criticisms with measured responses and results in internal suppression of dissident views. It resorts instead to bluster and xenophobia. Both such fears are equally overstated, whether they are from minorities, the civilian sector, or abroad, all of which the government suspects. These emotional attitudes will not be easy to erase even with positive political change.

Paranoia does not necessarily invalidate existential fears. But the geopolitical situation would seem to preclude any external threats to the regime except the more subtle one brought about not by aggression or economics but by insidious globalization that could transform Burman culture over time. The junta charges that criticism of Myanmar is excessive, and that other Asian authoritarian states are less subject to the unending complaints even when their human rights abuses are more dire or their lack of democratic actions and institutions more widespread. Where are, the junta asks, the emasculated opposition political parties in China, Vietnam, and Laos? In part, this discrepancy is accurate, because of two factors: the lack of immediate and perceived geopolitical and economic interests on the part of the West in Myanmar, thus the focus on one strand in their foreign policy agenda—human rights— while ignoring others.

The second factor is the image of Aung San Suu Kyi. This personalization of international political concern has been, of course, central to the formulation of policy toward the regime itself. However much foreign policy is subject to or analyzed through academic disciplines indicating rational choice or other schools of international relations and political science theory, the emotional appeal of a brave woman standing up to oppression and sacrificing her family in the process is a critical factor in the reaction of the world to Myanmar and its government. She has become the avatar of democracy and morality, perhaps creating impossible expectations. The military in a sense has created the international aura surrounding Aung San Suu Kyi by its repression. The military leadership dismisses this effect and concentrates instead on what it perceives to be her potential for disrupting the road to discipline-flourishing democracy through the 2010 elections and beyond, indicating an insular and imbalanced view of the state's needs that compromise might have precluded. Her trial in the summer of 2009 regarding violating the conditions of her house arrest is an ineffective junta effort to stigmatize her.

The dilemma for all groups and minorities in Myanmar as the 2010 elections approach is whether they will legally contest at the polls. Although that election will intentionally invalidate the previous 1990 elections that were won by the National League for Democracy (NLD), a new government, even if controlled by the military, will have a significant element of civilian authority (within strictures), that could provide more internal openness and even more freedom of expression, although within the ubiquitous "subject to law" provisions of the constitution. We are likely to witness the gradual attrition of stringent controls unless insurrection is believed to be imminent. Whether any such gradual change will satisfy internal needs or external demands is questionable. Tensions will probably continue.

Does the perceived internal and/or external legitimacy of the electoral process depend on the participation of the NLD? If it is invited to participate but decides not to do so, does that decision further marginalize that group (or even have it declared illegal) or delegitimate the whole elections to the Burmese or foreign states and observers? If officially precluded from running, what would be the effect of such a prohibition? It is possible that the NLD may split into a variety of fragments, with some of the younger members disagreeing with the "uncles"—the executive committee, composed of elder members.

The senior general at the Armed Forces Parade on March 27, 2009, while blaming the problems of Burmese politics on the colonialists and the egotism of civilian politicians, remarked that democracy was in a "fledgling stage," requiring nurturing, gradual growth, and tranquility. Quoting the Burmese proverb that "a recently dug well cannot be expected to produce clear water immediately," he implied that the *tatmadaw* would enforce those conditions and would take a long time to overcome past defects, implying the continuing need for military dominance. The *tatmadaw* will filter the water of the newly dug "democratic" well.

The efforts of the Obama administration to review policy toward Burma/Myanmar are welcome—this is the first significant indication of official U.S. dialogue on policy toward that country in some eighteen years. Such dialogue, let alone policy changes, will be resisted by those with vested interests in the present confrontation. Having imposed isolation, any significant U.S. retreat from that position without commensurate Burmese changes would be politically unacceptable. How the senior general and the junta will respond is unclear at this writing.

In discussing the role of the military in politics, years ago one distinguished Burman remarked, "The play is over, but the audience is forced to remain in their seats and the actors refuse to leave the stage." As 2010 approaches, we may see the on-stage chorus increased and diversified, but the usual actors (many in mufti) will still be in evidence both in front of the footlights, and now hidden in the wings as well and, most important, controlling the curtain.

As the political stalemate continues, as foreign pressures for reform seem ineffective, and as the internal conditions of the peoples in the country deteriorate, those outside of that benighted country can only hope that in some Burmese manner the people will, as U Nu once wrote, "win through."

# 9

# THE POWER OF
# POSITIVE CHANGE

## *Introduction*

Events in Myanmar since the elections of November 7, 2010, have profoundly altered the internal mood of much of Myanmar society and have surprised Burmese and seasoned foreign observers of the Myanmar scene. The pessimism that pervaded the society prior to the November 2010 elections, and the methodology and results of that voting, which prompted many foreign observers to call them a "sham," a "fraud," or, more discretely, "badly flawed," gradually gave way to the realization that for reasons, variously interpreted, positive change was in the air. During the inaugural address of President Thein Sein on March 30, 2011, the changes necessary for the government to undertake were first articulated; they constituted the most remarkable official and public self-criticism since the military coup of March 2, 1962. Many expatriate Burmese, antimilitary activists, and human rights specialists called them cosmetic and insincere, designed simply to ensure that Myanmar won the right to host the ASEAN summit in 2014. They pushed Burmese citizens and foreign governments to avoid being lured into alleviating political and economic pressure, including sanctions, on the military and its chosen government.

These critics have demonstrably been proven wrong, as reform policies mushroomed and foreign governments altered previously restrictive policies toward the newly named state: the Republic of the Union of Myanmar. A half-century of social and economic stagnation and decay, a difficult recovery from a taut military administrative command system, as well as cultivating attitudes of conciliation and compromise, hallmarks of the democratic process, prevent democracy——"discipline-flourishing" or otherwise—from immediately flowering in full bloom. Time is needed because essential power still remains in *tatmadaw* hands. Various systemic issues facing the administration remain unresolved and some are only partly addressed. Yet the progress begun should not be denied.

As this new edition goes to press, the implementation of reforms, even the articulation of some of them and the establishment of priority actions, are in process and their successes are subject to speculations. Foreign relations have dramatically evolved, especially with the West, with important implications for the China connection. The cautious pessimism that characterized the first edition of this volume must now be altered, and a new era of restrained hope instead reigns. To retain that flavor, so that the reader may judge how far society has progressed, the early commentaries remain in tact. In this new chapter, we catalogue three years of change, including two years of progress, and then we speculate on the future, especially on the next general elections that will be held in 2015 and beyond.

Changes are occurring rapidly, and the internal reform agenda has generated external dynamics that in turn reinfluence the domestic developments. This chapter is divided into three broad categories, which obviously overlap but which initially may be separated for clarity. These are the internal changes that have affected the society, the reaction to these changes by diverse foreign states and interests, and Myanmar's prospects. At the close, internal and external considerations will be melded.

### Internal developments

It is unlikely that any country in Asia in recent years has undergone such internal policy shifts in so short a time as Myanmar.

Although never "closed," as the popular international media has portrayed the state in its previous incarnations, the "opening" to the West was both cause and effect. Although the future remains unpredictable, the complete shutdown of the myriad reform policies initiated by President Thein Sein, with its potential destruction of the hopes so eloquently raised, seems politically unlikely. It would result in massive frustration threatening regime stability. The fulfillment of such hopes, however, is not an event, but a process of piecemeal progress that could unsettle the complex social fabrics that are Myanmar,

### How did the government prepare for the elections of November 2010?

The elections were part of the seven-stage plan toward what the previous government had called a "discipline-flourishing democracy." The government's corporatist-style political party was in place: the Union Solidarity and Development Party (USDP), transformed from a virtually ubiquitous mass organization and political home to a party for many of the ex-military. Inducements (public work projects, such as roads) were offered to the populace to ensure their support. Campaigning was restricted to give the state an advantage. Voting registers were compiled, and absentee balloting (called "advance voting" in Myanmar) encouraged; it often allowed mass voting in the USDP's favor. Although there were to be internal polling observers, the government was clearly able to manipulate the process for a decisive victory in its favor. It evidently was not about to allow the free voting and tabulation of results that gave the opposition a resounding victory in the May 1990 elections.

### Why did the National League for Democracy (NLD) decide not to participate?

The NLD was given the opportunity to participate in the elections, but several factors prompted their decision not to register. Aung San Suu Kyi, the effective and ultimate leader of that party, was under house arrest, and it was evident that the authorities would not release her until the elections were safely completed. The reason given publicly for her conviction was over the John Yetaw incident, and Senior General Than Shwe subsequently commutated her sentence by half, but this was all subterfuge, because some excuse would have been found to retain her. Aung San Suu Kyi was against registration. The costs of registration were abnormally high, the likelihood of free and fair voting and ballot counting was slim at best, and the oath of adherence to the 2008 constitution, which was a requirement of registration, was in the NLD view too restrictive. Participation would have destroyed the NLD claim of political legitimacy because of their victory in the May 1990 elections; the November 2010 elections were, in part, designed to eliminate that egregious military mistake.

Following the formation of the new government, by-elections had to be held for seats vacated by elected representatives that received cabinet posts, as joint appointments were illegal under the constitution. Aung San Suu Kyi had been released from house arrest in November 2010,shortly after the elections, and the beginnings of cooperation had occurred with NLD. The NLD then decided to contest the forty-five vacant seats, and Aung San Suu Kyi decided to run for one.

### How were the elections carried out, and what were the results?

The date for the elections of November 7, 2010, as for all important events in Burma/Myanmar, was likely chosen based on some astrologer's computations of the government's best chances for success. It is unlikely that they needed such assistance, because the effort to win was, using a basketball analogy, a full-court press. All the steps seemed to have been manipulated. Campaigning, registration, and the counting of ballots were controlled. The widespread use of absentee balloting and bloc voting seems to have been virtually ubiquitous. Some

3,071 persons in thirty-seven parties (plus independents) competed for 1,157 seats, of which the USDP won 875 (79.4 percent in the *Pyithu Hluttaw*—People's Assembly—and 77 percent in the *Amyotha Hluttaw*—the upper house (or in U.S. terms, a senate). Yet the triumph for the USDP also revealed some strains in the political fabric. In the seven minority areas, the USDP had a clean sweep in only one—the Kayah State. In the six other states, the USDP won between 30 to 46 percent of the votes, indicating that localized and ethnic issues remained contentious problems. With the infusion of the required 25 percent active duty military in all *hluttaws*, however, the government had a comfortable majority throughout the country. China regarded the peaceful electoral process as progress, although it was decried by most of the Western world. In spite of the obvious irregularities, the results produced a new dynamic in a society so long entrenched in the miasma of single-party military control (1974–1988).

**What was the configuration of the new government, the Republic of the Union of Myanmar, and who were its leaders?**

The outcome of the elections and the formation of the new government gave a new appearance to the state even though many believed this was, in effect, remembrance of things past. To all outward appearances, they were correct, but this familiar military overlay in mufti obscured the new dynamic that has since proven most important.

General Thein Sein (the former prime minister) was elected head of state, and General Tin Aung Myint Oo elected as vice president. Thura Shwe Mann, whom many thought might be president, was selected as speaker of the *Pyithu Hluttaw*, while a Shan USDP delegate became the speaker of the *Amyotha Hluttaw*. The cabinet was largely composed of former military officers, but there were a few civilians. Policies had been in the hands of the junta and thus under Than Shwe's control in the earlier period (1988–1992 under Saw Maung, 1992–2010 under Than Shwe), when the cabinet in that era basically carried out the junta's (Than Shwe's) pronouncements. The process seems to have been transformed. President Thein Sein has been remarkably open to contact and discussion, and yet he seems to have been able to bring a divided cabinet together in support for his reformist agenda. A partial cabinet reshuffle in the early fall of 2012 appears to have solidified his control. The vice president, publicly viewed as opposed to many progressive changes, retired because of "ill health," although this may have been a diplomatic nicety. His replacement was at first purported to be a former general, one of his family had foreign citizenship, and thus was ineligible under constitutional provisions. He was replaced by retired admiral Nyan Tun. Had the original choice remained, the constitution would have had to be amended. This would have served as a precedent for Aung San Suu Kyi to be elected to the presidency because her sons all have foreign citizenship.

### Why did the reforms take place, and why at that particular time?

This question, perhaps the most asked among foreign observers, is in part based on the external vilification of the previous regime and its military members who were considered the embodiment of political, social, and economic evil and from whom nothing positive could result. In some sense, reform was waiting to be born, having been quietly conceived over long periods in the minds of many patriotic, nationalistic members of the military who were forced to remain silent, stifled under the strict command system. They and their families silently watched the state and the lives of the peoples deteriorate.

With a new government, led by a president who had been exposed on his travels as prime minister to the visual and political effects of progress outside Myanmar, with the absence of the smothering and commanding presence of Senior General Than Shwe, with the experience of living through internal dissent in the streets, with the apparent need to reaffirm the classic

Burmese neutralist policies and balance Western and Chinese relations, and with the understanding that the U.S. could materially assist economic development bilaterally, and the opening of channels to multilateral donors, President Thein Sein seems to have recognized that reforms must start at the top or they might be demanded from the bottom. Only in Myanmar and Taiwan in East Asia did the leadership recognize the need for change before they were forced to acquiesce by the populace.

These may be proximate causes in some complex equation, but even more fundamentally change may have been, in part, an inchoate need to reassert the primacy of traditional Burmese autonomy that had been restricted by the colonial experience, Cold War dualism, and foreign ideologies and pressures. Those from abroad who credit sanctions and foreign pressures as catalysts for these changes, those who have decried them, and those who believe the Arab Spring forced reforms exhibit a hubris that denies the Burmese people the capacity to recognize their own needs and national interests.

### What have been the policies and the reform agenda of the new government?

During his inaugural address on March 30, 2011, President Thein Sein began to outline the deficiencies of the state and its government. He noted the need for improvement in health and education, he articulated the requirement for better relations with minorities, and he decried the prevalence of corruption. He soon launched an antipoverty conference and initiative, and he personally embraced popular criticisms of the state's lack of response to continuing, even accelerating, poverty and the deprivation of people's lives.

A wave of reforms followed. By regional standards, quite liberal labor legislation was enacted, allowing unions. The right to publicly demonstrate (subject to notification) was initiated. Censorship was greatly diminished. A human rights commission was established. A nongovernmental (yet authorized) think tank-cum-NGO called the Myanmar Development Resources Institute was formed that reported directly to the president and consisted of three components: economics, law, and security and political affairs. A new foreign investment law was passed, and foreign businesses invited into the country. Later, a Social and Economic Advisory Council was constituted to advise various ministries on needed changes and implementation. Importantly, hundreds of political prisoners were released. President Thein Sein has invited former dissidents to return to Myanmar, and some have responded, although a major response from the diaspora is likely to await indications of sustained reforms and legal protection.

Critically, a cease-fire was agreed in January 2012 with the Karen rebels—the longest insurrection in the modern world, which had started in 1949—and the government moved assiduously to garner foreign assistance (especially from the Japanese and Norwegians) to demonstrate both to the Karen and other insurgent or disaffected minorities the advantages of cooperation with the state. In the Kachin area in the north, however, fighting broke out in June 2011 that as of this writing has intensified, and involve airstrikes. The Chinese are concerned over this explosive border issue. The Myanmar government is attempting to resolve the problems, which undercut domestic and foreign support for the overall reform movement.

Reporting on various *hluttaw* (legislative) questions and debate, as outlined in the more open media, indicates that rather than being a rubber stamp of an admittedly overpowering executive branch, important questions were asked and discussed. A disagreement between the speaker of the *Pyithu Hluttaw*, Thura Shwe Mann, and President Thein Sein perhaps indicated both the possibility of a greater separation of powers and institutional and personal rivalries. Thura Shwe Mann called for a doubling of civil service salaries to cut corruption and improve services, but the president denied this challenge. The rather arcane dispute between the legislature—on the status of its committee structure—the executive branch, and the constitutional court, whatever their internal ramifications, was an indicator of increased pluralism in the political culture. It is widely expected that President Thein Sein may not run for reelection in 2015, but it is equally believed that Thura Shwe Mann may be a candidate.

A palpable change in the popular mood was also important, at least in the cities of Myanmar. People freely discussed their political views, journals and magazines publicly portrayed Aung San Suu Kyi, discussion of Aung San's historical role was more open, and criticisms of the government and past practices were evident. The changes in popular perceptions were widespread and welcome.

### What were the results of the by-elections of April 1, 2012?

By all internal and external accounts, the elections and vote counting were free and fair. Of the forty-five seats up for contestation, one was eliminated because of a technicality, and the NLD won forty-three. The NLD representation in the national parliament (*hluttaw*) was thus only about 8 percent, but it was a symbolic victory of major proportions. First, it seemed to indicate that if the 2015 national elections were conducted in an equally impartial manner, and the seats allocated as at present and not along the proposed proportional representation lines, the NLD might sweep the seats, as it did in the unrecognized May 1990 elections. Second, this was a major embarrassment for the USDP, the government's chosen political vehicle. Any casual visitor to Naypyitaw could not help notice the huge compound housing multiple grandiose structures of the USDP, located on the edge of the governmental section of the new capital. It indicated that the state had long ago determined that the USDP was to be a critical, military-backed political entity, and yet in its first free trial it had failed. Whether it becomes a vital party with an identifiable and separate agenda from the administration is unclear. Yet, the by-elections also indicated that if the government wished, it could conduct appropriate, internationally recognized elections meeting worldwide norms.

## What was, and has been, the role of Aung San Suu Kyi and the National League for Democracy?

In spite of her relative youth (she is sixty-seven as of this writing) compared with the "uncles" who had formed the NLD executive committee, which has now been revamped, Aung San Suu Kyi is the undisputed leader of that party. Her views prevail and are rarely questioned. Her internal support is widespread both because of her aura and because of the unquestioned reputation of her father. Her international reputation is untarnished, she is the avatar of democracy to the outside world, and has, in large part, determined U.S. and EU policies toward Myanmar.

She has assiduously been building the influence and reputation of the NLD and has campaigned throughout the state on its behalf. Her entry into parliament has created a new dynamic in the relationship. Her initial meeting with President Thein Sein in August 2011 went exceptionally well, and she has positioned herself in a potentially important role in the *hluttaw* in spite of the paucity of NLD-controlled seats.

Her external travels have been triumphal processions. In Bangkok, on her first trip abroad, she would have overshadowed President Thein Sein at the World Economic Forum, so he postponed his trip. Her next travels in the late spring to Europe (Switzerland, Norway, and the United Kingdom) were virtually regal tours. She finally personally received her Nobel Peace Prize in Oslo. She visited the United States in September 2012, addressing a U.S. joint session of Congress where she received a medal long awaiting her presence, and several cities. With some careful planning, President Thein Sein and Aung San Suu Kyi were generally scheduled in different cities on any one day, for their future cooperation, in part, depends on their amicable relations that would have been diminished by such popular rivalry. The adulation with which she was received in the United States indicated her influence both over public opinion and in policy circles.

In contrast to her external excursions, she walks a fine line domestically. She publicly called for constitutional amendments even before she was elected. To outside observers, she seems to have political ambitions beyond her current role and has not denied her potential interest in the presidency. Her ambiguity on the Rohingya rights issues has disappointed human rights advocates, but it is an indication of her political concerns and the political complexity of the problems. Yet to achieve those ambitions, she needs to build trust among the military; if she is to achieve her stated goal of making the constitution more democratic, then she needs military support to amend that document. To develop such trust, long lacking even though she has repeatedly talked about the importance of the military that her father founded, she must support the government's reforms. She has endorsed the reform effort generally and has finally indicated the era of sanctions should be over. But too strong an endorsement would mean that the government would get credit in any forthcoming election. Her comments on the reforms and foreign investment may have satisfied neither the military nor potential investors. Since she will be over seventy in 2015 when the next round of voting takes place, there is only a small window open for an enhanced personal political role (in contrast to that of the NLD).

### What has been the role of former Senior General Than Shwe since the formation of the new government?

Nothing is more subject to speculation in Myanmar than the opaque role of former head of state, Senior General Than Shwe, who ruled (1992–2011) according to his own whims and with whom disagreement was impossible. It is rumored that he has completely retired, but it is also rumored that he is in touch with key political and military actors. Although he has a state-supplied mansion in Naypyitaw, it is said he sometimes lives in Yangon. Some believe that he orchestrated a balanced new administration, with a clean, open president who believes in reform, and a hard-line vice president, who officially "retired" in July 2012. Some say that if Than Shwe's interests are protected, including the autonomy of the military, the unity of the state and its sovereignty, and the protection of his family's personal and financial interests, he is willing to see the country change course. In his perception, he may regard his rule as eminently successful. He has built a new national capital, vastly increased foreign exchange reserves, built up the infrastructure, joined ASEAN, established good relations with China and India, pacified (at least for a period) most of the major ethnic rebellions against the state, perpetuated effective military control while expanding the *tatmadaw*, constructed a major pagoda in Naypyitaw, and led the country to what he designated a "discipline-flourishing democracy." If he has done little to improve the lives of the diverse Burmese peoples, he may regard that as the task for the subsequent administration.

Than Shwe's former colleagues who might have threatened either his power or that of his successors are no longer influential. General Maung Aye, number two in the hierarchy, went to Singapore after a stroke and seems to have no influence, and General Khin Nyunt was charged with corruption in 2004, subjected to house arrest, and released in January 2012. He has been quoted as wanting to devote himself to social service activities.

### How have Burman-minority relations evolved under the new government?

The primary, fundamental issue facing any Burmese state, civilian or military controlled, has been the relationship between the dominant Burman population (some two-thirds of the population) and the diverse group of larger and smaller minority peoples (one-third of the population). No government since independence has resolved the issue, and military control has made this more difficult. After earlier demands for separation by some elements of the minorities, most wish for some type of federalism that would provide them with more autonomy within the Union and a greater share of the state's resources that they claim, with good reason, emanate from within their ethnic territories. From Ne Win on, the military has regarded federalism as anathema—the first stage toward secession. This may be changing, however, and a willingness to allow more local autonomy within the Union seems noticeable. The NLD is essentially a Burman party (there was a Shan NLD in the 1990 elections that won the second-highest number of seats), but it had in 1989 called for some form of federal structure.

The new administration quietly set aside the plan for integration of minority armies into Border Guard Forces—the major groups vehemently objected—and engaged in real negotiations with the remaining militias. As mentioned, in January 2012 a cease-fire was signed with the Karen in a milestone agreement. But negotiations with the Kachin Independence Organization in the north broke down and fighting continues as of this writing.

Although the government is intent on realizing peace with the minorities, and cease-fires are recognized as simply the first stage in building the mutual trust on which peace must be made, this is likely to be a protracted process. One hope for amelioration is the constitutional provision of seven "state" legislatures in major minority areas—this is the first time in Burmese history such local representation has been allowed, although their authority is unclear. Yet the state still regards any minority-language instruction in the official school curriculum as inappropriate, thus frustrating minority conceptions of their own ethnicity and identity, which has developed into a reified ethnic nationalism. Thailand, recognizing the issue as related to national unity, has at the discretion of local authorities allowed some modest percentage of the official curriculum to be taught in minority languages.

Although the government recognizes 135 groups (variously designated and actually based largely on language/dialect differentiation), one group has remained unrecognized since independence—the Rohingyas. Located along the East Pakistan-Bangladesh border, these Muslim groups have been excluded from all considerations of citizenship and are clearly the most deprived and controlled ethnic group within the state. Twice (1978 and 1991–92), over 200,000 each time fled into Bangladesh to escape police and military harassment; most returned under UN auspices.

Who these people are is a complex issue, relating to the precolonial history of the region, the first Anglo-Burman War of 1824–26, the possibility to freely migrate when Burma was governed from India, the role of the Indian army in World War II battles in the region, and subsequent migrations. Although a small number of Rohingyas was given citizenship and voted in elections, the Burman majority generally regard these people as Bengalis who should be in Bangladesh, and the prejudice against them is evident in public and officials statements. In the spring of 2012, Muslim-Buddhist riots broke out in the Rakhine area because of the alleged rape of a Buddhist girl by a Muslim man. Dozens were killed and martial law had to be imposed. The issue of the Rohingyas, who are not wanted in either Bangladesh or Myanmar, is the most poignant minority issue in that minority-prone state and remains unsolved. In 2012, the government established a commission to investigate the problem; their conclusions are still forthcoming. The government's concern is that anti-Muslim riots might spread to other areas of the country, which would set back reforms and progress.

## What is the continuing role of the military under the new government?

The *tatmadaw* under the previous SLORC/SPDC government had designed a constitutional system that would in theory allow them to retain essential control into the future over any new, representatively elected, civilian government. The active duty military legally comprises 25 percent of all national and local legislatures, and representatives are chosen by the military commander-in-chief who must constitutionally be an officer. This plan assumes the unity of the armed forces: any constitutional change requires a 75 percent legislative vote that is thus impossible to achieve if the military officers in the legislature remain united. The military is legally not subject to civilian scrutiny, although the *hluttaw* does currently review its budget. Constitutional provisions ensure that one of the three key leaders of the state—the president, vice president, or speaker of the parliament—and some key cabinet positions—defense, home affairs (control over the police), and border affairs—will be from the military. The military has the ability to declare a national emergency and revert to martial law. The majority of cabinet ministers are retired military personnel, and many retired military members in the legislature have been elected because they were eminent in their local constituencies.

The military academy is graduating larger numbers of officers than can presently be used in the *tatmadaw*, and it seems evident that many of them will eventually become civil servants, thus increasing military influence. In addition, the military conglomerates (the Myanmar Economic Holdings Corporation, the Myanmar Economic Corporation, and the businesses operated by the Office of Procurement of the Ministry of Defense) will retain powerful influence over elements of the economy, as the first two are not part of the public sector and are subject only to military control. Additionally, in a society in which power is highly personalized, retired military officers will continue to have prestige and influence in the society beyond institutional roles they might play.

If, under the SLORC/SPDC, the military had effectively conceived of and promulgated its role as the critical component of legitimacy (see the Coda in this book), under the new government this approach has been modified to incorporate the still-unwrapping reforms and the roles of the legislatures, with promise for a more balanced interpretation of Burmese history and power.

## How has civil society evolved in Myanmar under its new leadership?

The expansion of civil society internally started with the SLORC in 1988 and was greatly spurred by the public, spontaneous response to Cyclone Nargis in May 2008. With the new government and the lifting of many restrictions on censorship has come greater influence on state policies. The halt of the construction of the Myitsone Dam was credited by the president as his response to public opinion—that of civil society. These non-governmental Burmese organizations have become more active, and there is little doubt that their influence has grown with liberalization. The government is said to be planning revisions in the onerous registration processes that have hampered their growth.

In response to the democratic opening, international NGOs have been expanding their numbers and roles in the country, and the government has allowed many to operate without formal registration—demonstrating progress under the new administration is obviously more important than rigid adherence to past, formalistic requirements.

## How have human rights and societal restrictions changed under the new government?

The expansion of citizens' rights under newly passed laws has been a major element of the new government's policies. Most political prisoners have been released, although some groups claim some still are incarcerated. Censorship is now eliminated, and a new press law in the offing promises even greater freedom. A new human rights commission is actively engaged in considering transgressions, labor is freer, demonstrations are allowed with prior consent, and the atmosphere is markedly changed for the better. More space now exists between the people and the state administration; it is visible in the open discussions in the streets and teashops of the country. It is too much to expect, however, that after fifty years of constrained rights that all restrictions would be lifted across the states, as local administrations and agencies may be still fearful of exerting too much autonomy. The military command system may be long remembered. Yet the reforms are palpable, and probably cannot be overturned barring some exceptional catastrophe.

Problems beyond political rights abound and cannot be resolved quickly. They will also require deft foreign assistance. Solutions include reform of the educational system at all levels; the reinstitution of competence and support for improved medical services; reform of the agricultural sector, including agricultural credit; implementing regulations in two new land laws that will prevent the state's arbitrary land acquisition; and complete overhaul of the judicial system. Critical, as well, will be the opening of avenues of social mobility in the society. For fifty years, all these areas have been controlled by the military.

### How does the military view internal and external threats, and how have they responded?

Internal threats to any central Burmese government have been readily apparent since independence. All, except the Burma Communist Party, had localized goals and were not bent on overthrowing the central regime. They simply sapped state resources, denied official access to raw materials, and created regional instability. Aside from the expansion of the *tatmadaw* as a means to contain them, a generation ago some rebels claimed the state used weapons of mass destruction (gas) against them. Recently some opposition groups have resuscitated such charges, but none have ever been confirmed.

In the modern era, foreign perception is that Myanmar has no external enemies. This has not been the Myanmar government's view. In the 1950s and 1960s, China was perceived as a potential threat because of China's claims to northern Burmese territories, its intervention in the Korean War, and its ideological fervor. Since the SLORC/SPDC rule, that external danger has devolved to the United States. Palpable fears of a U.S. invasion resulted because of America's belligerent tone toward the regime, calls for regime change, and support of dissident groups in Thailand. Refusal to allow U.S. direct assistance to victims of Cyclone Nargis in 2008 was one result.

These perceptions have resulted in a buildup of armaments from China and a wide swath of other states, including some U.S. allies. On the other hand, some U.S. observers are now concerned that the Burmese government is interested in developing weapons of mass destruction, including nuclear and ballistic missiles, and they are worried about the government's relationship with North Korea. The Burmese government has tried to assure the United States that no nuclear weapons program exists and that military relations with Pyongyang would cease; although, an agreement between the two in 2008 indicated that North Korea would assist Myanmar in building medium-range missiles, presumably for use against U.S. bases in Thailand (a U.S. ally), from where an invasion would likely be launched. The U.S. State Department in July 2012 indicated that North Korea still provided arms technology to Myanmar, but this is said to be "winding down."

As one author earlier wrote, even paranoids can have enemies. How much the development of better relations with the United States has eased Burmese fears is unclear, but it no doubt has dampened them to an important degree. But colonial aggression, foreign support to ethnic rebellions, and a history of powerful bellicose actions by the United States against other states may still evoke even more than residual concerns.

### External response

Myanmar has become the newest Asian mecca for the foreign traveler, the potential investor, the nongovernmental humanitarian worker, and the foreign economic assistance government official. Hotels are overbooked, traffic is snarled, rental real estate prices and property values have astronomically risen. Monaco, London, and Hong Kong have the world's highest real estate values, but the boom (or bubble) in Yangon is apparent; prices have increased exponentially, threatening the real estate ascendency of those leading cities. Much economic assistance and humanitarian aid will be forthcoming, and a singular question is whether the state will have the capacity to absorb these funds wisely and effectively, and whether they will in turn raise living standards for the population. The question of state capacity rests not only on the internal degradation of education but also on nearly two decades of foreign prohibitions against state training that might have staved off the present crisis. In some sense, sanctions and enforced isolation have made the response to reforms far more difficult.

## What have been Myanmar's relations with ASEAN?

Although Myanmar joined ASEAN in July 1997 with the prospect of greater ASEAN investment in that country, and perhaps also to modulate Chinese influence, the Asian financial crisis of that year prevented such developments. Advocacy for joining ASEAN may also have been led by General Khin Nyunt, who was in charge of international relations and who recognized the need for improved foreign relations. After Myanmar, under pressure, agreed to abandon its rightful position of chair of ASEAN in 2006, and as the country moved to the transfer of power to the "civilianized" administration, Myanmar sought again the chair of ASEAN, and this was approved by ASEAN at the November 2011 meeting in Bali. The projected 2014 meeting, which will take place in Naypyitaw, will tax the Myanmar regime, for the chairmanship involves some 1,000 meetings at various levels, and there are questions whether Myanmar has the capacity, even with ASEAN administrative support, to cope effectively, and whether the Myanmar infrastructure can handle the influx of visitors and delegates. Chairing the summit in 2014 will certainly add internal and external political legitimacy to the administration.

## What were China's policies toward Myanmar, and how have they evolved?

Myanmar has erroneously been called in the media a "client state" of China. A prominent Chinese role is obviously in Beijing's national interest; it is even more important to the well-being of Yunnan province, which relies on Myanmar for trade. Myanmar in turn needs a friendly China, but how close a relationship is of concern to each. Some Chinese have called Myanmar a "beggar with a golden bowl" (a poor country with vast natural resources), while some Burmese have said that when China spits, Myanmar swims. China had officially become Myanmar's largest investor in 2011 with over US$15 billion, but this figure underestimates total Chinese influence, as smaller Chinese firms avoid the official foreign investment registration process. China may have as many as 2 million illegal immigrants in the country, and their control over elements of the economy has resulted in considerable popular anti-Chinese sentiment.

China has invested in two major pipelines from the Bay of Bengal across Myanmar to Yunnan Province—one for Middle Eastern and African crude oil, and the other for offshore Myanmar natural gas—to avoid, in part, the Straits of Malacca dilemma, which is a possible blockade that could affect the 80 percent of China's energy imports that pass through the Straits. Roads, ports and other infrastructure have also been constructed. In addition, China has invested in over three dozen dams, providing hydroelectric power that mainly will be sold to China. This has caused considerable consternation in local and national Myanmar circles.

In the spring of 2011, in his first trip abroad, President Thein Sein visited Beijing, and China and Myanmar signed a statement of a "Comprehensive Strategic Cooperative

Partnership." But bowing to popular opinion, President Thein Sein halted (for the period of his term in office—until 2015) construction of the Myitsone Dam on the Irrawaddy River in the Kachin State. Of a planned Chinese investment of US$3.6 billion, US$42.5 million had already been spent. The future of that dam is in doubt. Some in China suspect that opposition to the dam was fostered by the United States through international and local NGOs. China has indicated that it regards openings to the West, especially to the United States, as part of a "containment policy" against expanded Chinese influence in East Asia.

The official Chinese reaction was subdued, but the suspicion of Myanmar intentions caused consternation in Beijing, and the implicit trust that China had placed in a cooperative Myanmar relationship was shaken. It is evident that as China builds massive infrastructure in Myanmar, Myanmar has a greater say in the bilateral relationship because these are sunk costs that cannot be retracted. The dilemmas for China and Myanmar are to develop mutual relationships that recognize the national interests of both countries.

### What has been the changing role of the United States regarding the new government?

Beginning in 2009, the Obama administration began a review of Burma policy (that old name is still, as of this writing, the official U.S. designation of the state, but that is changing). This resulted in the formation of what was called "pragmatic engagement"—keeping the sanctions policies intact (at that time an internal U.S. political necessity) while engaging in high-level dialogue. Both sides sent signals that improvement in relations was desirable. Myanmar perhaps felt that economic development depended on better relations with the West, led by the United States, and that such relations would prevent what they may have felt was over-reliance on China. This may have been an attempt to revert to Burma's traditional policy of neutrality during the Cold War. The Obama administration may have felt that in all of East Asia, progress on U.S.-Myanmar relations was the most likely avenue of foreign policy progress. The Department of State designated Derek Mitchell as ambassadorial coordinator of U.S. policy toward Myanmar, and he was quickly confirmed by the Senate.

As internal reforms began to mushroom and as more political prisoners were released, the pivotal event was the visit of Secretary of State Hillary Clinton to Myanmar in early December 2011 with the explicit approval of Aung San Suu Kyi, who was personally called by President Obama. Given Aung San Suu Kyi's bipartisan influence in the Congress, this approval can be interpreted as political assurance of congressional support for her visit and administration policy. This was the first visit by a U.S. secretary of state since the 1950s, when a civilian government controlled Burma.

A wave of high-level international visitors followed as the Burmese administration released more political prisoners and the reform agenda expanded. By the summer of 2012, the United States had nominated, and the Senate had confirmed, Derek Mitchell as the first ambassador since 1990. The United States also modified its sanctions policies to allow appropriate investment and alleviated the financial restrictions on banking operations there. It still retained, however, an illogical ban on Burmese imports (previously estimated as about US$356 million in garments), and in August 2012 the president extended most of the sanctions and the ludicrous designation that Burma (Myanmar) was a threat to U.S. interests and security. President Obama met with Aung San Suu Kyi on her September visit to the United States, but he had no plans to meet with President Thein Sein when the latter addressed the UN General Assembly. Perhaps in an effort to assuage this important diplomatic discrepancy, upon President Thein Sein's UN visit, the United States eliminated the sanctions preventing Burmese imports into the country. This position was important for American businesses and for other countries that looked to the United States for leadership toward Myanmar.

Yet China viewed the closer relationship of the United States with Myanmar as part of the United States' "containment policy" that tried to limit Chinese influence in East Asia, and the secretary of state's Myanmar visit was (unofficially but in official channels) viewed as "undermining the [Chinese] wall in Myanmar." Myanmar thus was suspiciously viewed by the Chinese as included in the U.S. "pivot" to Asia, which involved U.S. marines stationed in Australia; policy toward the South China Sea; augmented naval forces in the region; and the alliances with South Korea, Japan, the Philippines, and Thailand.

### How have the European Union and Australia changed its policies, and how have relations with India and Japan developed?

With the continuation of the reforms, the EU's Common Position had evaporated, as individual countries began to eliminate the sanctions that had been imposed. In the spring of 2012, the EU formally suspended sanctions for a year; this seemed a political euphemism for their elimination, assuming no dire backtracking by the Burmese. Australia in 2012 also eliminated its sanctions policy.

India's good relations with Myanmar continued. Indian Prime Minister Manmohan Singh visited Myanmar in May 2012, the first Indian prime minister since 1987, and signed a variety of agreements and a US$500 million credit package. The theme was the "centrality of culture" in the relationship. President Thein Sein visited Delhi in 2011, and progress continued on the Keladan Multi-Modal Transport Project and the development of the port of Sittwe, through which India planned to increase its support of its northeast area on the Myanmar northwest frontier, and thus lessen political unrest there. Yet China-India relations, although formally correct, were still subject to some tension because of the disputed 96,000 square kilometers of disputed land of Arunchal Pradesh, where Myanmar borders both states.

Until 1988, Japan was the primary supporter of the various military governments of the country. Until the coup of that year, Japan had supplied some US$2.2 billion in foreign assistance—about half of all foreign assistance entering that country from all sources. Several factors caused the eclipse of Japanese influence after 1988. Japan had to re-recognize the new government (in contrast to other countries) causing a hiatus in their assistance and contracting. Japan then entered a period of economic stagnation, and their influence began to wane throughout Southeast Asia. Perhaps most important, Japanese relations rested on the personal rapport between General Ne Win, who had been trained by the Japanese as part of the "30 comrades" in 1941, and that government. As Ne Win's influence became marginal, and as China leaped into the breach, Japan's influence declined.

In part for security reasons and to contest Chinese influence, Japan had been seeking to restart its aid program, against U.S. pressures. It provided humanitarian assistance and debt relief. But the opening to Myanmar came under the new Myanmar government, and Japan is committed to a major assistance program to debt relief and in the areas of the former Karen insurgency.

### What are Myanmar's relations with South and North Korea?

In the last years of South Korea's "sunshine policy," the South Korean government officially informed the Burmese that they would have no objection to the re-recognition of North Korea after its attempted assassination of South Korean President Chun Doo Hwan in 1983. Shortly thereafter, Thura Shwe Mann, at that time military commander, paid a secret visit to the North, which was afterward leaked, and spurred rumors—compounded by local reports of secret buildings, North Korean tunnel construction in Naypyitaw, and the training of nuclear engineers in Russia—of a Burmese nuclear weapons program. The question of North Korean military relationships with Myanmar has been of concern to the United States, as was the possibility of a transfer of nuclear technology. Although Senior General Than Shwe may have had some interest in North Korea as a model of a state that with nuclear capacity was able to stand against the United States because senior military officials had been fearful of a U.S. invasion, the invasion fear was grossly inaccurate and the North's deterrent was also erroneous. The new government denied to the United States that Myanmar had such a program, and a North Korean ship was turned away from landing in Yangon. The United States has noted that complete normalization of U.S. relations with Myanmar would, in part, depend on Myanmar's adhering to UN-imposed sanctions against the North.

South Korean relations continued to be close in terms of trade and foreign assistance, but most importantly because of the role of the South Korean conglomerate Daewoo in exploring and negotiating for offshore Rakhine natural gas, which was eventually bought by the Chinese. Some foreign observers attempt to link both North and South Korea to events in Myanmar, saying that North Korea should follow Myanmar as a model of reform, and that Myanmar should study the South as a model of economic development (The South Korean government in 2012 agreed to fund a new Myanmar Development Institute, modeled on the very successful Korea Development Institute founded in the 1960s. Both comments, however, simplify history and ignore the unique Burmese experience.

### What are the prospects for the local private sector and foreign investment under the Republic?

The rush of international business interests since the formation of the new government has been overwhelming. The visit of the U.S. secretary of state and the easing of sanctions by the European Union and the United States prompted an outpouring of business explorations in all fields, including extractive industries. A new foreign investment law (the last one was promulgated in 1988) was passed, and nationalization of private industries is prohibited under the constitution. Hundreds of Japanese and Korean business firms have explored possibilities, and General Electric was the first U.S. company to invest after the lifting of those sanctions, followed by Coca-Cola. Many firms are waiting the formation of a new government after the 2015 elections to ensure that these reforms will continue to be endorsed.

### What has been the reaction of international advocacy organizations to the new government, its reforms, and foreign responses?

Many Burmese expatriates, human rights organizations, and Burma-specific antimilitary institutions have attempted in the early stages of the reforms to characterize them as ad hoc, superficial, and cynical attempts by the new government to win approval for both the lifting of sanctions and gaining hosting the ASEAN summit in 2014. As some of these reforms became law, and as the scope of positive, projected change became more secure, a concerted effort was made to lobby both the U.S. Congress and administration and the European Union to slow the process of policy change.

The initial response claimed that these efforts were not supported by Aung San Suu Kyi, but after her meeting with President Thein Sein, and her modest endorsement of changes, this approach became tenuous. Those groups had frequently advocated regime change; that is, recognition of the NLD victory in the May 1990 elections. While this clearly was a goal nearly impossible to obtain, after the NLD registered to participate in the by-elections of April 1, 2012, it became patently untenable. Yet the rear-guard action continued unabated, with efforts to continue the sanctions policy in some form while, almost reluctantly, recognizing some positive modifications of that policy.

## Myanmar's prospects

What are the prospects for Myanmar in 2015, the next half-decade, and into the future?

The scope and pace of liberalization in Myanmar since the inauguration of the "civilianized" Republic of the Union of Myanmar in March 2011 have been remarkable. These policy initiatives encompass a broad spectrum of the multicultural entity that is Myanmar. In politics, economics, governance, and in social arenas, President Thein Sein has articulated a reform agenda that is constantly expanding and has publicly acknowledged societal deficiencies that are real but were officially unacknowledged for a half-century of military-dominated rule. The state, under a military-scripted constitution overwhelmingly approved by a manipulated referendum in May 2008, has begun to move to a more pluralistic administrative system reflecting its pluralistic cultural, multiethnic base.

After fifty years of authoritarian control, about half of which was spent in relative international isolation, Western states have responded positively to these reforms. The European Union has suspended its limited sanctions policies, and even the United States, after two decades of the Clinton and Bush administrations ineffectively using sanctions to achieve the goal of regime change, has welcomed these events by suspending its more stringent sanctions. Japan is restarting its economic development assistance, and the multilateral aid agencies are beginning anew studies of this complex society's most urgent needs, which are virtually ubiquitous.

Observers of these reforms, from the U.S. secretary of state to seasoned specialists on Myanmar, and indeed to the citizens of that country, have questioned whether the reform agenda can be sustained and whether it is too fragile to continue. These issues are real, in contrast to the views of early foreign and domestic skeptics who believed the reforms were false or facades for continued authoritarian governance. The reality of the reforms has been generally accepted, but their continuity and potential effects are subject to question.

There is anecdotal evidence of resistance to the president's liberal agenda in his administration, among some higher level military officials, and from those strategically placed whose livelihood or monopolies on power or position would be threatened. Could these reforms, then, be reversed by such powerful elements?

Constitutional provisions exist for a return to strict military rule, which would stifle the reforms and return Myanmar to a garrison state where the military could claim a national emergency that warrants their control and retention of power. But the reforms have excited such internal optimism that the complete closure of the progress already exhibited might provoke a popular explosion of sentiment that could, in turn, evoke a national emergency, as viewed from the barracks. Thus, barring a foreign invasion or a nationwide natural disaster, either of which is most improbable, stoppage of the reform process as a whole is quite unlikely. The reforms are not likely to be torn asunder wholesale.

Observers, including some in the U.S. government, have called them "irreversible." As an overall process, this seems likely even though some might argue that they have been generated on a highly personal basis—by President Thein Sein. Power in Burmese political culture has been highly personalized, resulting in weak institutional authority. Should anything happen to him, or if the political process should substantially deteriorate when his presidential tour ends in 2015, the fragile reforms might slow. If President Thein Sein continues his measures through his presidency, having successfully administered the ASEAN summit meeting in 2014 and the Southeast Asian Games in 2013, then it is highly likely the reform process could not be completely undone. Should Aung San Suu Kyi publicly split with Thein Sein on the reforms or constitutional changes, this could slow the international support of such efforts.

More likely, however, is the persistence of problems inherent in the central government's capacity to implement the reforms and at speeds that deliver to the people the anticipated relief that they clearly have sought. The former strict military command system is no longer operative in civilian matters, in spite of the martial background of most of the leadership and the specified constitutional provision of military dominance. Changes in policy now must be legislated and then enforced through a system dominated by people who never have entertained liberalized ideas or procedures, or even had the legal opportunity to read about them during their lifetime. Articulation of policy changes is relatively simple compared with their implementation.

So the fragility of the reforms is less likely to become evident from their reversal than from their faulty implementation or unanticipated consequences. The reform process is also likely to be uneven, spotty, implemented in a less than ideal manner, and at paces that will probably cause frustration because the rate of change may be considered too slow or too fast.

As comprehensive as these changes sound, what will evolve will be a distinctly Burmese approach to liberalization. The military will control the constitution: Western concepts of civilian control over the military are anathema to the latter. The military will continue to influence and manage large segments of the economy through their conglomerates, which are not part of the public sector. The military will continue to train the "future elites," as the engraving on the Military Academy's gateway states, and perhaps not only in military institutions but throughout a civilianized administration. The private sector, starved of capital except to state-controlled enterprises, may well be in the hands of those who have nonbanking access to such funding—that is, the Chinese. Thus, the future middle class may be essentially Chinese and higher level military retirees. More broadly, complex problems and dangers will continue.

The apex of U.S. engagement with Myanmar came with the visit of President Obama to Myanmar on November 19, 2012. He discussed issues with President Thein Sein, saw Aung San

Suu Kyi at her residence, greeted staff at the U.S. Embassy and officially opened the USAID program, toured the Shwedagon Pagoda, and gave a lecture at the University of Yangon, all in the space of five or six hours. His eloquent talk stressed the need for reconciliation, improved minority relations, and continued reforms; his visit prompted considerable public enthusiasm. Some perennial critics called the trip premature and even dangerous, for some felt the momentum for the reforms might slowdown thereafter. Reports indicated that Aung San Suu Kyi was initially skeptical of the trip, but came publicly to support it. This symbolic venture, which increased the international and probably the internal legitimacy of President Thein Sein, highlighted that U.S. Burmese relations at this moment were the best they had been since Burmese independence in 1948. This probably increased Chinese anxiety about too great a Burmese reliance on the U.S., but perhaps the U.S. may have learned from the Chinese that too overwhelming a presence could sour even enhanced relations, and may be cautious of its future role.

How will the external world react to the vital elections of 2015 that will determine the state's progress over the next half-decade? Will the U.S. reaction on the validity of that election depend on the potential elected role of Aung San Suu Kyi and whether she could assume a presidential or vice-presidential position? The question whether such an overtly close relationship would be regarded as enhancing or undercutting her credibility in a nationalistic environment is important.

The most difficult task will be to find a quintessentially Burmese solution to the majority-minority tensions that since independence in 1948 have resulted in dozens of larger or smaller rebellions and, according to the estimate of a former head of state, the loss of some one million lives. Creating a nation-state is still an unfulfilled process. It never existed in the precolonial, the colonial, or in the independence period under either civilian or military regimes. It is the essential, most profound issue facing the country. It is on this solution that a brighter future for the sorry state of Myanmar rests. More positive initiatives have happened since March 2011 than in the proceeding half-century, but reaching an acceptable equilibrium of distributing power and resources among all ethnic groups will be difficult, involving changes in attitudes long engrained in the social fabric.

The interplay between internal reforms and foreign relations are intimate and complex. There are dangers of too much foreign aid that cannot be absorbed and of too many foreigners playing too large public roles. Strong nationalistic tendencies are evident, and not only within the *tatmadaw*. Real change must become apparent to the various peoples of the country, and the deftness of foreign support must be matched by nuanced governmental and social responses. These are complex relationships and much rides on their successful balance.

# SUGGESTED READING

Note: There are fascinating accounts of Burma in the nineteenth and early twentieth centuries by British and other travelers and officials, but they are too numerous to list here. For a taste, see Gerry Abbott's *Inroads into Burma: A Travellers' Anthology* (Kuala Lumpur: Oxford University Press, 1997). The interested reader should check the bibliographies in some of the listed volumes for their titles. For a more thorough list of contemporary Burmese materials, visit www.Burmalibrary.org. The most comprehensive, charming, and still relevant description of Burmese customs is: Shwey Yoe (Sir James George Scott), The *Burman His Life and Notions*. Originally published in 1882, it has been reprinted many times.

## Autobiography/Biography

Aung San Suu Kyi. *The Voice of Hope*. New York: Seven Stories Press, 1997.

Chao Tzang Yawnghwe. *The Shan of Burma: Memoirs of a Shan Exile*. Singapore: Institute of Southeast Asian Studies, 1987.

Ba Maw. *Breakthrough in Burma: Memoirs of a Revolution, 1939–1946*. New Haven, Conn.: Yale University Press, 1968.

Ba U. *My Burma: The Autobiography of a President*. New York: Taplinger, 1958.

Nu (U Nu). *Saturday's Son: Memoirs of the Former Prime Minister of Burma*. New Haven, Conn.: Yale University Press, 1975.

Wintle, Justin. *Perfect Hostage: The Life of Aung San Suu Kyi Burma's Prisoner of Conscience*. London: Skyhorse, 2007. (There are several other biographies.)

# Art

Fraser-Lu, Sylvia. *Splendour in Wood: The Buddhist Monasteries of Burma.* Trumbull, Conn.: Weatherhill, 2001.

Gutman, Pamela. *Burma's Lost Kingdoms: Splendours of Arakan.* Trumbull, Conn.: Weatherhill, 2001.

# Burmese Studies

Becka, Jan. *Historical Dictionary of Myanmar.* London: Scarecrow Press, 1995 (Asia Historical Dictionaries no. 15).

Seekins, Donald M. *Historical Dictionary of Burma (Myanmar).* Lanham, Md.: Scarecrow Press, 2006.

Selth, Andrew. *Modern Burma Studies: A View from the Edge.* Hong Kong: City University of Hong Kong, Southeast Asia Research Centre, Working Paper no. 96, 2007.

Selth, Andrew. *Burma Since the 1988 Uprising: A Select Bibliography.* Brisbane, Australia: Griffith Asia Institute, 2012 (published volumes only).

# Cuisine

Thanegi (Ma). *An Introduction to Myanmar Cuisine.* Yangon: Asia Publishing House, 2004.

# Economics

Khin Maung Kyi, Ronald Findley, et al. *Economic Development of Burma: A Vision and Strategy.* Stockholm: Olaf Palme International Center, 2000.

Tin Maung Maung Than. *State Dominance in Myanmar: The Political Economy of Industrialization.* Singapore: Institute of Southeast Asian Studies, 2007.

Turnell, Sean. *Fiery Dragons: Banks, Moneylenders and Microfinance in Burma.* 2008.

Walinsky, Louis J. *Economic Development in Burma, 1951–1960.* New York: Twentieth Century Fund, 1962.

# General/Contemporary Affairs

Charney, Michael W. *A History of Modern Burma.* Cambridge: Cambridge University Press, 2009.

Fink, Christina. *Living Silence: Burma under Military Rule*. Bangkok: White Lotus, 2001 2nd Edition, 2009.

Ganesan, N., and Kyaw Yin Hlaing, eds. *Myanmar: State, Society and Ethnicity*. Singapore: Institute of Southeast Asian Studies and Hiroshima Peace Institute, 2006.

Houtmann, Gustaaf. *Mental Culture in Burmese Crisis Politics*. Tokyo: Institute for the Study of Languages and Cultures of Asia and Africa, 1999.

Kyaw Yin Hlaing, Robert H. Taylor, and Tin Maung Maung Than, eds. *Myanmar: Beyond Politics to Societal Imperatives*. Singapore: Institute of Southeast Asian Studies, 2005.

Lintner, Bertil. *Burma in Revolt: Opium and Insurgency since 1948* (2nd ed.). Chiang Mai: Silkworm Press, 1999.

Lintner, Bertil. *Outrage: Burma's Struggle for Democracy*. Bangkok: White Lotus, 1990.

Mathieson, David S., and R. J. May, eds. *The Illusion of Progress: The Political Economy of Reform in Burma/Myanmar*. Adelaide: Crawford House Publishing, 2004.

Nash, Manning. *The Golden Road to Modernity: Village Life in Contemporary Burma*. New York: Wiley.

Pedersen, Morten. *Promoting Human Rights in Burma: A Critique of Western Sanctions Policy*. New York: Rowman & Littlefield, 2008.

Rotberg, Robert, ed. *Burma: Prospects for a Democratic Future*. Washington, D.C.: Brookings Institution Press, 1998.

Seekins, Donald M. *The Disorder in Order: The Army-State in Burma since 1962*. Bangkok: White Lotus, 2002.

Skidmore, Monique, and Trevor Wilson, eds. *Myanmar: The State, Community and the Environment*. Canberra: Australia National University Press, 2007.

Steinberg, David I. *Turmoil in Burma: Contested Legitimacies in Myanmar*. Norwich, Conn.: EastBridge, 2006.

Steinberg, David I. *Burma: The State of Myanmar*. Washington, D.C.: Georgetown University Press, 2001.

Steinberg, David I. (with Hongwei Fan). *Modern China-Myanmar Relations: Dilemmas of Mutual Dependence*. Copenhagen: Nordic Institute of Asian Studies, 2012.

Taylor, Robert H. *The State in Myanmar* (2nd ed.). Honolulu: University of Hawaii Press, 2009. [Earlier edition: *The State in Burma* (1988)]

Twawnghmung, Ardeth Maung. *Behind the Teak Curtain: Authoritarianism, Agricultural Policies and Political Legitimacy in Rural Burma/Myanmar*. New York: Kegan Paul, 2004.

Wilson, Trevor, ed. *Myanmar's Long Road to National Reconciliation*. Singapore: Institute of Southeast Asian Studies, 2006.

## Historical/Cultural

Aung-Thwin, Michael. *Pagan: The Origins of Modern Burma*. Honolulu: University of Hawaii Press, 1985.

Aung-Thwin, Michael and Maitrii Aung-Thwin. *A History of Myanmar Since Ancient Times. Traditions and Transformations.* London: Reaktion Books, 2012.
Bruce, George. *The Burma Wars, 1824–1886.* London: Hart-Davis, 1973.
Cady, John. *A History of Modern Burma.* Ithaca, N.Y.: Cornell University Press, 1958.
Collis, Maurice. *Last and First in Burma.* New York: Macmillan, 1956.
Furnival, J. S. *Colonial Policy and Practices.* Cambridge: Cambridge University Press, 1957.
Mi Mi Khaing. *Burmese Family.* Bloomington: Indiana University Press, 1962.
Shwe Yoe (Sir George C. Scott). *The Burman: His Life and Notions.* London: Macmillan, 1882; reprinted many times.
Thant Myint-U. *The Making of Modern Burma.* Cambridge: Cambridge University Press, 2001.
Thant Myint-U. *The River of Lost Footsteps: Histories of Burma.* New York: Farrar, Straus & Giroux, 2006.
Tinker, Hugh. *The Union of Burma: A Study of the First Years of Independence.* Oxford: Oxford University Press, 1957.

## Military

Callahan, Mary. *Making Enemies: War and State Building in Burma.* Ithaca, N.Y.: Cornell University Press, 2003.
Dittmer, Lowell, ed. *Burma or Myanmar? The Struggle for National Identity.* London: World Science, 2010.
Maung Aung Myoe. *Building the Tatmadaw: Myanmar Armed Forces since 1998.* Singapore: Institute of Southeast Asian Studies, 2009.
Selth, Andrew. *Burma's Armed Forces: Power without Glory.* Norwalk, Conn.: EastBridge, 2002.

## Minority Issues

Callahan, Mary. *Political Authority in Burma's Ethnic Minority States: Devolution, Occupation, and Coexistence.* Washington, D.C.: East-West Center, 2007.
Leach, E. R. *Political Systems of Highland Burma: A Study of Kachin Social Structure.* Cambridge, Mass.: Harvard University Press, 1954.
Silverstein, Josef. *Burmese Politics: The Dilemma of National Unity.* New Brunswick, N.J.: Rutgers University Press, 1980.
Smith, Martin. *Burma: Insurgency and the Politics of Ethnicity* (2nd ed.). London: Zed Books, 1999.
Smith, Martin. *State of Strife: The Dynamics of Ethnic Conflict in Burma.* Washington, D.C.: East-West Center, 2007.
Thawnghmung, Ardeth Maung. *The "Other" Karen in Myanmar. Ethnic Minorities and the Struggle Without Arms.* Lanham: Lexington Books, 2012.

# Narcotics

Lintner, Bertil. *Burma in Revolt: Opium and Insurgency since 1948*. Boulder, Colo.: Westview Press, 1994.
Renard, Ronald D. *The Burmese Connection: Illegal Drugs and the Making of the Golden Triangle*. Boulder, Colo.: Lynne Reinner, 1996.

# Novels/Essays

Aung San Suu Kyi. *Freedom from Fear and Other Writings*. London: Penguin, 1991.
Khoo Thwe, Pascal. *From the Land of Green Ghosts: A Burmese Odyssey*. London: HarperCollins, 2002.
Larkin, Emma. *In Search of George Orwell in Burma*. New York: Penguin, 2005.
Marshall, Andrew. *The Trousered People: A Story of Burma in the Shadow of Empire*. Washington, D.C.: Counterpoint, 2002.
Orwell, George. *Burmese Days*. New York: Harcourt, Brace, and Jovanovich, 1934.
Orwell, George. *Shooting an Elephant and Other Essays*. New York: Harcourt, Brace, 1950.

# Religion

Jordt, Ingrid. *Burma's Mass Lay Meditation Movement: Buddhism and the Cultural Construction of Power*. Athens: Ohio University Press, 2007.
Sarkiayanz, E. *Buddhist Backgrounds of the Burmese Revolution*. The Hague: Martinus Neijoff, 1965.
Smith, Donald Eugene Smith. *Religion and Politics in Burma*. Princeton, N.J.: Princeton University Press, 1965.
Spiro, Melford E. *Buddhism and Society: A Great Tradition and Its Burmese Vicissitudes*. New York: Harper & Row, 1970.
Spiro, Melford E. *Burmese Supernaturalism*. Englewood Cliffs, N.J.: Prentice Hall, 1967.

# Gender Issues

Harridaen, Jessica, *The Authority of Influence. Women and Power in Burmese History*. Copenhagen: Nordic Institute of Asian Studies, 2012.

# INDEX

# ABOUT THE AUTHOR

David I. Steinberg, Distinguished Professor of Asian Studies, School of Foreign Service, Georgetown University, was Director of the Asian Studies Program there for ten years, and prior to that Distinguished Professor of Korean Studies.

His career spans more than fifty years in dealing with Burma/ Myanmar. He was Assistant Representative of The Asia Foundation in Burma (1958–1962), and later Director for Philippines, Thailand, and Burma Affairs in the U.S. Agency for International Development, State Department. He led the team that negotiated the reentry of the U.S. aid program to that country in 1979 and has taught on contemporary Burma/Myanmar at Georgetown University and Johns Hopkins University. He is the author of seven volumes and monographs on Burma/Myanmar, and more than fifty book chapters and articles on that country in diverse publications, in addition to writing extensively for the press. He has visited Burma/Myanmar over sixty times since 1962. He has authored eight books and monographs on other topics, as well as one translation from the Korean, and over fifty published essays on Asia. He has been the editor of six volumes as well.

Professor Steinberg's career also includes service as Representative of The Asia Foundation in Korea and Washington, D.C., and as Assistant Representative in Hong Kong.

Professor Steinberg was educated at Dartmouth College, Lingnan University (China), Harvard University in Chinese studies, and the School of Oriental and African Studies, University of London, where he studied Burmese and Southeast Asia.